By Faith Alone

מגיד
MAGGID

Elyashiv Reichner

BY FAITH ALONE

THE STORY OF RABBI YEHUDA AMITAL

TRANSLATED BY

Elli Fischer

WITH AN AFTERWORD BY

Aviad Hacohen

Maggid Books

By Faith Alone:
The Story of Rabbi Yehuda Amital

First English Edition, 2011

Maggid Books
An imprint of Koren Publishers Jerusalem Ltd.

POB 8531, New Milford, CT 06776-8531, USA
& POB 4044, Jerusalem 91040, Israel

www.korenpub.com

Originally published as *Be'emunato* [Hebrew] by
Yediot Aharonot Books/Sifrei Hemed, 2008

ISBN 978-1-59264-731-6, *paperback*

A CIP catalogue record for this title is
available from the British Library

Printed and bound in Turkey

עשה לך רב וקנה לך חבר

This book is dedicated in tribute to
HaRav Yehuda Amital z"l
whose vision, ideology and warmth
transformed countless lives
and whose legacy
continues to inspire Am Yisrael.

The Moed Family

In honor of Leon Moed
and his longtime bond of friendship
with Rav Amital z"l

Contents

Preface to this Edition

On Friday, 26 Tammuz 5770 (July 9, 2010), Rav Amital returned his soul to its Creator. This edition, published after his passing, includes an additional chapter documenting the final two years of his life.

Since his passing, his Torah and his teachings have garnered renewed interest, and I believe that their relevance will only increase.

I wish to thank Rav Amital's family, Yeshivat Har Etzion, Yediot Aharonot Books, and Koren Publishers Jerusalem for their assistance in the publication of this edition.

Elyashiv Reichner
Yeruḥam
Tevet 5771 (December 2010)

Foreword

Shehehеyanu

A crowd of over fifteen hundred students and alumni of Yeshivat Har Etzion, members of the Meimad party, family and friends gathered at Jerusalem's International Convention Center on Friday, 18 Iyar, 5765 (May 27, 2005) to celebrate Rav Yehuda Amital's eightieth birthday. The event was meticulously planned, down to the minute. Rav Amital was to be called up on stage by the two emcees after a brief introduction, but he decided to ascend before being summoned. The hall was silent as he approached the microphone. "Since I see many friends and confidants here who I haven't seen for a very long time," Rav Amital began, "I wish to make the *berakha* of *sheheḥeyanu,* in accordance with the explicit ruling of the *Shulḥan Arukh.*" He began to recite the blessing: "Blessed are You, Lord our God, King of the Universe, who has given us life, sustained us…" His voice choked with emotion; he broke into tears and barely finished the *berakha*.

In the context of Rav Amital's life story, these words, "who has given us life, sustained us, and brought us to this time," take on a palpable, concrete meaning. How many times was young Yidele Klein's life in danger during his time in a Hungarian labor camp? In those fearful moments, it certainly never crossed his mind that sixty years later he

(photo: Ḥaggai M. Cohen)

With his son-in-law Rav Yehuda Gilad, on the occasion of Rav Amital's eightieth birthday.

would be standing on a stage in Jerusalem, the capital of the State of Israel, reciting *sheheḥeyanu* upon meeting hundreds of his nearest and dearest. Yidele Klein, the gaunt boy from Grosswardein (Oradea, Romania) and sole survivor in his family, became Rav Yehuda Amital, renowned educator and Rosh Yeshiva, communal leader, and minister in the government of Israel. His story is the story of holocaust and resurrection, of destruction and redemption, of a withered tree flourishing once again.

But his life story, as fascinating and astonishing as it may be, does not really tell the tale of Rav Yehuda Amital. His complex, multifaceted, and often contradictory personality is even more fascinating than his personal history.

He was the founder of an important stream within Religious Zionism, yet often swam against the current.

As an educator, he emphasized independent thinking and refused to become a Hasidic Rebbe, and yet his Hasidic spirit and charismatic personality made him just such a figure for hundreds of his students.

He was a rabbi who opposed the involvement of rabbis in politics, and yet he founded and headed a political party.

He headed the first *yeshiva* founded in Judea and Samaria, loved Eretz Yisrael, and spoke of messianic Zionism, and yet he expressed support for territorial compromise.

He was a courageous leader and original thinker who was not prepared to compromise in his commitment to halakha.

He was an optimist that many perceived to be hopeless, an innovator who was often inclined toward conservatism, a visionary as well as a sober realist, a man of penetrating truth who did not evade questions, but neither was he afraid of leaving them without answers.

This book would never have come about had Rav Amital not been prepared to sit with me for long hours and gladly answer all of my questions. In one of our conversations, when I presented him with an apparent contradiction between two statements attributed to him, he said: "I have many other contradictions that I haven't been able to reconcile."

Nevertheless, in this book I have tried to unravel a bit of the riddle that is Rav Amital. Readers may reasonably expect to be left with questions even after reading the book. But this, too, is an expression of Rav Amital's greatness. As he once said to me: "I went through the Holocaust; I can't say that every question has an answer."

It is my duty and pleasure to thank all those who helped me in the writing of this book: First, Rav Amital and his wife – Rabbanit Miriam – for opening their home to me, and to the entire Amital family, especially Rav Yoel Amital and Rav Shlomo Brin for their invaluable assistance in gathering source material. Dr. Aviad Hacohen advised, commented, and wrote the appendix for this work. Dr. Ezra Kahalani helped guide the project from its inception. The administration of Yeshivat Har Etzion and the staff of Herzog College gave me complete freedom to make use of their services. I am grateful to the dozens of interviewees who gladly gave of their time, to my close friend Yair Kleitman for his sound advice, and last but certainly not least, to my wife Dafna and to my children, for their cooperation and patience.

Rav Amital figured prominently in my own childhood. My father was a member of Yeshivat Har Etzion's first class, and he became a close disciple of Rav Amital. My uncle, Rav Yehuda Gilad, is married to Rav Amital's daughter Dina. As a student in Yeshivat Yeruḥam, I studied Torah under Rav Eliyahu Blumenzweig, a student of Rav Amital. After getting married, I learned at Yeshivat Har Etzion for a year, where I attended Rav Amital's classes and lectures. A few years later, after Rav Amital reached the age of eighty and took the rare and dignified step of appointing successors to head the *yeshiva*, I came to his home – now as a journalist – to interview him about this irregular step. Each meeting with Rav Amital left me with a thirst for more, so I was glad to have the opportunity to commit his life story to paper.

Elyashiv Reichner
Yeruḥam
Tishrei 5768 (September 2008)

Chapter One

Hearing the Baby Cry

I have a request to make of you, our alumni... you, our partners in this grand dream: Don't stop dreaming. Never should your children have to ask you, "Abba, did you once know how to dream?" Continue to live with the sense of mission with which you came here. Keep on feeling connected to the yeshiva and continue on its path. Stay inspired, and God willing you'll have help from Above, too.

Rav Amital to the first graduating class,
twenty years after the yeshiva's founding

Yeshivat Har Etzion officially opened on the chilly and damp evening of 3 Kislev, 5729 (November 23, 1968). Some thirty students reported to an abandoned Arab Legion barracks on Kibbutz Kfar Etzion. Rav Yehuda Amital, the head of the new yeshiva, did not make an appearance that night, nor did he take part in any activities on the inaugural day of the yeshiva that he ostensibly headed. He merely sent word to the astonished students that the following day he would deliver his first *shiur* on Tractate *Pesaḥim*.

(photo: K. Weiss)

The yeshiva's first days. The Jordanian Legion barracks in Kfar Etzion – the yeshiva's first home .

(photo: K. Weiss)

Religious Affairs Minister Zeraḥ Warhaftig (to the left of Rav Amital) visits the new yeshiva.

Rav Amital sent Kfar Etzion supporter Yedaya Hacohen of the Jewish Agency with the list of Talmudic sources for the students to prepare for the first *shiur.* Hacohen recalls that although he undertook the task, the manner in which the Rosh Yeshiva opened the yeshiva seemed odd to him. It was only years later, after he had become intimately familiar with Rav Amital's educational philosophy, that he understood; from Rav Amital's perspective, from day one the yeshiva revolved around its students and their studies – and not around him.

(photo: K. Weiss)

Rav Amital with his student Asher Yaron at the door to the beit midrash. Yaron fell in battle on the second day of the Yom Kippur War

* * *

On the day before Israel declared independence on 5 Iyar, 5708 (May 14, 1948), the four towns of Gush Etzion (the Etzion Bloc) south of Jerusalem fell to forces of the Arab Legion. They had been under siege for several months, during which time the women and children were evacuated secretly. The men stayed to defend the area and to keep open supply lines to Jerusalem. Many fell in defense of the Gush, and nearly all the survivors were massacred after they were taken prisoner by the Arab Legion. Moshe "Moshko" Moskovic had been a member of the religious Kibbutz Masu'ot Yitzḥak in the Gush, and had been on a mission abroad when it fell. After the War of Independence, he and the other remaining members established the coopereative Moshav Masu'ot Yitzḥak in the Laḥish region of southern Israel.

On 28 Iyar 5727 (June 7, 1967), Day Three of the Six Day War, Gush Etzion was liberated. That same day, Moshko filed proposals and plans for the reconstruction of the Gush. His primary objective was to resettle the Gush with as many Jews as possible. He wrote in his diary that a post-high-school *yeshiva gedola*, integrated within the framework of the Israel Defense Forces (IDF), must be established as part of the resettlement efforts. Ten days after the war, he had already presented his plans to Knesset members from the National Religious Party. His plans called for the yeshiva to stand at the center of a community, which itself would become a regional hub.

At the same time, members of Kfar Etzion, led by Ḥanan Porat, began arranging the reconstruction of the kibbutz that they had left as children and that many of their fathers had fallen defending. On 22 Elul, 5727 (September 27, 1967), the first community in the liberated Gush Etzion – Kibbutz Kfar Etzion – was launched.

Ḥanan Porat, then a student at Yeshivat Merkaz HaRav, also advocated the idea of setting up a yeshiva in the Gush. He felt that Torah study must accompany the community-building efforts.

The third person enlisted to promote the idea was Ya'akov Drori, the National Secretary of Bnei Akiva who helped found Yeshivat Kerem B'Yavneh, and a member of Kibbutz Sa'ad. Already at this early stage, it was clear that a Rosh Yeshiva would be needed. R. Moshe Zvi Neriya, the head of the Kfar HaRo'eh Yeshiva High School, advocated opening the new yeshiva with a nucleus of students even without a Rosh Yeshiva, but the other three believed that a Rosh Yeshiva would contribute to the stability of the conceived institution.

Ya'akov Drori was the first to mention Rav Yehuda Amital's name. Members of the Religious Kibbutz Movement were familiar with Rav Amital, who prior to the War of Independence had taught at Yeshivat HaKibbutz HaDati, then a branch of the Kletsk Yeshiva in Reḥovot.

In Shevat 5728 (February 1968), Ḥanan Porat visited Rav Amital's home for a preliminary meeting. Rav Amital spoke with his guest about the war's miracles and wonders and of God's grand scheme to return His Presence to *Tziyon*. "God did not perform all these miracles and wonders for us for nothing," he stated, "it was not so we would remain closed up in our homes." Porat recalls that these words left an opening that he boldly exploited, asking Rav Amital how he planned to actualize these ideas. "That's an excellent question," the host concurred, "what's on your mind, young man?" At that point Ḥanan proposed that Rav Amital head the new yeshiva planned for Gush Etzion. Rav Amital said that it was an excellent idea and that he would have to consider it. When he heard that the yeshiva was to open its doors that Elul, within six months of the meeting, and that an initial nucleus of students, alumni of Yeshivat Netiv Meir, had already committed to attend, he was very impressed.

In fact, Rav Amital had decided to accept the offer by the end of the meeting, even though he had not yet given a final answer. He saw this opportunity as a sort of restitution for not having been drafted to fight in the Six Day War, whose results had so inspired him. He refrained from giving a final answer until he was able to consult with his wife, Miriam. Miriam Amital also loved the idea and gave her consent. Rav and Rabbanit Amital were not interested in the conditions of his new job, nor did they ask about the sources of funding at the disposal of the yeshiva's founders.

Several days later, Rav Amital met with Ya'akov Drori and Moshko. I discovered a completely unique personality," Moshko recalls. "Passion for the idea under discussion had been ignited within him even before we visited. As a man of the Gush, I emphasized that the new yeshiva would be erected in memory of the Gush Etzion martyrs, and he was enchanted by the idea. We proposed a Yissakhar–Zevulun division of labor: he would engage in spreading Torah, and we would worry about finances. At that point, I realized that this man was completely grounded in reality. His questions were quite practical." Already then, Moshko recounts, Rav Amital made it perfectly clear that he intended to take charge of determining the culture and spirit of the yeshiva. He, and not the financial administrator. And indeed, from that point forward, the yeshiva was under his courageous leadership and responsibility.

Yoel Bin-Nun, now Rav Yoel Bin-Nun, a friend of Ḥanan Porat who helped to recruit students for the new yeshiva, also first met Rav Amital at that time. Bin-Nun was a student at Yeshivat Merkaz HaRav, where he had been studying under R. Zvi Yehuda Kook. At that first meeting, he realized that Rav Amital was unlike any other rabbi he had encountered. He recalls that Rav Amital cited a passage from *Ḥagiga*: "For a yeshiva, there is none better than an old man; for war, there is none better than a young man (*bakhur*)." According to Ḥazal, Rav Amital explained, the term "*yeshiva bakhur*" is an oxymoron. A *bakhur* belongs in battle, while the elderly belong in yeshiva. What, then, is a *yeshiva bakhur*? With this, Rav Amital expressed his idea of "*Hesder le-khatchila*," which sees the integration of Torah study with military service as an ideal. *Hesder yeshivot*, according to Rav Amital, were not designed merely to solve some technical problem; the IDF is the army of the Jews, not the Tsarist army that one would find every excuse to evade. When Ḥazal stated that "for war, there is none better than a *bakhur*," they meant that a *bakhur* is a combat soldier. Only one who combines military service with Torah study is worthy of being called a *yeshiva bakhur*; one who does not serve in the army is not worthy of the title "*bakhur*."

With this statement, Rav Amital articulated the abyss separating him from R. Zvi Yehuda. The latter's attitude toward military service was complex: there were periods when he instructed his students to serve, and there were situations in which he instructed them to defer their enlistment. He did not wish to connect his yeshiva to the military, preferring to keep them completely separate.

* * *

Rav Amital was the first to articulate, more than a decade earlier, the idea of combining military service with yeshiva learning.

"We must find an arrangement (a '*hesder*') with the army regarding the military service of yeshiva students," Rav Amital said to his father-in-law, R. Zvi Yehuda Meltzer, in the late 1950s. At the time, Rav Meltzer was working to create a *yeshiva gedola* program that would serve as the continuation of his Yeshivat HaDarom High School in Reḥovot. As one who served in the IDF for a year and a half, Rav Amital viewed military service as a crucial component of the Zionist yeshiva student's world. He was concerned that "if the religious don't serve in the army, there will be a schism in the nation." Additionally, he contended, if military service would not be integrated into Zionist *yeshivot*, no elite Torah scholars would be cultivated within the Zionist community. *Yeshivot* without military service, he explained, would produce non-Zionist Torah scholars, and the religious Zionist community would remain bereft of spiritual leadership. The only way to nurture Zionist Torah scholars is to make sure that yeshiva students serve in the army.

This situation is difficult to describe now that the religious Zionist community is large and strong, but during the first years of the state this community suffered from feelings of inferiority vis-à-vis both the *ḥaredi* (ultra-Orthodox) and *ḥiloni* (Secularist) communities. Graduates of public religious high schools and the fledgling yeshiva high schools were primarily concerned with establishing religious *kibbutzim* and Naḥal agricultural settlements. The few who considered yeshiva study were considered quasi-*ḥaredi* and suffered from a negative image within the religious Zionist community.

Rav Amital's explanation of the *hesder* idea fused ideology with practicality, a fusion that was very characteristic of Rav Amital's way of thinking; he always connected grandiose ideas to the practical world. Ephemeral ideals became grounded in reality.

The *hesder* idea posed an ideological alternative to *ḥaredi yeshivot*. The *ḥaredi* ideology maintained, and still maintains, that that any discipline can be studied while one is engaged in other matters, except for Torah, which must be studied continuously without distraction. Rav Amital saw this ideology as a diminution of the Torah's honor. "The occupation of Rabbi Yoḥanan the Shoemaker did not stand in the way of his greatness in Torah," he contended. He even used himself and his contemporaries as an example: people who "neglected" Torah study during the Holocaust but still became Torah giants.

Rav Amital was also the first, as far as anyone knows, to use the term "*hesder*" vis-à-vis the integration of yeshiva studies with military service. Years later, after the "*Hesder Yeshiva*" concept took root and became a brand name, he was sorry that he did not use a more meaningful name for the program. Nevertheless, the technical name given to this framework attests to the practical thinking of the man who first articulated it.

Rav Meltzer bought into his son-in-law's idea; he also ascribed great significance to military service by yeshiva students and had tried to establish, in the aftermath of the War of Independence, a military yeshiva under the auspices of the military rabbinate, in order to encourage students steeped in Torah to enlist.

The model for Rabbis Meltzer and Amital's idea was the IDF's Naḥal Brigade, which combined military service with agricultural settlement activity. Rav Meltzer proposed to Defense Ministry officials that yeshiva students be allowed to switch the agricultural aspect of the Naḥal program with yeshiva study.

Rav Meltzer was known for his tenacity in attaining goals he had set for himself. He went from door to door in the Ministry of Defense until his program was approved. In 5719 (1959), the IDF first recognized the special track to be known from that point forward as the *Hesder* program.

* * *

Even before the proponents of the planned Gush Etzion *hesder yeshiva* turned to Rav Amital, an initial core group of students had formed.

One evening during Kislev, 5768 (December, 1967), Ḥanan Porat visited Netiv Meir, then considered the top yeshiva high school, to recruit for the new yeshiva. Most of the students knew of the young man due to his involvement in the resettlement of Kfar Etzion. At the time, some of the students were considering joining, upon graduation, a Naḥal group being assembled and strongly promoted by the religious Zionist youth movement Bnei Akiva. Others were contemplating enrolling at Yeshivat HaKotel at the recommendation of Netiv Meir's Rosh Yeshiva, R. Aryeh Bina. Still others were choosing between the various *ḥaredi yeshivot* being touted by Talmud teachers of that persuasion and Zionist *yeshivot* such as Merkaz HaRav and Kerem B'Yavneh. The prospect of being a part of a brand new yeshiva in Gush Etzion and the centerpiece of a new community initially attracted those students who were debating between joining a Naḥal group and attending a yeshiva. They saw the new yeshiva's potential to create an ideal fusion of Torah study with pioneering new settlement in recently liberated areas. The post–Six Day War patriotic atmosphere also contributed to the appeal of Ḥanan Porat's gospel.

In that first meeting with Porat, five boys decided to join the yeshiva. One of them was Yeshayahu Yeḥieli: "That very evening we began converting other friends to the idea," he recounts, "we focused our efforts on the class's most sophisticated Talmudists. We knew that if we converted them to the idea, it would prove the seriousness of the yeshiva."

The initial meeting between the students and Rav Amital, which took place at the latter's home, was attended – in addition to the Netiv Meir students – by several students from Merkaz HaRav who planned to enroll in the fledgling yeshiva in order to bolster it.

Yeḥieli's most vivid memory of the evening is of Rav Amital being moved to the point of tears by the fact that he – a Holocaust survivor – was going to establish a yeshiva in Gush Etzion. When asked by the students what would make the new yeshiva unique, Rav Amital told them a Hasidic story that ultimately became the foundational narrative of Yeshivat Har Etzion. R. Schneur Zalman of Liadi – the founder and "Alter Rebbe" of Chabad and the author of *Tanya* – and his grandson, R. Menaḥem Mendel, known as the "Tzemaḥ Tzedek" after his *magnum opus,* were studying Torah in a three room house: the Alter Rebbe in an inner room and the Tzemaḥ Tzedek in a middle room. A baby slept in its bassinet in the outer room. The baby began to cry. The Tzemaḥ Tzedek, immersed in his studies, did not hear the cry. The Alter Rebbe heard the cry from the more distant room and went to soothe the baby. On his way back to the inner room, the Alter Rebbe reprimanded his grandson: "If someone is studying Torah and fails to hear the crying of a Jewish baby, there is something very wrong with his learning." So too, according to Rav Amital, one who is immersed in the world of Torah may not disengage from the world around him. He wished to impart this approach to his students at his very first meeting with them. Later on, he applied this outlook to himself when he entered the fray of public activism.

The boys asked Rav Amital numerous questions about the yeshiva-to-be. Many expressed concern that the yeshiva would not take root and that the Torah study there would not be sufficiently serious. They expected Rav Amital to placate them and assuage their doubts, but, to their astonishment, he refused to promise them anything. "I have no guarantees that it will succeed," he told them, "I have articulated my credo to you. Whoever wants to come is welcome. Whoever does not is invited to withdraw." Rav Amital even chose to use the biblical formula spoken by Jewish officers to their charges before battle (Deut. 20:8): "Is there anyone afraid and disheartened? Let him go back to his home." Thus, already at their first meeting with Rav Amital, the students were exposed to his honest and forthright personality and to the fact that he would speak his mind without worrying about the consequences. Yoel Bin-Nun, who was present at the meeting, was somewhat taken aback by Rav Amital's statements. "I thought that it's very risky to talk to the students like that. The rabbis at Netiv Meir were incessantly trying to convince them to go to Yeshivat HaKotel and not gamble on a new and unknown yeshiva. Instead of addressing their concerns, Rav Amital let them know that he, too, did not have all the answers. After the meeting, I stayed back with the boys to assuage those who were taken aback by the rabbi's responses and to persuade those who were still uncertain."

One of the uncertain students was Ya'akov Medan, later Rav Ya'akov Medan, one of Rav Amital's successors as Rosh Yeshiva. Ya'akov Medan was one of the most outstanding and sharpest students in that tenth graduating class of Netiv Meir. His elder brother, R. Barukh Medan, who had been Rav Amital's student at Yeshivat HaDarom, was then studying at the *ḥaredi* Yeshivat Azata, where he was eventually appointed to the faculty. Ya'akov, encouraged by the *ḥaredi* rabbis at Netiv Meir, was thinking about following in his brother's footsteps. Their father, Meir Medan, a Hebrew linguist and religious Zionist, was concerned that his second son would become *ḥaredi* as well and consequently tried to convince him to enroll in the yeshiva of Rav Amital, whom he knew and held in high regard. "Rav Amital was painfully honest about the state of the Torah world," recalls R. Ya'akov Medan, "he quoted Rav Shakh as having said, 'I wish my students knew Torah after five years in yeshiva like physics students know physics after a similar period.' We were used to pronouncements that were very different. Our Rosh Yeshiva, R. Aryeh Bina, was indeed inclined toward religious Zionism, but all of our teachers were *ḥaredi* and spoke of the Torah world as something completely pristine. For them there was a clear division between the wholly good Torah world and the suspicion–inducing secular world." According to Rav Medan, Rav Amital was the first rabbi to expose him to harsh criticism of the Torah world. He criticized the *yeshivot* that isolated themselves from the broader Jewish community; when addressing the new yeshiva, he barely offered any certainties, conveying to the students that there are no shortcuts in Torah and that they would have to work hard. "His honesty was overwhelming. His refusal to make promises and his statement that it all depends on our individual labors made quite an impression on me." In addition to the forthright statements about the Torah world, Ya'akov Medan was also impressed by the humanity and simplicity that Rav Amital radiated. Medan later recounted that in those days the prevalent assumption was that every rabbi is angelic and other-worldly. He could answer any question. Any incredulity or second-guessing was nothing but lack of comprehension on the part of the student. Medan was impressed with Rav Amital precisely because his bearing was not that of an angel. Medan was not looking for a mentor who would be an angel or a saint, but a human being who would understand his shortcomings and errors and his need for self-improvement. After some deliberation, Medan, too, decided to enroll in the new yeshiva. Classmate Yeshayahu Yeḥieli describes Medan's addition to the group of prospective students of the Gush yeshiva as a dramatic achievement. "Our greatest joy during those months was to enter the classroom in the morning and tell our *rebbe* that another boy committed to the new yeshiva. When we informed him one day that Ya'akov Medan joined, too, he went into shock."

Yeḥieli and his friends recorded another achievement on the day that Eliyahu Blumenzweig, later the Rosh Yeshiva of Yeshivat Yeruḥam, decided to join his classmates at the new yeshiva. Like Ya'akov Medan, Eliyahu Blumenzweig was one of the sharpest and most erudite students in the class. He did not attend the initial meetings with Rav Amital because he suspected that the yeshiva would become some sort of Torah–oriented Naḥal group for Bnei Akiva members, where the level of Torah study would not be serious. He was considering Yeshivat Kerem B'Yavneh and Yeshivat Merkaz HaRav. He joined the Gush group at a later stage, and the *ḥaredi* faculty members again let out a collective groan.

In the end, sixteen Netiv Meir students decided to enroll in the yeshiva. They were joined by three boys from the yeshiva high school in Kfar HaRo'eh, four from Or Etzion in Merkaz Shapira, several students from other yeshiva high schools, and four older students who had been studying at Yeshivat Merkaz HaRav. The future Rav Ya'akov Greenglick came to the yeshiva from Midrashiat Noam, the yeshiva high school in Pardes Ḥana. From his meeting with Rav Amital in Iyar 5768 (May 1968), he remembers only that Rav Amital instructed his son Yoel, then studying at the *ḥaredi* Yeshivat Kol Torah, to close his books on Yom HaAtzma'ut, Israel's Independence Day, and go watch the military parade. The IDF parade on Yom HaAtzma'ut of that year, the first parade after the victory of the Six Day Way, was especially grand. "Father said that it's a mitzva to go watch the parade," Rav Yoel recalls, "so I went with a friend and even gave notice that I'm attending because I think it's a mitzva." Yoel and his friend were the only two Kol Torah students who went to watch the procession.

* * *

That Iyar, Assistant Minister of Defense and former IDF Chief of Staff Zvi Tzur approved the "establishment of a yeshiva at Har Etzion, under an arrangement (*hesder*) similar to what is customary at Yeshivat Hesder Kerem B'Yavneh."

Due to the new *yeshiva*'s location over the Green Line, which mandated security patrols, the army required Har Etzion students to undergo four months of basic training prior to beginning their studies at the yeshiva. Rav Amital saw this as an ideal situation. "After a period of time in the army," he told his students, "you will know how to appreciate every moment spent studying Torah." On 14 Tammuz, 5728 (July 10, 1968), the students gathered in Kfar Etzion for two days of preparation for the military. Rav Amital gave halakha classes and addressed common halakhic questions faced by religious soldiers. R. Yoel Bin-Nun recalls that it was in those classes that he was first exposed to Rav Amital's impressive knowledge of the responsa literature and halakhic creativity. Rav Bin-Nun recognized Rav Amital's clear, straightforward, and original outlook and halakhic courage. In contrast to R. Shlomo Goren, then the Chief Rabbi of the IDF, whose bold halakhic rulings often felt contrived, with Rav Amital everything was straightforward, not tortuous. In addition to Rav Amital's creativity, Bin-Nun was also exposed to works of responsa that he had never heard of. Soon after becoming acquainted with Rav Amital, Yoel Bin-Nun met R. Akiva HaCarmi, the rabbi of Kiryat Shmuel, near Haifa, who had studied with Rav Amital in Yeshivat Ḥevron. "You have no idea who Rav Amital is," Rav HaCarmi assured him, "we were roommates in Yeshivat Ḥevron. There was always a stack of works of responsa next to his bed, which he would read before going to sleep like one would read a novel. He knows entire responsa by heart!"

Once Bin-Nun discovered Rav Amital's halakhic proficiency, he began pressing him to give more classes on the responsa literature, but Rav Amital refused. His refusal stemmed from his assessment that the students were not sufficiently mature. Years later he began giving classes on this topic, but he never saw himself as a halakhic decisor or *posek*. Even though he answered many of his students' questions over the years, he refused to publish his own responsa. His halakhic responses were always need-based, because his students required answers, and never with the goal of introducing halakhic novellae. R. Yoel Bin-Nun views this as a great opportunity wasted: "At Yeshivat Merkaz HaRav, where I was coming from, there is no place for halakhic decision making. The yeshiva has no obvious *posek*, and students had to look outside for practical guidance. I also think that had Rav Amital become established as a halakhic figure, firmly rooted in the Zionist Torah world, nurtured by the teachings of Rav Kook and Rav Ḥarlap, and knowing how to address philosophical matters in addition to rendering practical decisions, his subsequent political pronouncements would have been received completely differently."

After the military preparation days, the yeshiva students were enlisted for basic training. The yeshiva administration used this brief time period to arrange the physical aspects of the yeshiva's opening. An association affiliated with the yeshiva – the Har Etzion Yeshiva Association – was established, and Moshko began looking for a site for the yeshiva's permanent home. It was clear to everyone that the yeshiva's stay in Kfar Etzion would be temporary. Kibbutz members were not thrilled about hosting the yeshiva on their kibbutz, even for a short time. They were concerned solely with helping the fledgling kibbutz establish itself. Additionally, some members were worried about the effect that the strong presence of Torah-oriented yeshiva students would have on their kibbutz lifestyle. Only after some persuasion on the part of Ḥanan Porat was it agreed to lend the yeshiva, for one year, several structures that had been abandoned by the Jordanian Legion and that the kibbutz had designated for use as a youth hostel.

Moshko had a definite plan. He envisioned the yeshiva as the backbone of a regional community center. To that end, he set his sights on the hill with the lone oak tree, visible from Jerusalem. During the nineteen years of Jordanian occupation, the surviving women and children of Kfar Etzion had taken an annual pilgrimage to the border, and, gazing from afar at the hill with the oak tree, had sworn to return. In the summer of 1968, Moshko submitted a request to erect a regional center on that Gush Etzion hill. On September 1, the government decided that an interministerial committee would examine the possibility of establishing the center and submit its recommendation for government approval.

At the same time, Moshko was raising funds that would allow the yeshiva to commence operations once the boys returned from the army. At one point, they received an offer of a large donation from an American Jew, but on condition that the yeshiva be located in Jerusalem and not beyond the Green Line. Rav Amital and Moshko refused the contribution; their goal was not simply to build another yeshiva, but to build it in Gush Etzion.

Chapter Two

Mashiaḥ will Test the Yidele

Where I was born and lived until age eight, we never heard the term "Da'at Torah." *For halakhic questions we turned to the rabbi, of course. Occasionally he expressed outrage, and instructed about moral issues as well. But the idea that the rabbi sets all public policy? There was no such thing. That's a new phenomenon.*

One day in the early nineteenth century, a very strange man walked into the *beit midrash* of R. Moshe Sofer, known as the Ḥatam Sofer, in Pressburg, Hungary (today Bratislava, Slovakia), and asked for an urgent meeting with the Rosh Yeshiva. Some of the students wished the visitor well, others ignored him and continued studying, and a third group mocked the man's strange appearance and pretentious request.

When the Ḥatam Sofer exited his chambers after the meeting, he told his students that the strange man was none other than Elijah the Prophet, and that their behavior toward him would determine their futures: the mockers would not become Torah scholars; the ignorers would become Torah scholars but would not win any prestige; those who wished the stranger well and treated him with respect would grow in their scholarship of Torah and also win prestige and stature.

One of the students who ignored the tumult and kept studying was R. Yehuda Modren, the great-great-grandfather of his namesake, Rav Yehuda Amital. R. Modren indeed became a great Torah scholar, but as the Ḥatam Sofer prophesied, he never served in any rabbinic position. He authored novellae on the Talmudic tractate *Gittin*, glosses on *Sefer Terumat HaKri*, and a commentary on the Torah, but he never won any prestige. His great-great grandson, Yehuda Klein, born a century later on 3 Ḥeshvan, 5685 (October 31, 1924), frequently heard this story from his grandmother. The destiny that the Ḥatam Sofer charted for R. Modren was applied to his descendants by his granddaughter, Rav Amital's grandmother, as she charged them to become students and scholars of Torah, but to run away from honor, prestige, and other trappings of rabbinic aggrandizement.

Yehuda Klein was born in Grosswardein, Transylvania, a town

The Klein family in Hungary. Standing: Parents Yekutiel (Zalman) and Devora Klein. Sitting (from right): Grandfather Zvi Klein, the young Yehuda Klein (Amital), sister Ḥayya Sarah, Aunt Miriam and two cousins, grandmother Esther Klein.

Yehuda Klein (Amital) and his sister Ḥayya Sarah.

that changed hands between Hungary and Romania several times during the early part of the twentieth century. His storytelling grandmother, Dina Kanner, was a major figure in his childhood. After the death of her husband, Yeshayahu Kanner, a simple and unlearned man who earned a living from manual labor, she went to live with her daughter and son-in-law, Devora and Yekutiel Klein.

The Klein family lived in a building belonging to Grosswardein's Jewish community. Yekutiel, known to all as Zalman, was the community's bookkeeper. Devora ran a soup kitchen that operated mainly in the winter and fed three hundred paupers daily. The Kleins had three children: Yehuda, Ḥayya Sarah, and Yoel.

Grandmother Dina helped her daughter maintain her home. She slept in the family room, in a collapsible bed that she shared with her grandson Yehuda. Each morning she would arise early to recite supplications (*teḥinot*) and chapters of Psalms. Little Yehuda would wake up to the sounds of his grandmother's Psalm-reading. Each morning, polished shoes waited at his bedside. Despite his protestations, his grandmother insisted on shining his shoes and otherwise attending to her grandson, who spent his days studying Torah. Her many acts of kindness – she developed friendships with the numerous beggars who visited the house and always offered them a glass of tea while inquiring into their welfare – made an impression that stayed with Rav Amital throughout his life. The Klein family was not wealthy, but Zalman Klein nevertheless made sure to give his mother-in-law some small change to distribute among the mendicants.

In addition to her kindness, her asceticism left its indelible mark on her grandson. She would fast every Monday and Thursday from the beginning of Elul until the beginning of Nisan – more than half of the year – and when one of the regular fast days of the Jewish calendar fell out on a particular week, she did not give up her set fasts. She had accepted this practice when her son Yosef was conscripted into the Hungarian army during World War I, and she continued even after his safe return home.

Despite her personal piety, Grandmother Dina imparted to her grandson a critical attitude toward being excessively meticulous in mitzva observance – *frumkeit* in Yiddish. Many years later, he would frequently warn his students of the dangers inherent in the over-cautiousness and anxiety that often accompanied mitzva observance.

The Klein family was Ashkenazic and religious, but not Hasidic. Zalman Klein was clean-shaven, and he and his sons covered their heads with caps. Once, when Yehuda returned from the barber with longish sidelocks, Zalman made sure to trim them. "I'd rather cut them myself than wait for you to cut them when you get older," he explained. Although the family did not belong to any Zionist movement, it was Zionistic in spirit and Eretz Yisrael permeated the atmosphere at home. Grandmother Dina always spoke about her dream of making a pilgrimage to Eretz Yisrael, and other members of the household were certain that they would eventually immigrate. Most of Zalman's brothers realized their dream and made *aliya* to Palestine in the 1920s. Later, his parents, Zvi and Esther, followed in their footsteps. Zalman and two other brothers with families remained in Hungary for economic reasons. Yehuda was eight years old when his grandparents made *aliya*. He recalled the Hebrew newspapers that his father received weekly. Although several weeks had elapsed between their publication and their arrival in Grosswardein, his father showed great interest in them and read them thirstily.

Yehuda attended *ḥeder* like the other boys in the community. The curriculum was individuated; the boys would play in the courtyard as the teacher, the *melamed,* called each boy in turn to study the letters of the Hebrew alphabet and to learn to read. Little Yehuda had a frail constitution and did not excel in sports. He made up for his physical weakness with academic excellence and a developed imagination. He grew up with a profound spiritual awareness. The *melamed* often told the boys that when *Mashiaḥ* comes, he would test the Torah knowledge of each *yidele,* each boy. Yehuda, who everyone called Yidele, was convinced that the *melamed* was talking specifically about him. He occasionally dreamt of the Messiah's arrival and subsequent assessment of Yehuda's Torah knowledge. One day, while playing in the schoolyard, Yehuda thought he saw a shooting star. The young boy was convinced that it portended the imminent arrival of the Messiah, about whom he had heard so much in *ḥeder.* Within seconds he had gathered his friends, and they burst into song and dance around one of the trees. They sang "*vetaher libeinu le'ovdekha be'emet*" ("Purify our hearts to serve You in truth"), the song that eventually became the anthem of Rav Amital's spiritual approach. The boys, led by Yehuda, quickly went to wash their hands in anticipation of the *Mashiaḥ*'s arrival, but the *melamed* came out and put an end to their celebration. Little Yehuda felt terribly disappointed. For a long time, he remained convinced that had the *melamed* not intervened, he and his friends would have met the Messiah himself.

At the age of six, Yehuda began to attend the Jewish public school in the community. After school, he would return to the *ḥeder* for more Torah study. Four years of public education was the extent of his formal education.

As he neared his Bar Mitzva, Yehuda had to prepare a sermon, as was customary. His father even conditioned the celebratory meal on the delivery of a worthy *derasha.* Yehuda asked his father to hire a tutor to help prepare the *derasha,* but his father refused. Yehuda's tears and pleas made no difference; Zalman Klein wanted to teach his son independence.

As the celebration drew near, Yehuda, left with no choice, began to peruse the books in the house in search of a suitable sermon. He decided on a nice essay on the topic of *ḥadash* (the season's new grain, which was forbidden until the second day of Pesaḥ) that he found in a halakhic work. In addition to the halakhic idea, he was also expected to prepare a homily on the weekly Torah portion. He had an idea: he would ask his paternal grandfather, a Torah scholar in his own right, for help. Zvi Klein already lived in Jerusalem at that point. Twelve year old Yehuda wrote his grandfather a letter full of flowery phrases in which he outlined the halakhic components of his speech, and concluded with a request for a few homiletic ideas on the *parasha* of *Noaḥ*. To the best of his recollection, Yehuda never got a response.

There was no money to buy Yehuda new clothes in honor of the Bar Mitzva. Instead, his mother promised to sew a particularly colorful patch onto his old and already patched jacket. In those days, it was customary to celebrate a Bar Mitzva with a communal kiddush hosted by the family. The highlight of the kiddush was, of course, the Bar Mitzva boy's speech. The Kleins' small apartment could not accommodate everyone who wanted to hear Yehuda's *derasha*. Those who could not squeeze their way into the home positioned themselves under the window so that they could hear. "They all stood there," describes Leah Chen (nee Fuchs), who grew up in the same community, "so that they could hear that brilliant boy. Later, they spoke about his *derasha* with amazement." Zalman made sure that his son's success in his studies did not translate into excessive pride. "Here you are exceptional," he would say, "but when you get to yeshiva in Eretz Yisrael you won't stand out like you do here." Yehuda Klein believed his father.

When Yehuda was fourteen years old, R. Ḥayyim Yehuda Levi arrived in Grosswardein. R. Levi was the grandson of R. Moshe Shmuel Glasner, author of *Dor Revi'i* and the rabbi of the Transylvanian city of Cluj (Klausenberg). After studying and obtaining his rabbinical ordination in Hungarian yeshivot, Rav Levi decided to become familiar with the Lithuanian yeshivot was well, and went to study in the Mir Yeshiva. In contrast to the Hungarian yeshivot, the Lithuanian yeshiva emphasized penetrating analysis over mastery of large quantities of material. Rav Levi was one of the most outstanding students in Mir, and after two years there he resolved to disseminate the Lithuanian style of learning in his native Hungary. In order to establish a Lithuanian-style yeshiva, he needed the support of local rabbinic and lay leaders. Many people in the community did not look kindly on the innovations that this young new rabbi brought with him from Mir, but several Torah scholars gave him their support, and the yeshiva opened its doors. By that time Yehuda Klein had completed his studies in *ḥeder* and was looking for a yeshiva. His father, who had heard Rav Levi speak, was impressed by his personality and decided that this yeshiva would be suitable for his son.

The Lithuanian yeshiva did not have an easy time at first. For two years, only four or five students, aside from Yehuda Klein, placed their trust in the young rabbi. The students felt a strong sense of responsibility towards the yeshiva. Yehuda felt as though the yeshiva's very existence depended on his presence and studying there. He was afraid to leave the yeshiva even for five minutes. Over time, the yeshiva grew, reaching a peak of forty-five students – but by then it was too hard for Yehuda to jettison that heavy sense of responsibility that had weighed upon him during those first years.

Rav Levi's impact on Yehuda was inestimable, opening him up to an entire world of Torah that he had not known before. It was from Rav Levi that he first became familiar with the novellae of R. Ḥayyim Soloveitchik and R. Isser Zalman Meltzer, whose granddaughter Yehuda eventually married. Yet Rav Levi's influence on Yehuda went beyond study methods; he had a decisive influence on Yehuda's decision to dedicate his life to studying and teaching Torah. Rav Levi's iconoclasm and willingness to buck trends – evidenced by his call for Lithuanian-style Torah study in Hungary – left their mark on his disciple.

The Jewish community of Grosswardein numbered approximately thirty-thousand individuals – about a third of the city's total population. It was the second largest Jewish community in Hungary. The vast majority of Jews in the community affiliated with the Ashkenazic *ḥaredi* Orthodox stream, under the leadership of the heirs of the Ḥatam Sofer. A minority affiliated with the liberal Neolog community, roughly equivalent to the contemporary Conservative movement. In 1916, at the height of World War I, R. Yisrael Hager, the Vizhnitzer Rebbe, arrived in Grosswardein and began to establish a Hasidic court in town. The *ḥaredi* and Hassidic communities generally maintained a relationship of mutual respect. This is attributable to Rav Hager, who was known for his easygoing personality. R. Yisrael Hager died in 1936 and was succeeded by his son, R. Ḥayyim Meir Hager. The court of Vizhnitz was physically close to the Klein home, so on Friday nights, when Yehuda wished to continue studying even after the gentile maid extinguished the lights, he made his way to Vizhnitz, where the lights stayed on until late. Out of curiosity, Yehuda would join the Hasidim at their *tisch*. Tzipora Friedman-Ben Shalom (nee Hager), the daughter of Rav Ḥayyim Meir, remembers him well: "He stood out because the Hasidim would be wearing black hats or *shtreimlach*, while he wore a hat of a lighter color." Rav Amital later said that these *tischn* did not succeed in making him a Hasid. Already then he had begun to develop his dual approach to the Hasidic world. Yet despite all of the criticism that he later leveled against various phenomena within Hasidut, he never denied the Hasidic aspect of his personality.

One incident in particular set Yehuda Klein and the Vizhnitzer Hasidim in opposition to each other. R. Dov Berkowitz, one of the greatest Torah scholars in the city and a proponent of Rav Levi's yeshiva told Yehuda – as he pored diligently over a tome of the Talmud – that some students from the Vizhnitz yeshiva were disparaging Rav Levi's novellae. Yehuda swiftly went over to the *beit midrash* of the Vizhnitz yeshiva and found the students who had badmouthed his teacher studying a passage from *Tosafot* on *Bava Kama*. Within seconds he began a scholarly debate with them regarding the interpretation of the passage, and he showed them that they misunderstood it. He then grew agitated and rebuked them: "You're incapable of grasping the straightforward meaning of the *Tosafot*, but you allow yourselves to scoff at Rav Levi's novellae?"

The four years during which Yehuda imbibed Torah from his mentor, R. Ḥayyim Yehuda Levi – the years of his spiritual development in a new yeshiva – overlapped with the first years of World War II. During the fourth year, just as the status of the yeshiva and its leader were becoming established in the community, everything collapsed as the skies of Hungary darkened.

Chapter Three

No Interest in Little Amitals

In every yeshiva there is the risk that the students will become clones of their rabbis: identifying with everything they say, responding how they respond, and emulating their style. They lose their individuality to become shadows and replicas of their mentors. Is that our goal? To create four hundred clones?

Yeshivat Har Etzion indeed opened its doors in Kislev, 5729, in the absence of its new Rosh Yeshiva, who felt that his presence was unimportant.

Those first few days, the students saw other demonstrations of Rav Amital's approach, according to which the heart of the yeshiva is its students. That first evening, as they prepared for Ma'ariv, the first prayer service in the yeshiva, the question arose as to which custom the yeshiva would follow, Ashkenaz or Sefarad. The students called Rav Amital from the reception area of the adjacent military base, and he answered them: "You are the yeshiva; you decide. If you can't decide, take a vote and follow the majority."

He answered them similarly when they asked him how often it was appropriate for them to go home for a visit. It was then customary in yeshiva high schools for students to spend Shabbat at home every third week. The students debated whether to adopt the custom of the high schools or to extend their stay in yeshiva and go home only once a month. On this matter as well, Rav Amital responded: "You are adults. Decide for yourselves."

Moreover, the students' decisions were binding on their teachers. In those days, many students at post high school *yeshivot* would smoke as they studied. The students of Yeshivat Har Etzion decided right away that smoking would be prohibited in the *beit midrash*. Rav Amital, then a smoker, honored their decision. Whenever he wished to smoke a cigarette, he left the *beit midrash*.

(photo: K. Weiss)

Teaching a class in the old beit midrash (now the Zomet Institute/Makhon Tzomet) in Alon Shvut.

Giving responsibility to the students did not stem from any evasion of responsibility on Rav Amital's part. He insisted on involvement in every decision that he considered important, but also constantly imparted to the students that the yeshiva was theirs and that it was primarily their responsibility to shape it. At the same time, Rav Amital did not want to create a situation in which senior students, "*alter bochrim*" in Yiddish, involved themselves in areas that really were the domain of the administration. As the yeshiva began to expand, the decision was made to appoint a manager to oversee the yeshiva's maintenance staff. A veteran maintenance man complained to the older students about his relative demotion, and these students approached Rav Amital to protest the "injustice" that they felt was done to this man. Rav Amital gave them a stern reprimand for interfering where they did not belong. He explained that *alter bochrim* who intrude into areas outside the purview of their authority can cause the ruin of a yeshiva. Another time a student approached Rav Amital to complain about some aspect of the yeshiva that, in his mind, had to be changed. Rav Amital brought the student over to the window, pointed to a barren hilltop, and said: "You see that desolate *jabla'a* (hilltop)? If you'd like, you can go there and build whatever kind of yeshiva you want. This hilltop is already taken."

The personal responsibility toward which Rav Amital educated his students was not limited only to the yeshiva curriculum. Many times he refused to answer his students' personal questions, out of a desire to teach them responsibility and independence of thought. "I'm not your *chasidishe rebbe*," he constantly reminded them as he declined to answer questions that he thought they should be deciding for themselves. He was known to ridicule the widespread phenomenon of yeshiva students asking their rabbis extraneous questions that have nothing to do with halakha and everything to do with using common sense. Thus, for example, he liked to tell about one young scholar who asked his rabbi whether it was becoming for a man of his station, a Torah scholar, to take out the garbage in his house. "The rabbi permitted it," Rav Amital scoffed.

Even with regard to halakhic questions, Rav Amital tried to teach his students to take personal responsibility by studying the halakhic issue themselves. When a student once asked him a simple question whose answer could be found in any book of halakha, Rav Amital answered him, "Pardon me; I'm not a library." Occasionally, when a student asked him whether a certain activity was permitted or prohibited, Rav Amital would prefer to lead him toward the answer: "Why do you think it's forbidden? Why should it be permitted? Tell me what you yourself think."

Even when he did give a student an answer, he tried not to present it as a communal directive. He sometimes even explicitly asked the student not to publicize the given response, so that it would not be construed as a ruling. He wanted the students to clarify the halakha for themselves; he did not want them to imitate him: "I have no interest in little Amitals," he used to tell them on various occasions.

Although he refused to be a Hasidic rebbe, it did not take long for the students to discover that Rav Amital possessed rebbe-like qualities. His overflowing charisma, rhetorical skill, Hasidic soul and inspiring leadership won him the adoration of his pupils, even if he refused to admit it. Other characteristics that turned him into a reluctant rebbe were the Hasidic tunes that he taught, the stories with which he peppered lectures and communal meals, and of course his penchant for singing and dancing. When he stood at the center of a circle of dancing students, eyes closed, singing solo, he looked, to an observer, exactly like a Hasidic master surrounded by his devotees.

Rav Amital's attitude toward religious ecstasy induced by singing and dancing was ambivalent. On one hand, possessed of a Hasidic soul, he certainly recognized the existence and even importance of religious experience in the service of God. On the other hand, he taught that one could not achieve awe of God through experiential tools alone; service of God demands an intellectual component in addition to the emotional one. Another reservation expressed by Rav Amital about the experiential realm stemmed from his suspicion of the artificialness that often characterizes outward enthusiasm. He frequently spoke with his students about the importance of sincerity in the service of God, and cautioned them against exteriorization and phoniness. It is therefore no wonder that in the view of the students of Yeshivat Har Etzion, the song most identified with Rav Amital is "*vetaher libeinu le'ovdekha be'emet*." His revulsion of anything counterfeit in the service of God also found expression in his critical attitude toward excessive swaying and *shokeling* during prayer. "One could run an electrical generator off of these impressive oscillating movements that I sometimes see students making as they pray," he once told his pupils. He acknowledged the need to sway slightly during prayer to increase intensity, but on the other hand, he noted, one cannot solve the soul's troubles with mere physical movements.

Another phenomenon that Rav Amital frequently criticized, already in the first years of the yeshiva's existence, was the tendency toward halakhic stringency that often characterizes yeshiva students. When a student consulted with him about the proper size of fringed *tzitzit* garment, Rav Amital told him: "The *Mishna Berura* writes that pious individuals adopt a more stringent position. I don't think that I'm on the level of the 'pious individuals' that the *Mishna Berura* is talking about, but you, no doubt, wish to be stringent like them." He expressed opposition to students accepting stringencies, superfluous in his opinion, that ran counter to their family traditions. Thus, for instance, he became furious at a student who had accepted the custom of *gebrokhts* – abstaining for the full week of Pesaḥ from matza that had come into contact with water – and therefore planned to "purify" all of the utensils in his house. Rav Amital contended against this student that such actions equate non-acceptance of these stringencies with eating non-kosher food. More generally, Rav Amital feared that the yeshiva would create different halakhot from those practiced by laypeople, which would in turn cause those in the orbit of the yeshiva to look down upon the lay "*baalebatim*," as had happened in Lithuania. "In Hungary, *baalebatim* were treated with respect as well," he made sure to note in the presence of his students.

* * *

The curriculum selected for the fledgling yeshiva can also shed light on Rav Amital's objectives as he charted its spiritual course. A letter sent to the students prior to their arrival in yeshiva asked them to bring a complete Tanakh, the books of Psalms and the Early Prophets with commentaries, a *Midrash Rabba*, a Torah with commentaries to study the weekly portion, a set of *Mishna Berura* for the study of halakha, and several works of Jewish thought: *Kuzari*, the Rambam's *Shemoneh Perakim*, and Rav Kook's *Orot*.

The emphasis on the study of Tanakh, which eventually became a trademark of Yeshivat Har Etzion, was then considered innovative. At Yeshivat Merkaz HaRav, for the sake of contrast, there were Tanakh classes, but in practice they became classes on Jewish thought and philosophy since they were not overly concerned with understanding the straightforward meaning of the verses or biblical realia. In his initial discourses about the character of the yeshiva, Rav Amital declared that the study of Tanakh would be a significant part of the curriculum. He viewed the study of Tanakh as an integral part of what a yeshiva student ought to study. "The Talmudic debates of Abaye and Rava are not enough to become a Torah scholar," he said. The revolution in Tanakh study wrought by Yeshivat Har Etzion and the affiliated Herzog College was the brainchild of R. Yoel Bin-Nun. Yet Rav Amital provided its impetus and the legitimacy by giving the study of Tanakh pride of place in his yeshiva.

From the outset, the yeshiva's classes in Jewish thought prominently featured the related philosophies of the *Kuzari,* the Maharal, and Rav Kook. Rav Amital himself taught classes on the *Kuzari,* the Rambam's *Shemoneh Perakim,* and the philosophy of Rav Kook. His classes were unique in their existential and personal approach. He always made sure to connect highly theoretical ideas to concrete reality. R. Uzi Friedlich, a member of the yeshiva's first class, arrived after a year studying at Yeshivat Merkaz HaRav. He describes significant differences between the Jewish thought classes at Merkaz HaRav and Rav Amital's classes:

> R. Zvi Yehuda Kook's classes frequently spoke about the people of Israel as a collective entity; I didn't always understand his language. When I heard Rav Amital's first *Kuzari* lesson, it was like a cold drink for a thirsty soul. When he spoke about the king of the Khazars, who was informed in a dream that his intentions were noble but his actions lacking, Rav Amital addressed man's thirst for God. I sensed that this was exactly what I had been missing at Merkaz – attention to man and his personal relationship with God. The Jewish collective is certainly important, but it must be approached by way of the individual and personal. Rav Amital represented a different doctrine, one with its feet on the ground and with a human face. He taught us to use our own words even when expressing ideas in the name of Rav Kook or the Maharal. He would tell us: "If you're studying the Maharal and you sense that you grasp it, try formulating the idea in your own words.

Don't mindlessly recite the ideas. If you don't understand – say so!" Rav Amital himself was not ashamed to occasionally admit this about himself.

* * *

In addition to Rav Amital, the yeshiva faculty that first year included R. Yehuda Shaviv, Yoel Bin-Nun, and Ḥanan Porat, who taught in the yeshiva in addition to his capacity as secretary of Kibbutz Kfar Etzion. Initially, there was a single daily Talmud class, taught by Rav Amital. It soon became clear, however, that the student body was too diverse for a single *shiur*. Ten days after studies commenced, Yeshayahu Yeḥieli wrote in his diary: "The situation in Rav Amital's *shiur* has recently taken a turn for the worse; the outstanding students participate in the thrusts and parries while the simpletons struggle to follow the discussion and remain attentive. For that reason, it was decided to split the group in two, and from now on R. Yehuda Shaviv will also deliver a regular *shiur* in Gemara." R. Shaviv had arrived from the Kollel at Yeshivat Kerem B'Yavneh to serve as an instructor in the new yeshiva.

Yoel Bin-Nun served as resident advisor and his wife Esther as house mother; together, they became the first and only family to move to Kfar Etzion because of the yeshiva. The Amital family never lived near the yeshiva. During the first few years, the official reason was the Amital girls' education, as they attended schools in Jerusalem. Yet nothing changed even after they graduated. In truth, Rav Amital wished to separate the yeshiva from his home life. He was concerned that the yeshiva's strong physical presence in his home would disrupt his family life. On a personal level, he wished to maintain some independence and not get completely sucked in to the yeshiva's routine. Rav Amital's daughters say that it was important to their father that he lived in a community among *baalebatim* (laymen). Rav Amital's positive attitude toward *baalebatim* was made manifest on various occasions.

Although they never moved to Kfar Etzion, the Amital family spent every second Shabbat there with the yeshiva, which required no small amount of dedication. Rabbanit Amital describes those first Shabbatot as a special experience: "We bunked in one large and cold room that had mold on the walls. We slept on cots arranged side-by-side. The bathrooms were outdoor. Yet I never felt one bit like I was suffering or sacrificing, because I loved the idea of the yeshiva. I am incapable of describing those Shabbatot as harsh because I enjoyed them very much."

Rav Amital was aware of the price paid by the young Bin-Nun family for living so close to the yeshiva. He also understood that it was not easy for Esther Bin-Nun as the only woman on the staff. He made sure to take stock of her needs and offered to shop for her in Jerusalem. When Esther complained, as house mother, that the students left their rooms messy, he reprimanded them. Once he even posted a note on the bulletin board informing the students that if their tidiness and cleanliness did not improve starting Sunday, he would come clean their rooms.

* * *

In early March 1969, the ministerial committee assigned to examine the yeshiva decided to recommend to the government the construction of a permanent yeshiva building on the hill with the lone oak. It was also decided not to publicize the recommendation yet. The problem that the

Celebrating Purim at the yeshiva.

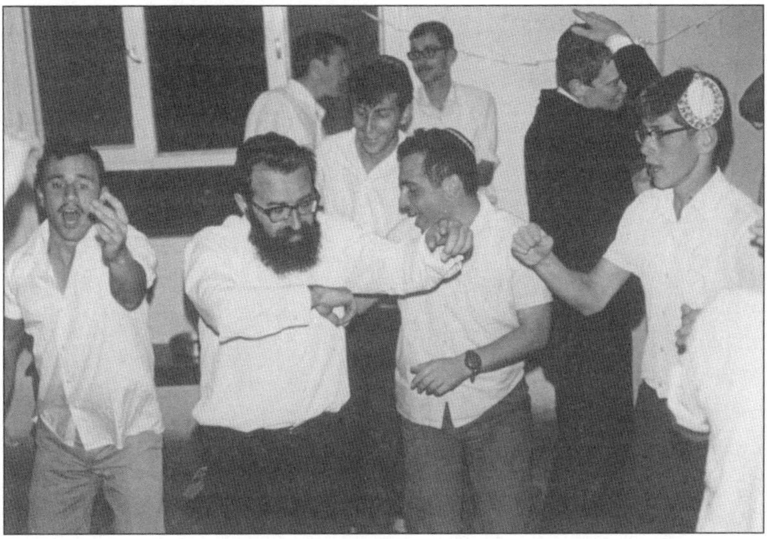

Celebrating Purim at the yeshiva.

government faced was that in order to execute the committee's decision it first had to expropriate lands where there had been no Jewish settlement prior to the fall of the Gush in 1948. The political ramifications of expropriating Arab lands to establish Jewish settlements delayed the decision. The yeshiva's contract with the kibbutz expired in February 1969, but it remained in Kfar Etzion.

The first Purim celebrated in the yeshiva showed the students new facets of their Rosh Yeshiva's colorful personality. During the lead-up to the festival, the boys and their teachers deliberated how to celebrate Purim in a *hesder yeshiva,* and how they would ensure that the joyous atmosphere would differ sufficiently from the jovial ambience of Purim celebrations in yeshiva high school. Yehuda Schwartz, a member of the first class, described in his diary how Rav Amital reacted to his students' misgivings: "We don't need to plan anything. We don't need to wonder whether or not this or that '*shtick*' will work. We don't rejoice in order to make the *shtick* work. We need to learn to rejoice out of inner elevation and a palpable sense of the miracle." The students had again been shown that for Rav Amital, divine service should be natural and not artificial. There is no need to plan too much, and indeed true joy cannot be planned. When the Holiday began, the students discovered that Rav Amital knew how to drink and become intoxicated. The joy that he exuded immediately became the focus of the celebration. Yeshayahu Yeḥieli described the events of that Purim in one brief line of his diary: "Rav Amital and Yedaya are going wild, and we, following them, are going all around the farm." Yehuda Schwartz wrote: "At the end of the meal, Rav Amital got up on someone's shoulders. We all closed our eyes and danced." Later, Schwartz recounts, Rav Amital went to put a drunk student to bed. The next day, Shushan Purim, all of the students joined Rav Amital for the Holiday feast at his home in Jerusalem. That too was a special experience whose centerpiece was an inebriated Rav Amital. It became a yeshiva tradition. Over time, the students discovered that Rav Amital appreciated a strong drink not only on Purim. A particularly good mood or even a mild dolefulness constituted ample justification, from his perspective, for a shot or two.

* * *

Soon after Pesaḥ, the ministerial committee visited the designated hilltop for an on-site examination of the possibility of putting the yeshiva

At the Purim feast. To the left of Rav Amital is Ḥanan Porat. To his right is Rav Moshe Levinger.

there. Rav Amital joined the ministers during their inspection. Encouraged by their visit, he returned to the students and announced to them, in the name of Minister Yigal Allon, that "progress is expected in the near future." On the night of Yom HaAtzma'ut, Rav Amital delivered an emotional speech. He explicated verses from the Song of Songs and spoke about how a "pleasing time," the time of redemption, had arrived. Addressing the momentous events of the past generation, he grasped his beard and cried out: "I don't have a single gray hair in my beard, and yet I have witnessed the Holocaust and the rebirth with my own eyes!" His emotion-laden words astonished the young men. They sensed that this man in front of them experienced these events with a rare intensity that they had never encountered before. During those first years, Rav Amital discussed the Holocaust only in the context of the rapid shift to rebirth. He never described in detail what he had undergone and never addressed questions of faith post-Holocaust. He only emphasized the magnitude of the miracle by virtue of which he was saved. Ḥanan Porat tells of a particular discourse delivered by Rav Amital in which he applied the verse from Lamentations (3:1), "I am the man who has known affliction," telling the students: "Had someone told me in my youth, when I was in a labor camp, that in another x number of years I would be a Rosh Yeshiva in Eretz Yisrael, in the liberated Gush Etzion, I would tell him that one must not mock another like that, even about something imaginary. And yet, here I stand before you today, fulfilling that imaginary script."

Yehoshua Cohen, a former Stern Gang member, a member of Kibbutz Sdeh Boker, and a friend of Israel's first Prime Minister David Ben-Gurion, was at that time temporarily staying in Kfar Etzion to promote an idea that he had pitched to the young kibbutz – opening a field school there. Cohen became friends with some of the yeshiva students, notably Yoel Bin-Nun and Ya'akov Medan, and spoke a common language with Rav Amital as well. On the other hand, Cohen could not wait for the yeshiva to leave the kibbutz, since the buildings occupied by the yeshiva were designated as the lodgings of the field school that he hoped to establish. On April 28, 1969, Cohen reported to the students, based on his sources in the government, that the government had decided at that stage not to establish the regional center and the yeshiva on the hill with the tree. This information generated a sense of despair among the students. Yoel Bin-Nun recalls that Rav Amital assembled the students and, for the first time, raised the idea of giving up the fight and closing the yeshiva until the decision was changed. The students were dumbstruck, and some of them rose up in opposition. Bin-Nun proposed that they take over the site without a permit. It had not been long since members of the Beitar movement were forcibly removed from Mt. Gerizim and Shilo. Bin-Nun planned to set up a tent camp on the hilltop in order to exert public pressure on the government to approve their move there. Rav Amital viewed this proposal as a futile demonstration. He was not prepared to fight against the government. "In my opinion," Rav Bin-Nun propounds, "already then one could discern Rav Amital's opposition to messianic–ideological efforts to settle Jews in Judea and Samaria, of the type developed several years later by the Gush Emunim movement. I believe that he even saw in my proposal the first signs of a dangerous anarchism. I, however, viewed setting up an encampment on that hill-top as a legitimate protest measure. One might say that I identified our differences through that debate and realized that I speak a different language. Nevertheless, he did not try to shoot down my plan. He agreed to go home and wait to see how things developed."

Ultimately, Yoel Bin-Nun's pirate plan was never realized. Rav Amital obtained a reassuring letter from Minister Zeraḥ Warhaftig according to which the ministerial committee actually decided in favor and passed the recommendation on to the government. A cabinet vote was expected soon.

Even before the proposal was put before the government, Moshko managed to add to the text – which until that point addressed only the approval to build a yeshiva – the significant words "regional center." It is doubtful that the ministers who voted in favor of that draft could foresee that these two words, which enabled the construction of Alon Shvut, would be such an important step in the development of Gush Etzion.

To ensure a majority in the cabinet vote, Rav Amital and Yedaya Hacohen paid a visit to the leader and senior government representative of the Ḥerut party, Menaḥem Begin, and confirmed that he would support and vote in favor of the proposal. Begin did not know either of them but still welcomed them late one evening into a narrow corridor of his home in Tel Aviv. He listened to them, and as he escorted them to the door, he reassured them: "You have my voice and my vote." The proposal won a majority, and the students received word that the construction work would soon commence.

The students celebrated Yom Yerushalayim, the anniversary of Jerusalem's liberation and reunification, on 28 Iyar of that year together with the members of Kfar Etzion in the kibbutz dining room. Rav Amital again spoke about the events of the Six Day War in terms of redemption. *Shir HaShirim* was read, Ḥanan Porat told stories about his experiences in the battle to liberate Jerusalem. Those present were surprised in the middle of the party by the sudden appearance of the Chief Rabbi of the Israel Defense Forces, R. Shlomo Goren. That evening, the students got the privilege of hearing Rav Goren talk about his participation in the conquest of Ḥevron. Rav Amital described that speech with a smile. "Rav Goren told us how he single-handedly conquered Ḥevron; the army did not show up until a few hours later."

Over the years, Rav Goren and Rav Amital developed different approaches to Yom Yerushalayim and the Six Day War. Rav Goren thought that the primary achievement of the war was the reunification of Jerusalem and the liberation of the territories of Judea, Samaria, and Gaza. Rav Amital, on the other hand, saw salvation and rescue, from death to life, as the great miracle of the Six Dar War.

Chapter Four

A Yeshiva Establishes a Community

> *When I established the yeshiva, the architect designed a* beit midrash *like a concert hall, without windows. I told her the story of a certain righteous man: A shofar blast was heard throughout the town, and the townsfolk thought that* Mashiaḥ *had arrived. The* Tzaddik *stuck his nose out the window, sniffed slightly, and proclaimed, "No; when* Mashiaḥ *comes, we will be able to feel it in the air."* A beit midrash *needs windows so that we can sense* Mashiaḥ's *arrival.*

On Rosh Ḥodesh Elul, 5729 (August 15, 1969), the yeshiva inaugurated its second year in Kibbutz Kfar Etzion. *Elul zeman,* the brief semester that extends from the beginning of Elul until after Yom Kippur, is the most intense time of year in yeshivot as it builds to the crescendo of the High Holidays. This was Yeshivat Har Etzion's first *Elul zeman* and the first opportunity for the students to get to know Rav Amital during the Days of Awe. In every subsequent year, Rav Amital delivered inspirational discourses on three occasions: on the Saturday night before Rosh HaShana, prior to the first recitation of the penitential *Seliḥot* prayers; on Rosh HaShana; and on Yom Kippur just before the closing *Ne'ila* prayer. His *Seliḥot* discourse tended to focus on the humility and self-abnegation required of man. "Needy and destitute, we knock at Your door," Rav Amital said at one of those discourses, "each of us must develop a sincere sense of being needy and impoverished, a true feeling of inadequacy, and then resolve to improve and perfect something in ourselves." On the second day of Rosh HaShana, prior to shofar-blowing, Rav Amital often discussed the Binding of Yitzḥak, specifically emphasizing the motif of Avraham's suffering and the inner turmoil that raged within him on his way to offering his son. "One who considers the Binding superficially would conclude that it constitutes nothing but the silent and submissive acceptance of the divine command… all at once, everything is dismissed, everything evaporates: fatherly love, compassion, humanity, morality… I believe that such a conception is completely erroneous. I believe that Avraham's love for his son never disappeared and never wavered. On the contrary: its intensity was a condition of his offering." Rav Amital liberally cited midrashic comments from *Yalkut Shimoni* that dramatically describe Avraham as one who "was swimming in tears." He brought further evidence of his view that Avraham did not accept God's decree with equanimity from the realm of halakha. In the past, several additional blessings were added to the *Amida* on public fast days. One of them contained the following formulation: "He Who answered our father Avraham on Mt. Moriah will answer you and hear the sound of your cries today. Blessed are You, God, Redeemer of Israel." Rav Amital viewed this as proof that Avraham never made peace with the commandment to sacrifice his son and continued to cry out and beg for the cancellation of the decree.

Rav Amital regularly opened his pre-*Ne'ila* homily with a midrash on *Shir HaShirim* 5:5 that appears in *Kad HaKemaḥ* by Rabbeinu Baḥya:

> "I rose to let in my beloved; my hands dripped myrrh – my fingers, flowing myrrh – upon the handles of the lock." "I rose to let in my beloved" – this refers to the Shaḥarit prayer. "My hands dripped myrrh" – refers to the Musaf prayer. "My fingers, flowing

myrrh" – refers to the Minḥa prayer. "Upon the handles of the lock (*man'ul*)" – this is *Ne'ila*.

The passage in *Shir HaShirim* describes how the beloved woman procrastinates and misses the time of favor during which her beloved knocks at the door of her home and the gates of her heart, begging to be let in. During these sermons, Rav Amital often spoke of the need to open one's heart during the last moment of Yom Kippur, before the gates of heaven closed. "God is knocking at the door to man's heart, asking to be let in," he said to his students in those final moments of the Days of Awe.

In addition to the discourses, there were the High Holidays prayers that Rav Amital led, stirring the hearts of his students: Musaf on both days of Rosh HaShana, Kol Nidrei and Ma'ariv, Musaf, and *Ne'ila* on Yom Kippur. Over time, Rav Amital's *nusaḥ*, the singular way in which he sang and chanted the prayers, became the model and ideal High Holiday prayer among his students. Many alumni recount that many years after they left the yeshiva, Rav Amital's prayers – clear, sincere, and deeply connected to his audience – continue to resound in their hearts each year. "In addition to his pleasant voice, warmth, and the fact that he *davened* from the heart," says Dr. Tovah Lichtenstein, the wife of Rav Aharon Lichtenstein, "Rav Amital did not include many tunes, and thus his *nusaḥ* connected more easily to the prayer of generations of Jews everywhere who *davened* like this." Some of Rav Amital's students, who themselves eventually led the High Holiday prayers as *sheliḥei tzibbur*, adopted his *nusaḥ*, imparting it to many others in the process.

Rami Yanai, a student during the early years of the yeshiva and himself a *shali'aḥ tzibbur*, once tried to characterize the singularity of Rav Amital's prayer: "Rav Amital's prayers offered the rare opportunity to peer deep into his soul. His prayer came from so deep inside that the difference between what was inside and his exterior was erased. This is what gave it its special power."

* * *

That same Elul of 5729 saw the beginning of Kibbutz Rosh Tzurim, the second Gush Etzion community. Two months later, in Ḥeshvan 5730 (October/November 1969), the cornerstones for a regional center and

(photo: K. Weiss)

Groundbreaking ceremony for Yeshivat Har Etzion and Alon Shvut.
Seated (from right): Welfare Minister Yosef Burg, Housing Minister Mordekhai Bentov, Interior Minister Moshe Ḥayyim Shapira, Deputy Prime Minister and Immigrant Absorption Minister Yigal Allon, MK Michael Hasani. Standing: Rav Amital.

(photo: K. Weiss)

Ḥanan Porat, representing Kibbutz Kfar Etzion, speaks at the groundbreaking ceremony.

for the yeshiva's permanent home were laid amid great fanfare. At the ceremony, it was officially announced that the regional center around the yeshiva would be called Alon Shvut, meaning "oak of return," after the lone oak tree nearby. Representing the government at the ceremony were Deputy Prime Minister and Immigrant Absorption Minister Yigal Allon, Housing Minister Mordekhai Bentov, and two ministers of the National-Religious Party: Interior Minister Moshe Ḥayyim Shapira and Welfare Minister Yosef Burg. Minister Yigal Allon, of the Labor party, said at the ceremony that the reconstruction of the Gush "is the most moral and constructive form of revenge in the repository of Jewish values... military presence is no substitute for civilian presence." He characterized the new communities emerging beyond the Green Line as a "set of great acts" that "reinforces Jewish presence along vital frontiers and at strategic junctures." Minister Bentov, who belonged to the left wing Mapam party, said to those present: "You are blessed with outstanding youths who are willing to undertake pioneering tasks." Bentov made it known at the ceremony that his ministry would allocate two million liras for the construction of Gush Etzion. Rav Amital thanked those who helped establish the yeshiva and the regional center and posited in his speech that "the order of the day is to expand the notion of security, to integrate it with Jewish values, and to find the appropriate balance between physical and spiritual power." He also declared that the time had come for a "*mamlakhti*" yeshiva, one in which the students viewed Torah study and army service as going hand-in-hand.

Since the ceremony took place just two weeks prior to the elections for the seventh Knesset, the National-Religious Party fully exploited it for political purposes. The party bussed in hundreds of Bnei Akiva yeshiva high school students, transforming the ceremony into a show of political strength. Rav Amital was revolted by the political nature of the gathering. He felt that the religious politicians unjustly stole the show from the yeshiva. His treatment at the hands of the organizers served as a painful reinforcement of this feeling: on a raised platform next to the dais sat government ministers and Knesset members. The organizers did not reserve a seat for Rav Amital, the head of the yeshiva in whose honor the ceremony was ostensibly held. The humiliation reached its peak when a *ḥaredi* rabbi arrived and was immediately given a place of honor on the platform.

Rav Amital's reaction was not long in coming: he cut off all ties to the wheeler-dealers who organized the event, for better or worse.

Ḥanan Porat, who later became a Knesset member as part of the National-Religious Party, also opposed the political exploitation of the ceremony. Representing the members of Kibbutz Kfar Etzion, Porat expressed his satisfaction that the rebuilding of the Gush won support from various political quarters. "Thank God, Gush Etzion is not a narrow NRP issue!" Porat exclaimed, incurring the wrath of the NRP ministers. Rav Amital, on the other hand, appreciated Porat's statement.

* * *

The yeshiva continued in its temporary quarters in Kfar Etzion through the winter of 5730. That Adar (February/March 1970), Prime Minister Golda Meir visited the yeshiva. Rav Amital, who wanted to accelerate the construction of the yeshiva's permanent building in Alon Shvut, requested that the government invest in the students of Yeshivat Har Etzion, who combine military service with Torah study, no less than it invested in Naḥal settlements, like Kalya on the northern shore of the Dead Sea. "What these students produce will be no less important than the settlements that will flower as a result of the Dead Sea outposts," he claimed. Golda agreed with him but maintained that the yeshiva must first lay the groundwork thoroughly. "I truly hope that we can do that," Rav Amital replied.

Despite promises, the new buildings in Alon Shvut were not ready by Pesaḥ, and the yeshiva began its summer session in Kfar Etzion. Given the increasing pressure from the kibbutz to vacate the yeshiva buildings so that they could turn it into a guest house, Moshko proposed that the yeshiva temporarily move to the distant campus of Yeshivat Or Etzion. The boys completely dismissed the proposal. They were concerned that the temporary relocation would become permanent and that the yeshiva would never return to Gush Etzion. Yoel Bin-Nun again gravitated toward a pre-emptive move to Alon Shvut, whatever the cost. He recalls that this time Rav Amital agreed with him, though he conditioned the move on the completion of the floors of the new buildings.

The day before Yom Yerushalayim 5730, Bnei Akiva yeshiva high school students came to tour Gush Etzion. Rav Amital met them by the lone oak and told them: "It is said about our patriarch Avraham that on his way to sacrifice Yitzḥak he 'saw the place from afar.' The Midrash explains that Avraham saw a cloud covering the mountain, and he asked Yitzḥak and his servants if they too saw the cloud. Yitzḥak saw it, but Yishmael and Eliezer did not. Can you see the cloud on the mountain?" Rav Amital asked the students, "Do you believe that there will be a beautiful yeshiva on this mountain?" The students did not fully understand Rav Amital, who was pointing to a barren hilltop. "I see a vibrant yeshiva here, with dozens of students milling about," he told them confidently.

The day before Shavuot, Rav Amital announced to the yeshiva that they were leaving Kfar Etzion. A similar notice was given to the kibbutz administration. On 20 Sivan 5730 (June 24, 1970), the yeshiva moved to its new home and thus founded the community of Alon Shvut. That afternoon, the students convened in the new *beit midrash* and affixed a *mezuza* to its door. "We recalled the stories about the tower and stockade[1] communities," explained Yoel Bin-Nun, who was in charge of all of the move's logistical aspects. "Of course, there was no real comparison. Yet we felt that we were but a drop in the bucket of a much grander operation: the revival of Jewish settlement in the Land of Israel. The added aspect of Gush Etzion gave a reddish tinge to that revival – the tinge of the sun rising, after it had set nineteen years earlier." The community of Alon Shvut, founded by the yeshiva, now includes seven-hundred families, including the families of three of Rav Amital's daughters.

1. Tower and Stockade: Settlement method used during the period of the British Mandate. Since the establishment of new Jewish communities was restricted by the Mandatory authorities but existing ones were not subject to dismantling, these settlements were hurriedly constructed, often overnight.

Chapter Five

A Two-Headed Yeshiva

A Jew once knocked on the door of the Maggid of Mezeritch. The Maggid asked, "Who's there?" The answer came: "It is I." The Maggid was shocked that a Jew could so simply say "It is I." "It is I? How is it possible to say such a thing?" He opened the door and invited the man in. He asked: "Have you eaten yet?" The man shook his head. The Maggid told the Jew: "Go to such-and-such place, several miles away from here, and eat there." After an arduous journey, the Jew reached the designated place, dusty and worn out. Just then, a wedding was taking place in the village, and as usual a place was set up for paupers to take part in the feast. The Jew joined the paupers and feasted with them. At the end of the meal, it was noticed that a silver spoon was missing. Suspicion immediately centered on that Jew, and they yelled at him, "Thief! Thief!" The Jew responded: "Not I! Not I!" He eventually was able to run away from them and start making his way back to the Maggid. The whole way back he was thinking about why the Maggid sent him to that feast. When he finally arrived at the Maggid's home, he knocked on the door, and the Maggid again inquired, "Who's there?" The Jew wished to answer "It is I," as he had always done, but he suddenly stopped himself and instead responded, "It is not I." Through the beatings and suffering that he had sustained, the lesson penetrated his heart: there is only one "I" – "Him."

During the yeshiva's second year, Rav Amital asked R. Aharon Lichtenstein, a senior Talmud teacher and the head of the Kollel at Yeshiva University in New York, to join him as co-Rosh Yeshiva at Yeshivat Har Etzion.

The model of multiple simultaneous Rashei Yeshiva had already existed in the yeshiva world. In Yeshivat Ḥevron, where Rav Amital had studied, three Rashei Yeshiva, the three sons-in-law of the prior Rosh Yeshiva, R. Moshe Mordekhai Epstein, all served together. Their co-appointment was mainly designed to prevent family tension and battles of succession. But Rav Amital's decision was extraordinary since he was under no such constraints. He explained his bold step as follows: "I never thought that I could run a yeshiva alone, and I had heard that Rav Lichtenstein is a great Torah scholar of sterling character."

Rav Lichtenstein was born in France in 1933. In 1940, a few months after the Nazi occupation, his family escaped to the United States. He was a close disciple of R. Joseph B. Soloveitchik, who ordained him as a rabbi. He later married Rav Soloveitchik's daughter, Tovah. After completing a doctorate in English Literature at Harvard, he took a position at Yeshiva University. In addition to his Talmud lectures and heading the Kollel, he also taught literature.

Already in 1968, R. Ḥayyim Druckman, the Rosh Yeshiva of Yeshivat Or Etzion, told Rav Lichtenstein that a Rosh Yeshiva was sought for the planned Yeshivat Har Etzion, but it was not a good time: a year earlier, his mother-in-law had passed away, and the young family did not want to leave Rav Soloveitchik alone so soon after he was widowed. Two years later, in the summer of 1970, the time was right.

Rav Amital sent Rav Lichtenstein a handwritten letter on simple lined paper. He did not mention his own role in the yeshiva. Rav Amital thought that it would be impossible to offer a Torah figure of Rav Lichtenstein's caliber anything less than the position of Rosh Yeshiva. As such, he agreed to step aside and give up his share, leaving the position of Rosh Yeshiva to Rav Lichtenstein alone.

Rav Amital's son Yoel recounts that he was shocked when he saw the letter. He knew that his father intended to invite another rabbi to join him, but this total self-effacement, as though he did not exist, astonished Yoel. "I asked him, 'Abba, do you really intend to do what you wrote in the letter?' He answered in the affirmative." Yedaya Hacohen also did not understand Rav Amital's actions. "I did not understand his openness. I thought that he was shooting himself in the foot with that offer."

Rav Lichtenstein was very impressed by Rav Amital's generous offer. He also understood from the letter that, if he wished, he could serve as the sole Rosh Yeshiva. Nevertheless, once he came to Israel and met with Rav Amital, he insisted that if he would accept the offer, they would serve as co-Rashei Yeshiva. "Very few people in the Torah world have done what Rav Amital did," Rav Lichtenstein said, "I think he was very clever; he understood that if he added me, I would not be taking away half of his kingdom. Rather, the two of us together would comprise the kingdom."

Rav Lichtenstein visited Israel in the winter, when the yeshiva was still on Kibbutz Kfar Etzion. He delivered a *shiur* to the students and made a strong impression on them. So that Rav Lichtenstein, too, would be impressed, Rav Amital asked Eliyahu Blumenzweig, now the Rosh Yeshiva of the *hesder* yeshiva in Yeruḥam and then one of the most outstanding and sharpest students in that first class, to engage Rav Lichtenstein in erudite conversation (in yeshiva-speak, to "talk in learning"). Rav Amital then took his guest to a spot overlooking the barren hilltop and told him that the yeshiva would be there soon. Rav Lichtenstein was impressed, but being cautious and deliberate by nature, he did not rush to give an answer. He planned to return in the summer with the rest of his family and to make a joint decision with them. For Rav Amital, the decision-making process was always quick and resolute, free of prolonged indecision. Over the years, he learned to cope with his colleague's more measured style of decision-making.

Closer to the summer, Rav Lichtenstein received another offer, from Yeshivat HaKotel, a *hesder yeshiva* that had been established after the Six Day War in the Jewish Quarter of Jerusalem's Old City. He decided to take a closer look at both yeshivot over the summer and then make a decision. All through the summer, Rav Lichtenstein gave three *shiurim* a week at each yeshiva. Yeshivat HaKotel had clear advantages over Yeshivat Har Etzion: it was more economically established and was safer, from security and national perspectives. Despite it all, at the end of the summer Rav Lichtenstein decided to join Yeshivat Har Etzion. The main reason for his decision to join the new yeshiva in the Gush was Rav Amital, who had made a very strong impression on him. "I was enthralled by Rav Amital's personality," Rav Lichtenstein confesses, "beyond his intelligence and his greatness in Torah, he had a captivating personality. I'm saying this as someone who does not have such a personality." Rav Lichtenstein's one abiding concern was that

(photo: Reuven Kopitchinsky)

A yeshiva with two heads: Forty years of partnership with Rav Aharon Lichtenstein.

the students' surplus of pioneering spirit would come at the expense of the caliber of their Torah study. "I considered their pioneering attitude to be a double-edged sword. On the one hand, it was intriguing to participate in building up an area of the Land of Israel. On the other hand, I feared that the yeshiva would attract students whose primary interest was building the land and not studying in yeshiva." Rav Amital also said that from his perspective the main challenge was to establish and strengthen the yeshiva. He set a goal of imparting this lesson to the students: with all the importance of pioneer spirit, the main spiritual challenge was Torah study.

Even after reaching a decision, it was another year before Rav Lichtenstein joined the yeshiva in practice. He wanted to put his affairs in order in the US and prepare well for moving a family of six to Israel. By the time he arrived and settled in Jerusalem, the yeshiva was already in Alon Shvut.

For nearly forty years, Rav Amital and Rav Lichtenstein co-headed the yeshiva, demonstrating an amazing and awe-inspiring partnership. Though they would never have admitted it, the reason for the success of the co-Rosh Yeshiva model was undoubtedly their deep and innate humility. Their modesty found expression in the genuine mutual respect they had for each other even behind closed doors. The Rashei Yeshiva themselves explained the secret of their success as having to do with the differences in their personalities, which created a healthy harmony and prevented tension. Rav Amital, typically, explained these personality differences pithily: "We are very different. We have completely different backgrounds. He has a doctorate, while my general education was all of four years of grade school. I thought it would be a good combination for the yeshiva." Unsurprisingly, Rav Lichtenstein's explanation is more detailed: "Each of us brought something different to the table. I would not have presumed to compete with Rav Amital in his areas of strength. He was warm and clever; he combined vision with practicality. In terms of his learning, he was fully conversant in the areas of practical halakhic rulings and responsa. I am not. Another element of his personality, which also manifested itself in his learning, was his propensity for flashes of halakhic and Talmudic insight. I am more stable. My method of study is more organized. I am more cautious by nature and in my mode of expression. He had warmth and exuberance, songs and stories. He could also occasionally erupt like a volcano and soon thereafter be cool and composed again. That type of intensity does not characterize me. With regard to Torah study, we were not merely complementary, we made each other better."

Rav Amital learning in the beit midrash.

Above all, the fertile learning environment that they created benefited the students, who were presented with two different models of Torah study. The difference between the Talmud lessons of the two Rashei Yeshiva was obvious from the outset. One prominent difference pertained to the importance of the *shiur* (lecture) in the yeshiva's overall objectives. Rav Lichtenstein came from an American "Brisker" background in which the *shiur* is the centerpiece of the curriculum. A student at a Brisker yeshiva knows that his teacher has an articulated body of ideas that he wishes to impart to his students, and all study revolves around the *shiur* and its contents. For that reason, Rav Lichtenstein's *shiurim* have always taken place relatively frequently. At Yeshiva University's Kollel, Rav Lichtenstein delivered a *shiur* daily, and he continued to do so at Yeshivat Har Etzion. Rav Amital, on the other hand, came from the Lithuanian-Hungarian *beit midrash*. In Yeshivat Ḥevron, his alma mater, *shiur* did not occupy a central place, meeting infrequently and garnering sparse attendance.

The content of Rav Amital's and Rav Lichtenstein's *shiurim* differed greatly as well. Rav Amital felt that no *shiur klali,* weekly lecture to the entire yeshiva, was justified without some novel point, a *ḥiddush*. Once, he even cancelled the *shiur* at the last moment because he discovered a rationale which undermined the *ḥiddush* that he planned to propose. He generally based his *shiurim* on the works of recent sages – the *Aḥaronim* – and on responsa. Rav Lichtenstein's tightly structured *shiurim,* on the other hand, presented the students with a highly organized and comprehensive overview of the topic the yeshiva was then studying. His sources were the works of the medieval sages, the *Rishonim,* and the main part of the *shiur* was the penetrating analysis of the various positions of the *Rishonim,* and sharpening subtle differences between their respective understandings of the issue.

The different styles of *shiur* had ramifications for their length as well. Whereas Rav Lichtenstein's regular Talmud *shiur* lasted close to two hours – longer for a *shiur klali* – Rav Amital's *shiur klali* generally ended an hour to an hour and a half after it began. His other *shiurim* could end after less than half an hour. "Whatever can be said in an hour, can be said in half an hour," he would often quip.

The variance in the length of their respective *shiurim* further attests to their different demeanors. Rav Amital did not speak long and also educated his students to speak concisely. One Shabbat, a student got up at a meal and said a short idea related to the weekly *parasha*. Afterward, Rav Amital said to his students, "That's how one should speak, short and sweet." The following Shabbat was Rav Lichtenstein's turn to spend in yeshiva. Again a student said a short *devar Torah* at a meal. Rav Lichtenstein, however, told the student that his speech was too short, that a *devar Torah* should be structured and organized, from top to bottom.

One time, Rav Lichtenstein needed his colleague's brevity. At the bar mitzva of one of his sons, he asked Rav Amital to speak instead of him. "But it's your son!" Rav Amital pointed out, astonished. "Yes," replied Rav Lichtenstein, "but the family wants me to speak briefly, and I am simply incapable."

Even though Rav Lichtenstein's *shiurim* were very long, the students grew very fond of them, often fonder than they were of Rav Amital's *shiurim*. Predictably, this did not bother Rav Amital.

The contrast between Rav Lichtenstein's and Rav Amital's methods had ramifications in other aspects of the yeshiva as well. One of the dilemmas that the yeshiva faced when it moved into its permanent building was how the *beit midrash* would be furnished. Would the students study at desks, like in a classroom or library, or would they use *shtenders* (lecterns) as was practiced in the European *yeshivot*. Rav Amital considered installing the familiar *shtenders*, but Rav Lichtenstein insisted on desks and tables. For him, it was not merely a question of style; his method of learning required the immediate availability of reference material, including entire miniature sets of the Babylonian Talmud and Rambam's *Mishneh Torah*. In the old *beit midrash* there were only *shtenders*, which could accommodate only the single volume of text being studied. Rav Lichtenstein had a hard time without other volumes nearby, and so he sat near the *bima*, the table used for public Torah reading, in lieu of a desk.

Ultimately, Rav Lichtenstein's request was accepted, but only because the issue was more important to him than it was to Rav Amital. This was their unwritten agreement: in the event of a difference of opinion, if the issue was more important to one than to the other, the other would acquiesce. Rav Lichtenstein saw similarities between the unwritten agreements that governed his relationship with Rav Amital and the relationship between two spouses.

* * *

Nevertheless, Rav Amital was very concerned about other matters of furniture and décor.

When the new yeshiva building was inaugurated in 1977, and the selection of an ark, curtains, and a *bima* came to the fore, Rav Amital involved himself in every detail. He chose the curtain that would adorn the ark and insisted that the ark and *bima* not be too big.

The disciplines of art and design were never foreign to Rav Amital. Whoever visited the Amital home would be introduced to his love of art. The walls of the home were covered with original portraits that Rav

Rishon LeTziyon Rav Ovadia Yosef and President Ephraim Katzir at the inauguration ceremony for the yeshiva's new beit midrash. To the right of Rav Amital is Moshe (Moshko) Moskovic, the yeshiva's director.

Amital carefully picked out himself. Earlier in his life, he alternated the paintings every now and then, like in a gallery. He acquired most of his art directly from the artist. One portrait of Binyamin Avniel (who served as a Knesset member for the Ḥerut party) was given to him by the artist after he expressed interest in it. He purchased other portraits from an artist in Safed named Bianca Tauber. Tauber was a Holocaust survivor, and in one of the works that Rav Amital bought from her, a blackened tree appears as a symbol for the Jewish people during the Holocaust. Rav Amital also owned art books, and during his visits abroad he visited quite a few museums. His favorite artistic movement was Impressionism. Many students love to mention this hobby of Rav Amital's as evidence that their Rosh Yeshiva knew how to appreciate aesthetics.

* * *

If the furniture was the province of the two Rashei Yeshiva, the exterior magnificence and beauty of the new yeshiva building was the subject of a large disagreement. The building, still home to the yeshiva today, was painstakingly designed by a team of architects, with input from the

Rashei Yeshiva and the administration. It is comprised of a network of integrated and connected buildings – a dining room, offices, classrooms, lobbies, and a library. The student dormitories were designed as pavilions surrounded by well-kept gardens. The crown jewel was the main sanctuary of the yeshiva, the *beit midrash*, visible for miles around. The greatest advocate for building such an impressive campus was Moshko, the yeshiva's director, who felt that the students should be able to study magnificent Torah in a magnificent setting. A visitor touring the yeshiva once asked Moshko why the yeshiva needed a sanctuary as large as a theater. Moshko abruptly responded: "Listen to your own words! People rarely visit the theater, but it warrants a beautiful building. In this yeshiva, people will be studying Torah twenty-four hours a day! Doesn't it deserve the same?" Yet there were students and alumni who did not look favorably on the massive investment of designing new buildings for the yeshiva. Many of them thought that such magnificence and beauty was not becoming of the Torah world. After all, the Mishna in *Avot* (6:4) says about those who study Torah: "This is the path of Torah: Eat bread with salt, drink water in measure, and sleep on the floor." Some of them even boycotted the inauguration ceremony.

(photo: Yosef Cohen)

Yeshivat Har Etzion

Rav Lichtenstein, who certainly appreciated the magnificence of the new building, nevertheless had reservations about the fish ponds that were installed adjacent to the yeshiva. Rav Amital, on the other hand, fully supported Moshko's vision every step of the way. He explained why to his confidant, Yedaya Hacohen: "I saw that this issue was very important to Moshko, so I decided to give him my support. There will be other times when I have to back Rav Lichtenstein and oppose Moshko."

Another significant difference between the two rabbis was their philosophical worldview. Two spiritual giants outlined religious Zionist philosophy in modern times: R. Avraham Yitzḥak Kook and R. Joseph B. Soloveitchik. Rav Lichtenstein is the son-in-law of Rav Soloveitchik and faithful to his teachings, whereas Rav Amital formulated his philosophical worldview in the spirit of Rav Kook's teachings, to which he was attracted even as a youth in Hungary. There are numerous differences between Rav Soloveitchik's dialectical worldview and Rav Kook's harmonious worldview. One such difference pertains to the conception of the State of Israel. Rav Kook's view, as interpreted by most of his students (Rav Kook died before the founding of the state), is that the state is the "beginning of redemption," a significant phase in the messianic process. Rav Soloveitchik, in contrast, described the establishment of the state as a great opportunity, one that was squandered in many respects. During the early years of Yeshivat Har Etzion, Rav Amital often spoke about the establishment of the State of Israel in terms of the messianic redemption. Even after he began to question his own certainties about the redemptive process, it was not because he was gravitating toward Rav Soloveitchik's ideas, but for other reasons, that will be discussed later. Rav Amital viewed himself as a student of R. Ya'akov Moshe Ḥarlap, who was a disciple of Rav Kook. Rav Soloveitchik's teachings never spoke to him and he never related to them in his *shiurim* and discourses. Rav Lichtenstein, as a disciple of Rav Soloveitchik, was skeptical of characterizing the state as the "beginning of redemption." Addressing the messianic atmosphere that prevailed after the Six Day War, he frequently told students – in a somewhat cynical tone – that he had not seen *Mashiaḥ* roaming the streets of Jerusalem. The students had difficulty accepting his position; some of them even engaged in heated debates with him on the issue. Uzi Friedlich, a member of the yeshiva's first class and currently the yeshiva's *mashgi'aḥ ruḥani* (spiritual supervisor), described the students' frustration with Rav Lichtenstein's positions. They went to "complain" about Rav Lichtenstein to Rav Amital, who promised that he would address the issue in one of his discourses. He gave a fiery speech that went directly against Rav Lichtenstein's positions. But the students were still not satisfied; they wanted Rav Amital to call Rav Lichtenstein to order for his views. To this Rav Amital responded: "Rav Lichtenstein is a great man. He should say what he feels he should say. Listen to him, listen to me, and decide for yourselves."

In addition to the vast differences that contributed to their harmony, Rav Amital noted another reason for the success of his partnership with Rav Lichtenstein: "The secret of our success is that we never divided different areas of activity between us. When there is such a division, it creates problems at the boundaries of the different areas. We have no problem of boundaries because we both deal with everything, which suits our personalities." As Rav Lichtenstein described it, "Each of us gravitated toward where he wanted to be."

As a pragmatic thinker, Rav Amital was more involved in making practical administrative decisions for the yeshiva. With his knowledge of the IDF's structure, Rav Amital also took responsibility for issues relating to the students' military service. Rav Lichtenstein's dominance found its expression in the yeshiva's exacting standards of Torah study. He set a very high bar – some have said too high. He did not articulate his high standards by making direct demands on the students, but through personal example; he was always very demanding on himself. His own perfectionism when it came to Torah study radiated outward and affected the students and the environment of the yeshiva as a whole. "The yeshiva benefited from a miracle – Rav Aharon joined it," Rav Amital stated. "If we managed to maintain the primacy of Torah study, it is largely to his credit."

Rav Lichtenstein occasionally felt called upon to safeguard the primacy of Torah study at the yeshiva. Although Rav Amital also frequently spoke to the students about the importance of diligence and industry in their studies, he was by nature more open to other, more practical courses of study within the yeshiva, and was less concerned about their undermining the study of Torah for its own sake. The clearest example of this was the respective attitudes of the two Rashei Yeshiva to Herzog College, the teachers' college that was established as a small institutional affiliate of the yeshiva and became, over time, a large college with a fine reputation. Although Rav Lichtenstein had the stronger academic background of the pair, he actually displayed excessive caution and hesitancy regarding the integration of collegiate studies into the yeshiva curriculum. He supported the establishment of the institute-cum-college and continues to serve as its rector, and yet, at certain critical decision-making points pertaining to the college, his deliberate and conservative character was more in evidence than his academic background.

Discussions about opening a teachers' institute next to the yeshiva began shortly after the yeshiva's establishment. The dearth of teachers with a Torah education and a religious Zionist worldview generated pressure from the religious school system on the *hesder yeshivot* to quickly produce capable teachers. The high expectations of *hesder* alumni came not only from the field of education, but also from other systems that wished to avail themselves of *hesder* graduates.

During those first years, Rav Amital often had to curb the grand expectations that had developed around his students. Shortly after the yeshiva's move to Alon Shvut, it hosted a conference of major religious-Zionist communal figures to discuss its objectives. Yosef Goldschmidt, director of the religious public school system at the Ministry of Education, spoke about the need for religious, yeshiva-educated teachers. Professor William Low (Ze'ev Lev) – the physicist who had recently founded Makhon Lev, a college of technology that included Torah studies – spoke of the need for yeshiva-oriented scientists. A representative of the Chief Rabbinate in attendance spoke of the need for rabbis and rabbinical court judges who had served in the IDF. When everyone was finished, Rav Amital said to them: "I have heard what you have to say. With God's help, all of your expectations will yet be fulfilled. But first let us study Torah." Nevertheless, he did not dismiss overtures from the Ministry of Education, and he saw the importance of opening a teachers' college alongside the yeshiva. Aside from the needs of the education system, the establishment of the teachers' college was another expression of Rav Amital's practical thinking. He certainly placed great ideological value on working in the field of education, but more than that, he wanted his alumni to get jobs. The college allowed the students to complete their years in yeshiva with a teaching certificate, enabling them to join the education system immediately. The teaching certificate also served as a tranquilizer for many of his students' parents, who were loath to see their sons dedicate their best years to the study of Torah for its own sake, without gaining any practical rewards from it. R. Yoel Bin-Nun recalls Rav Amital saying during the yeshiva's first year of existence: "We cannot go to the parents of the students, ask them to support the yeshiva, and then, after five years, turn their sons out of the yeshiva without any sort of certificate." Yet despite his support for the establishment of the college, Rav Amital was adamant that its courses should not come at the expense of the regular yeshiva schedule. This was mainly accomplished by recognizing some of the yeshiva's *shiurim* as college classes as well. Yehuda Schwartz, a member of the yeshiva's first class and later the director of the college for seventeen years, recalls Rav Amital's insistence that the college classes be on a high level: "He said to us, the college faculty, 'Take as much time as you need away from the students, but do good and serious things.' He despised trivial matters. When students came to him to complain that a particular college class was boring and unnecessary, he would fly off the handle. He was furious whenever he got the feeling that time was being wasted on nonsense."

* * *

Rav Amital always exhibited great openness regarding the types of *shiurim* given in the yeshiva. The traditional yeshiva world has an innate fear that foreign ideas will penetrate the *beit midrash* from the academy. R. Uzi Friedlich, *mashgi'aḥ* of the yeshiva, tells how the yeshiva once hosted the father of one of the students, a professor of Jewish thought, and the students asked him to give a *shiur* on the topic of kabbalistic doctrine: "It was during the yeshiva's early years, and Kabbala was outside our purview; it was a deep and serious discipline, not to be studied lightly. I was concerned that as a result of the *shiur* students would be attracted to philosophical studies at the university. I shared my concerns with Rav Amital. 'Don't worry,' he assuaged me, 'our crowd knows full well how to discern quality. If the *shiur* is good, then great! If not, it won't impress them.'"

Another time, some of the yeshiva's older students asked Rav Amital to teach them the Rambam's *Guide of the Perplexed*. Rav Amital refused to give the *shiur* himself, so instead it took place at the home of the author and philosopher Dr. Naḥum Arieli. R. Hillel Raḥmani, who heads the yeshiva's Jewish Thought department, also describes Rav Amital's open-mindedness with regard to what could be taught in *shiurim*. "It was important to him that there be variety in the yeshiva. He was not afraid that someone would come and attract the students away, because he never felt threatened. He trusted his students and his educational method." Rav Amital's openness ended, though, when it came to closed ideological conceptions that he felt claimed a monopoly on truth. He would tell his students that he wanted his yeshiva to remain free of the teaching and influence of Chabad adherents or "Merkaznikim" (those in the orbit of Yeshivat Merkaz HaRav), since those two groups are unprepared to listen to any opinions but their own.

The open-mindedness that Rav Amital exhibited with regard to *shiurim* also characterized his attitude toward the substance of what his students were learning. When he identified certain students' need to diverge from the regular framework – for instance, to limit their study of Talmud in favor of other disciplines – he understood and supported them. One such student was Yosef Avivi, a member of the yeshiva's second class and now a scholar of Kabbala: "Rav Amital allowed me to study whatever I wanted. At first, during the afternoon break, I studied the *Shelah* – R. Yeshaya HaLevi Horowitz's *Shenei Luḥot HaBerit*. He knew, but did not object. Slowly but surely, these subjects began to fill my regular *sedarim* (study sessions), not just break times, until my entire afternoon and evening *sedarim* were spent studying books that could not be found on many desks in the yeshiva. Rav Amital knew of this, and encouraged me." Avivi once told Rav Amital about a certain work that he had seen in manuscript at the National Library and wished to edit, but could not due to lack of funds for the large amount of photocopying it would entail. Rav Amital granted Avivi some financial assistance from a discretionary fund of his and encouraged him to work on the manuscript. "More than the financial assistance," Avivi says, "he provided spiritual assistance and support. Rav Amital's enthusiasm encouraged me to review the manuscripts; all of my work, from then until now, is because of him, and to his credit." In the introduction to a work published in 5737 (1977), *Signonot HaKodesh BaTorah*, Avivi wrote: "My gratitude and appreciation goes to the Rosh Yeshiva, Rav Yehuda Amital, who allowed me to study my part of the Torah and did not impose the yeshiva's framework on me." More than a decade later, Avivi published a new edition of R. Moshe Ḥayyim Luzzatto's *Mesilat Yesharim* (*Path of the Upright*). He inscribed the copy that he gave to Rav Amital with the following message: "To Rav Amital, who taught me that a man can be *upright* even if he does not follow the *path*."

Rav Amital also allowed a student from the yeshiva's first class, Asher Yaron, who later fell in the Yom Kippur War, to take university courses as a member of the Kollel in the yeshiva. This was quite an exceptional arrangement in the yeshiva world at the time. Yaron studied mathematics at Hebrew University in the morning and then diligently studied Torah in the *beit midrash* every afternoon.

At the same time, Rav Amital limited his openness to the desires of his students only to instances where he felt that there was a real need that justified deviating from the norm. When he felt that there was no such justification, he did not hesitate to rebuke those who independently adopted a schedule that differed from their peers' or spent their time on unusual learning material. He once caught – and castigated – a first-year student devoting the majority of his morning *seder* to the study of Rav Kook's *Orot HaKodesh*. If that student would revert to Talmud study in the wake of the rebuke, Rav Amital said, it indicates that he did not really need to study *Orot HaKodesh*. And if he would persist with what he was doing despite the reprimands, then apparently it was a real need, in which case Rav Amital would let him continue.

Chapter Six

An Educator with Proportions

> *The greatest educational impact is achieved when the teacher is unaware that he is teaching and the student is unaware that he is learning. This is the meaning of "the name of Heaven shall become beloved through you" – a person through his ordinary conduct should bring about a sanctification of God's name, without even being aware that he is influencing others through his behavior.*[1]

Rav Amital received rabbinical ordination from R. Isser Zalman Meltzer, his wife's grandfather, at the age of twenty-five, having just completed seventeen months of military service during the War of Independence. Meir Ḥovav, who had been with Rav Amital since his days as a student in Yeshivat Ḥevron soon after the latter's arrival in Israel,

1. Rabbi Yehuda Amital, *Jewish Values in a Changing World* (Jersey City, NJ: KTAV Publishing House and Yeshivat Har Etzion, 2005), p. 151.

A soldier in the War of Independence.

and who then had served in the same brigade during the war, recalls that after the war various bodies from within the religious and secular communities began to take interest in the young Torah scholar. Members of the farming community of Meron, who had become acquainted with Rav Amital during his military service in the Galilee, proposed that he become their rabbi. But Rav Amital wished to return to Torah study and so preferred work that would allow him to do so. His father-in-law, R. Zvi Yehuda Meltzer, found him work as a court clerk in the Reḥovot rabbinical court that he founded and headed. The job of the rabbinical court clerk is to help the rabbinical court manage its cases. His responsibilities include preparing case files, recording minutes, and writing verdicts. Rav Amital worked as a clerk for two years, until he could no longer bear the bickering of the married couples suing for divorce. "I can already prepare a fixed transcript for the judges," he joked, "the wife curses and the husband beats…" It took some courage to leave his position. It was clear to those on the rabbinical court that if he would want to, he would have a future appointment as a judge on his father-in-law's court. Rav Meltzer urged his son to remain in his position, which

Teaching at Yeshivat HaDarom in Reḥovot.

Top center: Rav Zvi Yehuda Meltzer, the head of Yeshivat HaDarom. Beneath him is Rav Amital. Rav Mordekhai Breuer is in the top left corner.

allowed him to continue studying Torah, and eventually become a rabbinic judge, but Rav Amital remained obstinate.

He joined the yeshiva that his father-in-law founded in Reḥovot, Yeshivat Kletzk, and began giving *shiurim* there.

In Elul, 5713 (August 1953), Yeshivat HaDarom opened its doors. Yeshivat HaDarom is a yeshiva high school founded by R. Zvi Yehuda Meltzer to complement Yeshivat Kletzk, a post-high-school yeshiva. Eventually, Yeshivat Kletzk was merged into Yeshivat HaDarom. Rav Meltzer headed the yeshiva high school, and his son-in-law, Rav Amital, was appointed on Ḥanukka of its first year to be its spiritual supervisor. One year later he became the *ram*, the primary religious studies teacher, of its first class. That first class was composed of twenty students, half born in Israel and half immigrants, mostly from Yemen. Among those first students was Moshe Ben-Arush, who became Professor Moshe Bar-Asher, Israel Prize winner and the president of the Hebrew Language Academy. From his first meeting with Rav Amital, he mainly remembers his delightful countenance. Professor Bar-Asher, who had moved to Israel alone from Morocco, recounts:

> That first year, he would speak to us on Friday night after *Kabbalat Shabbat*. He often quoted Rav Avraham Yitzḥak HaKohen Kook and frequently referred to *Klal Yisrael* and the trauma of the Holocaust. The Israelis would go home for Shabbat, but we immigrants would stay in yeshiva and Rav Amital would invite us to his home. "My home is your home," he would tell me. I once absented myself from yeshiva to visit my bedridden grandfather. The next day, on my return, Rav Amital announced that he would review the *shiur* that he gave the previous day – for my sake.

Another student was Zvi Thau, later R. Zvi Yisrael Thau, Rosh Yeshiva of Yeshivat Har HaMor, which broke away from Merkaz HaRav in the 1990s. Zvi Thau was born in Vienna and grew up in the Netherlands in a modern Orthodox home. He was involved in Dutch culture and world literature, thirstily read the works of Martin Buber, wrote poetry, and even recited his poems while standing on a chair in Dutch coffeehouses. At the age of seventeen he lost his mother, and soon after he exploited his father's visit to the U.S. by running away from home and making *aliya* alone. Based on a cousin's recommendation, he came to Yeshivat HaDarom, where he was taken in by Rav Amital's warm embrace. "He was very kind to me," Rav Thau relates, "I was like one of his family." At some point, Thau learned that a relative abroad had taken ill, and there was nobody to help him. He decided to bring the relative to Israel, and to that end he sought a home where his relative would be taken in, and a doctor who could treat him. Rav Amital left his work at the yeshiva and traveled all around Israel with his student, helping his in his search. "He was prepared to do anything for me," Rav Thau recalls, "his embrace built me up, allowed me to stand on my own two feet." Rav Amital also introduced the young and well-educated Zvi Thau to the world of Torah. "When he brought me into the world of Torah, I did not feel any constriction or contradiction. This says a lot about him. I do not know if someone else could have introduced me to the world of Torah like that."

At one point, Zvi Thau's father demanded that his son complete his high school matriculation, even making his continued financial support contingent on it. Rav Amital traveled to Jerusalem to try to convince his student to acquiesce to his father's demand and take the matriculation exams. The student refused. His father never made peace with the fact that his son would never get a high school diploma until he was on his deathbed in Amsterdam, when his son came to help take care of him. "He finally understood that I had chosen a different path, and told me that he is happy to have children and grandchildren engaged in Torah and mitzvot."

Because of Rav Amital, after a year at Yeshivat HaDarom, Zvi Thau chose to continue his studies at Yeshivat Merkaz HaRav, where he became one of the closest disciples of its Rosh Yeshiva, R. Zvi Yehuda Kook. "I knew a snippet of R. Avraham Yitzḥak Kook's writings from my rabbi back in Holland," Rav Thau relates, "but my first significant introduction to his writings was from Rav Amital. His *shiurim* on Rav Kook's philosophy were amazing. I especially remember his *shiurim* on *Orot HaTeshuva*. Because of him I arrived at Merkaz with a lot of knowledge and was able to understand Rav Zvi Yehuda."

Ultimately, Rav Amital and Rav Thau became disputants on a long list of issues relating to Torah study and questions of policy and society.

Despite their disagreements, Rav Thau guarded his old teacher's honor and refrained from attacking him. Once, in the late 1970s, he tried enlisting Rav Amital into a battle being waged by Merkaz HaRav to cancel a concert at which Handel's *Messiah* would be played, as it depicts the life of the Christian messiah. Rav Amital did not join them, disappointing Rav Thau. Another time, they met by chance and Rav Amital invited Rav Thau to travel with him so that they could talk en route. Rav Thau avoided doing so, later explaining: "Since he was my *rebbe* and teacher, I did not want to clash with him, and I knew that if we started speaking we would argue. I, of course, don't agree with his positions, but that doesn't affect the gratitude I owe him and the appreciation I have for what he did for me."

Another disputant of Rav Amital's from those days was R. Elazar Menaḥem Shakh, who would later become the leader of Israel's *ḥaredi* community. Rav Shakh was a student of R. Isser Zalman Meltzer (R. Zvi Yehuda Meltzer's father), at his yeshiva in Kletzk, Poland. He married Rav Meltzer's niece and followed him to Palestine in 1940. At that time, Rav Shakh's attitudes toward Zionism and the state were moderate, and he saw no problem with teaching in Zionist *yeshivot*. Despite their age difference (Rav Shakh was already over fifty whereas Rav Amital was closer to twenty-five), they became quite friendly. Rav Amital would praise Rav Shakh's *shiurim* and add some ideas of his own, and Rav Shakh would share his cigarettes with his junior colleague. Once, in the middle of Rav Shakh's *shiur*, Rav Amital posed a challenge that wrecked his hypothesis, and he stopped the *shiur* in the middle. Rav Amital saw this as a sign of Rav Shakh's greatness. Later, according to students, Rav Amital did the same thing when confronted with a similar situation in *shiur*.

Rav Shakh and Rav Amital would occasionally debate their attitudes about Zionism, the military, and the fledgling state. Years later, when he was already the *ḥaredi* leader, the two met. Rav Shakh embraced Rav Amital and said, "Reb Yehuda, Reb Yehuda, we're so far apart now that we don't even argue."

* * *

Rav Amital's students at Yeshivat HaDarom especially recall his reaction to the March 1953 execution in the United States of Julius and Ethel

Rosenberg, a Jewish couple convicted of espionage relating to passing nuclear secrets to the Soviet Union. Rav Thau remembers Rav Amital's tears on the day that the couple was taken for execution. "It was inspiring to see how he took it all to heart, how he experienced everything." Yedael Meltzer, brother-in-law to Rav Amital and then a student in Yeshivat HaDarom, relates how that morning Rav Amital entered the *beit midrash* upset and agitated. He went up to the *bima* and, choking back tears, said to the students:

> This morning a Jewish couple was murdered in the United States. They were sentenced to death because they were Jews. The world has learned nothing from the terrible, horrible, Nazi anti-Semitism that was revealed in all its shocking ugliness during World War II, just a few years ago. Anti-Semitism still operates at full power and has now broken out in the United States, ostensibly the most tolerant nation in the free world.

Yedael tells that Rav Amital claimed that the entire judicial proceeding against the Rosenbergs was a perversion of justice and that anti-Semitism and Jew-hatred oozed out of every word uttered by the prosecution and the judges. He contended that if the Rosenbergs had not been Jewish, they would not have been sentenced to death, since many of the reasons for their conviction were baseless. "Fifteen years after the Rosenbergs' execution, U.S. newspapers began to publish serious allegations about the handling of the case, and the claim was raised that the conviction stemmed from anti-Semitism and not from the search for truth. Everything that the American press discovered fifteen years after the trial," Yedael concludes, "Rav Amital discerned at the time."

* * *

Professor Ya'akov (Gerald) Blidstein, winner of the Israel Prize in Jewish Thought in 2006, studied at Yeshivat HaDarom in 1954–55 as part of a group of students from the United States who came to Israel to spend a year studying in yeshiva. In those days, he recounts, it was customary for students to devote fifteen minutes a day to the study of *mussar* – self-improvement – from R. Moshe Ḥayyim Luzzatto's *Mesilat*

Yesharim. Blidstein, with whom this treatise did not particularly resonate, approached Rav Amital to discuss the issue even though Rav Amital was not his teacher. "He told me, 'It's okay. You can read R. Luzzatto's plays, or anything else, if you prefer. Whatever speaks to you.' He communicated to me that it's not the end of the world if I don't study *Mesilat Yesharim*." On another occasion, Blidstein complained to Rav Amital that he was bored in yeshiva. "'Go travel for two weeks and then come back,' he advised me. His willingness to say something like that was typical of his educational approach."

Even at home, Rav Amital's educational philosophy was characterized by keeping things in proportion. His daughters tell about how he never attributed much importance to test grades. Ayelet Yishai, the youngest Amital daughter, recalls that he commented on a test result of fifty, "Amazing. You knew half the material…"

* * *

As Yeshivat HaDarom's high school grew and developed, its *yeshiva gedola* program faded. The combination of young boys with untrained minds and young men who wished to immerse themselves in the world of Torah did not succeed, and in 1957 the *yeshiva gedola* ceased to exist. Rav Meltzer did not despair and decided to re-open the yeshiva, this time as the continuation of the high school, although it would have separate dining facilities. It was at this moment that Rav Amital proposed a combination of Torah study and military service – a *hesder* track.

Years after Rav Amital first proposed the idea, R. Aharon Lichtenstein penned an essay entitled "The Ideology of *Hesder*" in which he described, at length, the halakhic and Torah-based rationale for a combined framework. Commenting on his colleague's essay, Rav Amital quipped, "When I suggested the idea to my father-in-law, I didn't think about anything written in Rav Lichtenstein's article. I only though about one thing: how to cultivate a rabbinic elite in the religious Zionist community."

For Rav Meltzer, the idea of combining Torah study and military service was not foreign. In the aftermath of the War of Independence, he wanted to establish a military yeshiva under the auspices of the military rabbinate, in order to encourage students steeped in Torah to enlist. He presented the idea to the Minister of Education and Culture, Zalman Shazar, who later would become President. Meir Ḥovav, who was present at the meeting, recalls that Shazar demonstrated a real grasp of the matter and promised to take the issue up with Ben Gurion. In actuality, though, nothing came of the meeting. Several years later, when Rav Amital proposed the idea of *hesder*, he found a willing ally in Rav Meltzer.

This time, Rav Meltzer did not let up. He went from door to door in the Ministry of Defense until his program was approved. In 5719 (1959), the IDF first recognized the *hesder* track of Yeshivat HaDarom, and its students began to combine their studies with military service.

The new *yeshiva gedola* at Yeshivat HaDarom did not last long, but students at the teachers' seminary established at the yeshiva by R. Ya'akov Berman continued – and continue – to benefit from that *hesder* track.

Over time, a dispute has broken out between Yeshivat HaDarom and Yeshivat Kerem B'Yavneh regarding the identity of the first *hesder* program. Both of these venerable *yeshivot* stake a claim to that distinction. This dispute can be resolved in a few ways. One way is semantic – distinguishing between a *hesder* track and a *hesder* yeshiva. Kerem B'Yavneh, the first *hesder* yeshiva, was founded in 1954 by graduates of Bnei Akiva, with the assistance of Rav Ḥayyim Druckman and Ya'akov Drori, and it was the students who demanded that military service be integrated into their studies. The solution they found was that their military service would be through Naḥal: the students were classified as members of a Bnei Akiva-affiliated Naḥal group, not as *hesder* yeshiva students. Kerem B'Yavneh was only officially designated a *hesder* yeshiva in 1965, some six years after the *hesder* track at Yeshivat HaDarom began to operate.

The other resolution to this dispute is more fundamental, since it distinguishes between *hesder* as an ideal and *hesder* as a compromise. Even if Kerem B'Yavneh was indeed the pioneer *hesder* yeshiva, there is no doubt that the attitude of its Rosh Yeshiva, R. Ḥayyim Ya'akov Goldvicht, toward the military aspect of the program differed greatly from that of Rav Amital, who articulated the idea, and Rav Meltzer, who implemented it. For Rav Goldvicht, military service was not the ideal. For Rav Amital, however, it was a paradigm of integration – a *le'khat'ḥila* solution. In an interview that Rav Goldvicht granted to *Hazofe*'s Ḥaggai Hoberman in 1991, he acknowledged that his attitude toward combining yeshiva with military service was never positive, saying: "I worried that if the students would all go to the army, we would be left without a yeshiva." Rav Amital and Rav Meltzer had a completely different attitude toward the military framework: the desire to combine military service came from them, not the students, and consequently they did not fear, as Rav Goldvicht and others did, the impact that integration would have on the yeshiva's stability.

In 1991, the *hesder yeshivot* won the Israel Prize for Special Contribution to State and Society. Rav Goldvicht accepted the award on behalf of all the *hesder yeshivot*. At one point it was proposed to Rav Amital that he too represent the yeshivot at the ceremony, but he refused. He suggested that Rav Goldvicht should be joined by R. Yuval Cherlow – an alumnus of Yeshivat Har Etzion and one of the first officers to come from a *hesder* yeshiva – and a *ram* at Yeshivat HaGolan – a *hesder* yeshiva. Ultimately, Rav Cherlow indeed sat among the honorees, but Rav Goldvicht alone accepted the prize. Many felt at the time that Rav Amital would have been a more appropriate choice to accept the award.

* * *

Rav Amital was a *ram* at Yeshivat HaDarom for ten years. All of his children were born during that decade in Reḥovot. The oldest child of Rav Yehuda and Miriam Amital was their son, Yoel, born in 1950 and named for Rav Amital's younger brother, who was killed at Auschwitz. Two years later their oldest daughter, Devora, was born, named for Rav Amital's mother. Three more daughters followed: Dina, named for Rav Amital's venerated grandmother, Tali, and Ayelet.

In 1965, Rav Amital left Yeshivat HaDarom and moved with his family to Jerusalem, settling in the relatively new neighborhood of Givat Mordekhai. When Rav Meltzer came to visit them in their new home, he was shocked at the home that his daughter and son-in-law chose to invest the bulk of their funds in. Its infrastructure was not yet developed, and the two apartments that the Amitals bought, to combine into one large apartment, were on a basement floor. "I'll help you financially," Rav Meltzer promised his daughter and son-and-law, "as long as you get out of here."

The Amitals did not take Rav Meltzer's advice, and lived together

With his firstborn son, Yoel.

in that apartment on Shaḥal Street in Givat Mordekhai for forty-five years, until Rav Amital's death. Mordekhai Koren, one of the neighborhood's old timers, describes Rav Amital as someone who was very involved in the community. "Modestly, quietly, he always greeted fellow worshippers. If someone was absent from *shul,* he inquired into his wellbeing. Even as he pored over whatever volume he was studying, he kept an eye on whatever was going on. He was in no way disconnected from communal life." One of the daily prayer services at the central synagogue of the neighborhood – the *netz minyan* that started at sunrise – has been known for decades as "Rav Amital's *minyan.*"

During the late 1960s, Yeshivat Ḥevron, then located in Jerusalem's Ge'ula neighborhood, commenced construction on its new building in Givat Mordekhai. Around the same time, rumor began circulating in Givat Mordekhai about plans to build a local center for Christian missionary activity. When community activists tried to enlist Rav Amital's support in their fight against the mission's construction, he promised them that Givat Mordekhai would be a poor choice of location for the missionaries. "In a few years, Yeshivat Ḥevron will move into the neighborhood," he explained with a twinkle in his eye, "and those boys know just how to deal with missionaries."

Rav Amital took a big gamble on his future when he decided to leave his teaching position at Yeshivat HaDarom to move to Jerusalem. No serious or permanent job awaited him in the capital, and as the head of a family of seven, it was not a simple move from an economic perspective. He began teaching on a part-time basis at a variety of educational institutions. He served as a *ram* in a Sephardic yeshiva founded by R. Ovadia Yosef, taught classes on the *Kuzari* at Mikhlalah in the Bayit VeGan neighborhood, taught at a leadership training seminar run by the Jewish Agency in the neighborhood of Beit HaKerem, and taught Talmud at Yeshivat Merom *Tziyon*, a vocational yeshiva in Bayit VeGan. Avraham Ron, then the director of public-religious education at the Ministry of Education, offered him jobs at the ministry, but Rav Amital was not interested. Soon after the Amitals moved to Jerusalem, the chief rabbi of Reḥovot, R. Elimelekh Bar-Shaul, passed away. Reḥovot's religious leadership offered the job to Rav Amital, but he refused. The rabbinate did attract him; he did not find it to be a spiritual challenge that would suit his personality.

As an official rabbi, he knew he would have to disconnect from the community, from the *baalebatim*. Rav Amital's positive attitude toward *baalebatim* was made manifest on various occasions. At one of the many festive Purim banquets held at his home over the years, he cited a midrashic interpretation of the following verse (Deut. 11:22): "to love the Lord your God, walk in all his ways, and adhere to Him." According to the Midrash, the way that one "adheres" to God is via Torah scholars. "But what does one do if there are no Torah scholars to cling to?" Rav Amital asked those present. One of them answered that in such a situation one must cling to God directly. "When there are no *talmidei ḥakhamim*," Rav Amital stated, "one must cling to the simple *baalebatim*."

Since he saw his place as being among *baalebatim*, Rav Amital never had excessive expectations of his children. This, too, set him apart from his colleague, Rav Lichtenstein, who expected his children to become Torah scholars. Rav Amital expected his only son to "be a good *baalebos*." "I had no dreams of him being a Rosh Yeshiva or a *talmid ḥakham*," Rav Amital said of Yoel, who now serves as a *ram* at Yeshivat Sha'alvim, "I wanted only that he become a good, God-fearing Jew who sets aside time to study Torah. I married into a rabbinic family in which they say to a boy that he should be a Torah giant. I don't have such pretensions. Why should I have such pretensions? My father was not a Torah giant, and neither was my grandfather. I wouldn't care if my son became a shoemaker, as long as he's a good Jew."

When it came to educating the girls, the gap between Rav Lichtenstein and Rav Amital was even greater. Long before the revolution in women's Torah study, Rav Lichtenstein insisted that his daughters should study Torah. He studied Torah regularly with his two daughters, and they each marked their entry into Jewish adulthood at age twelve by completing an entire order of the Mishna. The Amital family did not invest great significance in the "bat mitzva" concept. "He joked about the importance that I ascribed to the issue of women's education," Rav Lichtenstein tells about his colleague.

On this issue of the religious status of women, there is no doubt that Rav Amital's position changed significantly. Toward the end of his life, he viewed the phenomenon of women's Torah study positively and recognized the need for a stronger female voice in the Torah world. "I view it as a sign of greatness when someone is capable of changing his mind about such fundamental issues," notes Rav Lichtenstein.

* * *

Two years after the move to Jerusalem, in Iyar 5727 (June 1967), the Six Day War broke out. Rav Amital, then forty-three years old, was not called up, to his profound frustration. He helped the war effort by providing relief on the home front, assisting those stuck in bomb shelters, but it did not really displace his frustration about not being called up. Many citizens felt deeply anxious about the war, but not Rav Amital, who was very optimistic. Yoel, who was then studying at Yeshivat Kol Torah in Bayit VeGan, recalls his father speaking about that period as a "great time" and citing a statement by Rav Kook about war in the time of redemption: "When there is a great war in the world, the power of the Messiah is awakened." His daughters remember him sitting in an armchair at the door to the communal bomb shelter, listening to a transistor radio, reporting on events to the others in the shelter and calming people down. The results of the war put him on a great spiritual high. In a speech he gave years later to his students, he said about those times: "Are there words to describe how our hearts fluttered when we reached the Temple Mount?" As a Holocaust survivor, he often spoke about the fear of a second Holocaust that gripped the nation on the eve of the war, which only heightened the sense of great rescue after victory. He defined the outcome of the war, like the establishment of the state, as a great sanctification of God's name, a *kiddush HaShem,* before all the nations of the world. He called for viewing the events in a messianic vein, offering two reasons for his contention. The first was the comfort that it would bring to the people of Israel – "There is nothing more comforting than starting to move along the messianic track," he told his students, "and we are entering the phase from which there is no going back, a phase that will have suffering, a phase that will unfortunately see more war; the process of redemption is in perpetual motion. It is no mere one-time episode." The second reason was the call to action – "When we look at the events of our time in the messianic vein, it makes a claim on us. It obligates us. If we know that we are living in the generation of redemption, it gives us added strength. Indeed, we are capable of bringing about the complete redemption. Our actions have a different gravity...the redemption is slowly unfolding before us, and it obligates us. For that reason, we should mention and emphasize *Mashiaḥ* constantly."

Chapter Seven

Eight Princes of Men

It says in Psalms (145:18): "God is near to all those who call Him – to all who call Him in truth." Anyone who truly calls, whether religious or not. Neither I, as a Rosh Yeshiva, nor my students and friends, your comrades-at-arms, represent God any more than you do. Whose prayer comes nearer to God – the prayer of someone like me who was trained in it from childhood, or your prayer, which you discovered in the heat of battle? Only God knows… a sincere prayer that originates in the depths and flows forth from there, even if the words are stammered, is heard at the highest heights. King David wrote in one of his psalms (ibid. 130:2), "God! Listen in to my voice (HaShem shema be-koli)*; may Your ears be attentive to the sound of my supplication." A great Hasidic master once pointed out that it does not say "listen to my voice* (shema koli)*," rather "listen in to my voice* (shema be-koli)*" – listen to what is hidden within the notes of my voice, what I could not articulate in words.*

Speech to Yom Kippur War combat soldiers,
HaMa'alot MiMa'amakim, 5734 (1973)

The 5734 (1973–74) academic year, the sixth year of Yeshivat Har Etzion, began normally. More than two-hundred students were studying in the yeshiva that year, and it had become one of the most outstanding and popular Zionist *yeshivot*. On the eve of Yom Kippur, Rav Amital delivered a discourse, as he did every year, on a theme of the day. He cited the prophecy of Yeḥezkel (33:1–3), which warns the people of impending war if they do not repent:

> Son of man, speak to your countrymen and say to them: When I bring the sword against a land, the people of that land take one of their number and appoint him their watchman, so he sees the sword advancing on the land, and he blows the shofar to warn the people.

Later in that chapter (v. 11), a well-known verse appears: "Say to them: As I live – declares the Lord God – I do not desire the death of the wicked, but the wicked man's turning from his ways. Turn back! Turn back from your wicked ways! Why should you die, O House of Israel?"

Some of the students saw this, in retrospect, as a foreshadowing of what happened the next day.

War broke out on the afternoon of Yom Kippur. Many students were called to report to their units even before the fast ended, and they went to take leave of the Rashei Yeshiva. They left the yeshiva's *minyan* and convened their own, completing *Ne'ila* early. They were led in their prayers by Moshe Tal, a fourth-year student and a newlywed, having been married less than two months earlier. At the yeshiva's main *minyan*, Rav Amital gave an emotional speech before *Ne'ila*. He quoted the Rambam's *Hilkhot Melakhim* (7:15) regarding one going out to battle:

> Once he enters the heat of battle, he should rely on the Hope and Rescuer of Israel in its time of distress. He should know that he is doing battle for God's sake, and he should place his life in his hand. He should not be afraid or scared; he should not think of

> his wife or children, but rather should erase their memory from his heart, and turn his attention from everything else to war.

These words made a profound impression on the students.

Right after the end of the holy day, R. Yoel Bin-Nun, then Alon Shvut's security coordinator, among other things, urged the students not to wait for their orders, but to report to their units independently. He even shared with the students his assessment that the Bar-Lev line, the string of fortifications along the Suez Canal, had already fallen – and was reprimanded by Rav Amital, who expressed faith in the IDF's steadfast durability. On the other hand, Rav Amital was not euphoric, either. When one of the students proposed reading the Song of the Sea, which expresses gratitude to God for His miracles, Rav Amital rejected the idea, saying: "Slow down. First let's hear what's happening."

The yeshiva – which was about to break for Sukkot anyway – was emptied of students, and Rav Amital went home to Jerusalem.

It was not long before terrible tidings began to arrive, one after the other. During the first twenty days of the war, Yeshivat Har Etzion lost eight of its students.

Amatzia Ilani, a second-year student in the yeshiva's fifth class, only studied there for ten months. He was sent to the canal fortifications before the High Holidays as an emissary of the military rabbinate and was killed at the Budapest outpost, the stronghold commanded by Motti Ashkenazi, on the day of Yom Kippur.

Asher Yaron and Sariel Birnbaum, members of the yeshiva's first class, were called up right after Yom Kippur and were killed the next day, in the holding defense battle against the Syrians on the Golan Heights. Birnbaum died still wearing his Yom Kippur clothes. Yaron was counted amongst the missing-in-action for a long time before his body was found. He left a wife and daughter.

Danny Ehrlich and Benny Gal were killed on the Egyptian front on the third day of the war. Ehrlich was a member of the yeshiva's fourth class. Gal was a member of the fifth class, a second-year student, all of nineteen years old. Like Amatzia Ilani, Gal, too, was sent to the canal fortifications as an emissary of the rabbinate and was killed after he insisted on remaining with the wounded who had served with him in the outpost.

On the seventh day of the war, the first of the intermediate days (*Ḥol HaMo'ed*) of Sukkot, Avner Yona and Rafi Neuman, members of the yeshiva's third class, were killed on the Golan Heights.

Twenty days after the outbreak of war, the day after the cease-fire declaration, Moshe Tal, the *ḥazan* of the call-ups, was killed in the Sinai. Tal, the son of Supreme Court Justice Zvi Tal, left a pregnant wife.

In most cases, Rav Amital heard about the loss of the student immediately, sometimes even before the parents. The tidings wounded him deeply, but outwardly he kept conveying optimism. One external sign attested somewhat to what was going on in his soul: after quitting for several years, he started smoking again during the first days of the war. It was a long time before he quit smoking again. A student who was a guest in Rav Amital's house that Sukkot experienced more evidence of what Rav Amital was going through. One night, as they slept in the *sukka*, he heard Rav Amital moaning in grief, heartrending moans that reminded him of the whimper of the shofar. Yoel Amital, who was called up on Simḥat Torah, later asked his father how he felt and what he had to say about the loss of his eight students. Rav Amital sorrowfully answered his son: "What did the Alter of Slabodka say after the events of 1929, when so many of his students from Yeshivat Ḥevron were killed? He cried."

In addition to the eight students who fell, several yeshiva students were wounded in the war, some of them severely. Meeting them was also traumatic for Rav Amital. Yehuda Schwartz, a member of the first class, was very critically wounded on the Golan Heights the day after Yom Kippur. Five days after being wounded, Rav Amital and Yedaya Hacohen went to visit him at Rambam Hospital in Haifa. Schwartz recalls:

> Rav Amital didn't recognize me. I was completely bandaged and the prognosis was very bleak. He knew it was me only because he saw my wife sitting next to me. I couldn't see the Rav because my eyes were covered, but they told me that he was worried by what he saw. Some say that he started smoking again because of that visit with me. The next time he came to visit, my legs were covered by a device designed to keep the sheets away from the burns on my body. Rav Amital saw the device and became very

> alarmed. He thought that something terrible had happened to my legs and immediately lifted the sheets to see that everything was okay. The first day that I was able to put on *tefillin,* I called him to tell him the news. I could feel him crying into the phone.

Immediately after Sukkot, Rav Amital informed Rav Lichtenstein that he was incapable of functioning as a Rosh Yeshiva for the time being, handing over all authority. Once *ḥoref zeman* (winter session) began on the first of Ḥeshvan, Rav Amital barely visited the yeshiva. Instead he traveled frequently to the front, to visit his students. The few students who remained studying in the yeshiva characterized Rav Amital during that period as the yeshiva's 'foreign minister'.

In his travels to the front, Rav Amital found some healing for his wounded soul. Wherever he went he encouraged his students, but he also drew strength from them. Once, on a radio show, he recounted the experience of his first encounter with his combat-soldier students, during a lull between battles:

> We came to them as Rashei Yeshiva, but there were moments that we were cut down to size in their presence, and we stood like students before their masters, awestruck by their greatness… we stood dumbfounded in the presence of students who, a few days earlier, were engaged in resolving the Talmudic debates of Abaye and Rava and clarifying Talmudic discussions, and now they were waging war with all their heart and soul, believing that they were indeed fighting God's wars and that God was fighting for them. I would not be exaggerating if I said that we felt that we were breathing the air of the Tanakh.

The students also experienced something special when Rav Amital came to visit them on the front, during battles. R. Hillel Raḥmani, a member of the yeshiva's third class who was then fighting on the Golan Heights, describes the meeting with Rav Amital as a spiritual experience:

> Right after Sukkot, he came with several other rabbis. We gathered in the synagogue and Rav Amital asked to speak last. When

> he got up to speak, everyone felt like he was going to prophesy, not merely speak. I have no idea what he spoke about. I don't remember a single word. But it was truly prophetic. He spoke with all his heart. I think that just a few minutes earlier he was informed that Rafi and Avner fell, and he was caught up in an extraordinary storm of emotions. He spoke about the war, about vision, about the Jewish people. Silence descended on the whole crowd. This was not just another speech by a Rosh Yeshiva, but something much more.

Some of the Har Etzion students fought on the Golan Heights in the 679 (reserve) Brigade, commanded by Ori Orr. Orr remembers well Rav Amital's visit to his students during a lull between battles.

> We were regrouping between battles when they told me that a group of rabbis wanted to visit the yeshiva students in the brigade. Of course this made me happy – anything that could bolster the spirits of the fighting men was important. Rav Amital radiated serenity and equanimity, and I saw the high regard in which the students held him. When he finished making his rounds among the students, he approached me and told me that the students are full of vigor, and value my leadership. I thanked him. He then added that the students believe that there will be victory, and with God's help we'll get to the outskirts of Damascus. I told him that we would win and that God's help is very important, but that we're at least forty tanks short, and would be in a much better state if we had them. Rav Amital emended his statement and said to me: "You know what? I accept that. I hope that you get your forty additional tanks, and then, with God's help, you'll reach the outskirts of Damascus."

During the cease-fire, the nature of Rav Amital's visits to his students changed. The students, and many other soldiers, even those who were not religious, wanted to hear words of spiritual encouragement from him and from other rabbis who came to visit. "It turned out," Rav Amital recounted, "that when it comes to thirsting for God's word, the differences between soldiers who are yeshiva students and other soldiers, religious and non-religious, become somewhat blurred." He began shuttling from unit to unit to meet combat soldiers, to hear their experiences, and to strengthen them with words of encouragement. When he returned from his visits to the front, he would encourage the soldiers' families in the home front. R. Ya'akov Fisher, a member of the yeshiva's third class who fought on the Northern Front against the Syrians, got married during the months of the war. About a week before the wedding, Rav Amital came to visit his unit. "He understood that there was no chance that I would be released to go home for my *aufruf* on the Shabbat before the wedding, so he lifted my spirits. When he got home, he called Tzippy, my fiancée. Instead of telling her that I would not be home for Shabbat, he said, 'Don't worry. The equipment compartments of the tanks are filled with candy. The guys will make him a great *aufruf*. It'll be fine.'"

During those visits, Rav Amital got to know Moshe (Musa) Peled, later to become the commander of the IDF Armored Corps but then a division commander, and the two became friends. Peled asked Rav Amital to devote more of his visits to pep talks with the officers. Rav Amital reached the officers' hearts using original methods that typify his personality. Yedaya Hacohen, who accompanied Rav Amital on many of those visits, tried to illuminate the secret of Rav Amital's magic, as expressed on one of those visits:

> We got to one of the large bases in the Sinai and found students from the yeshiva there. After speaking with them, Rav Amital wanted to meet with the battalion commanders and the brigade commander. He entered the officers' tent and tried engaging them in conversation, but they could not find a common language. When Rav Amital saw that there was no chemistry, he left. That evening they gave us a tent and sheets, and we began preparing for bed. Seconds before I fell asleep, I noticed Rav Amital leaving the tent. I didn't follow him. He returned at two o'clock in the morning, his face radiating happiness. "Yedaya, you missed out," he told me. Later it became clear to me that I had indeed missed out. Rav Amital had gone back to the officers that he had met

> during the day. I don't know what he said to them, but he managed to get them to open up. At some point, someone brought out a bottle of booze, and at that point the ice was completely broken. The officers began to pour out their hearts talking about the harsh battles they had gone through, and the conversation continued into the middle of the night. That's how Rav Amital's good relationship with the officers began.

Rav Amital attributed the great personal admiration that he won from many of the commanders to his students. He claimed that the commanders attributed to him, as a teacher, all of the traits exhibited by his students in battle.

The harsh result of the war impacted Rav Amital on the personal level, but his spiritual worldview was not altered, at least not for the first few years after the war. Despite the war, he continued to maintain, with perfect faith, that the present period is the "beginning of redemption." In a discourse in Ḥeshvan 5734, a month and a half after the war's outbreak, he said: "We are commanded to live with the faith that there is no going back since the return to *Tziyon* began. There may be temporary setbacks, but there is no retreat. All roads, paved and unpaved, lead to the redemption of Israel." On another occasion he said: "What we are witnessing is the first realization of the prophetic vision of the return to *Tziyon*. The steps are the steps of *Mashiaḥ*, and although sometimes accompanied by suffering, the steps are sure and the way is clear…"

Rav Amital defined the war as one of the phases of redemption, saying that "it is forbidden to look at it in the way we looked at tragedies that occurred during the long exile." He testified about himself that during the Holocaust he had hoped that if death had indeed been decreed on him, he preferred to die fighting in Eretz Yisrael. He believed that the war must be viewed in a messianic vein because it broke out in the context of the resurrection of Jewish sovereignty, because of its universal ramifications, and because of the great salvation that it included. Even the fact that the war broke out on Yom Kippur was viewed by Rav Amital as a sign that it was a messianic war.

On the other hand, Rav Amital conceded that war is not a necessary phase of the redemption process. "Based on everything that is currently happening, it is clear that we are in the process of redemption through the path of suffering," he said. "The fact that redemption can come without suffering but nevertheless is accompanied by it obligates us in the mitzva of crying out, of introspection, of contemplating our actions, so that we know that God awaits our repentance." Nevertheless, in the context of this introspection, Rav Amital rejected the idea that was being sounded that the war broke out as a punishment for the military's hubris, fueled by the euphoria that followed the Six Day War. Rav Amital claimed that sins should first be sought "among us," the *beit midrash* community, and added that the soul-searching should begin with an examination of interpersonal and social behavior.

In addition to introspection, Rav Amital thought that war should inspire spiritual awakenings and investigation of Jewish identity. He asked the combat soldiers to engage without prejudice in the search for identity – not to investigate "who is a Jew?" but rather "what is a Jew?" What is our destiny, what is our fate? What are the reasons for our wars? What is the secret of our existence? And what power is hidden in the fact that we are "a people that dwells alone and shall not be counted among the nations" (Num. 23:9)?

Most of the students who remained in yeshiva during the war were not Israeli and thus not drafted. They were part of a special program for foreign students, which began in 1972 and continues today. One of those students from abroad, Nissan Zisken, performed the chores of several students who were responsible for various aspects of the yeshiva's functioning, but who had been called up to the front. One day, one of the younger students in the group met Zisken and complained about how the war harmed the yeshiva's study sessions. "What a lousy year it's been," the student said, "I came here to study, and all of a sudden war breaks out. How can someone learn like this?" Zisken boiled with rage, thinking, "This yeshiva lost eight of its students; the Jewish people has lost almost three thousand of its sons, and this boy only cares about his own studies?" Zisken decided to hold his tongue, but approached Rav Amital to tell him what the student had said. Rav Amital convened the foreign students for a talk and told them, "I want you to know that this year you will learn very little in the way of the Talmudic debates of Abaye and Rava as you planned. However, here you will learn one thing that you will never find in the Gemara or the Shulḥan *Arukh* – the value of the people of Israel."

During the course of the war, students at the front were sent a leaflet produced by the yeshiva called *Alon Shvut* (the word "*alon*" means "leaflet" in addition to "oak tree"; though they sound the same, the two "alons" are spelled differently in Hebrew). The leaflets included updates from the yeshiva and from the front, summaries of discourses, and letters. Until the beginning of Shevat, the editors, Nissan Zisken and David Weg (Nativ), refrained from relating to the deaths of the eight yeshiva students. At first, the omission stemmed from the fact that some of the fallen were still MIA. But even after their bitter fate was learned, the editors preferred to skip difficult tidings so as not to harm the morale of the students at the front. By the beginning of Shevat, however, it had been nearly four months since the outbreak of the war, and it was impossible to ignore the rumors that had made their way to the front as well; the editors decided finally to address the fallen students. The leaflet opened with an obituary that began: "The bitter tidings began arriving even as the battles raged, but our sorrow and pain were mixed with anxiety and hope about the fate of those of our beloved friends who had been declared missing. They have now unfortunately been added to the list of the fallen." In that same issue, Rav Amital wrote to his students:

> Our hearts are torn eight times, tears that will never be mended. Our cries, bursting forth from the walls of our hearts, are as silent as the cries of every stone in the *beit midrash*. Who can express our grief? Who can count our tears? Who can measure our pain?

In Adar 5734, toward the end of *ḥoref zeman*, the first students began returning to the benches of the *beit midrash*, and Rav Amital began to visit more frequently as well. The first Purim after the war was charged with mixed feelings. The joy of the holiday was mixed with anguish over the war's victims. A particularly emotional moment occurred on one of the nights before Purim, when all the rabbis and students sat together at a *tisch*. Rav Amital began softly singing familiar tunes, and the atmosphere began to heat up. Later, he told the students the well-known story of a Jew trying to remember the origins of a certain tune, and whose searches led him ultimately to the tune of Kol Nidrei. "At the root of every tune," Rav Amital told his students, "we eventually reach Kol Nidrei." He began humming Kol Nidrei, from the night of Yom Kippur, and suddenly Purim had been transformed into *Yom HaKippurim*. Decades later, when Rav Lichtenstein described those moments, tears fill his eyes. "It was a moment of spiritual exaltedness, and suddenly it linked back to the moment of departure for the battlefield. Whoever experienced those moments will never forget them. They say that some earn their share in the world to come in a single moment; that entire winter – in which Rav Amital was not present in yeshiva – he acquired in that moment."

As Adar gave way to Nisan, the last of the students who had been called up were discharged, and they returned to the yeshiva. On 2 Iyar, 5734 (April 24, 1974), the yeshiva held a memorial service for its eight slain soldiers, at which Rav Amital eulogized them. He began by saying that the grief over the Yom Kippur War fallen was so great that it obscured the great salvation that the war wrought.

> The combination of salvation and sorrow in this world of ours, in which God's Name and God's throne are not complete, is a too-common combination. Salvation and sorrow usually co-exist. It is the way of the world that every great salvation in battle comes with sorrow, and usually at the price of sorrow. But sometimes the grief is so great, so all-encompassing, so deep, and so galling, that a man's heart is too narrow to include both feelings – the feeling of salvation alongside the feeling of sorrow. Then it is as though the salvation is dwarfed, until even it becomes grief.

For this speech Rav Amital sustained severe criticism. Many in the religious-Zionist world classified this statement, according to which the sorrow over the fallen obscures the feeling of salvation, as defeatism. Looking back, they assessed this statement as the beginning of the changes that occurred, or so they claimed, within his nationalist ideology.

Later in the same speech, Rav Amital wished to express the feelings of those who were able to return from the battlefield yet experienced psychological distress over the death of their peers. "The question that preoccupies them, steals their rest, and bothers them incessantly...is the question, 'Why did we come back, but not them?'" Rav Amital was well acquainted with the question of survivor's guilt. It had been with him ever since he survived the Holocaust.

Rav Amital referred to the eight fallen students as "eight princes of men," an epithet he borrowed from the prophet Micah's eschatological prophecy of restoration (Micah 5:4–5):

> Should Assyria invade our land and tread upon our fortresses, we will set up over it seven shepherds and eight princes of men. And they will shepherd Assyria's land with swords and the land of Nimrod with a keen blade. Thus he will deliver from Assyria, should it invade our land, and should it trample our border.

Rav Amital explained that the prophet described fighters not as military men, but as shepherds and princes, symbols of tranquility, delicacy, and nobility.

After this general opening, Rav Amital proceeded to eulogize each of his eight students at length. He spent a lot of time during the week leading up to the commemoration writing these personal eulogies. His daughters describe how he spent long hours toiling over each and every eulogy. In his great sensitivity, he made sure that each eulogy was the same length, so that no family would feel slighted. His sensitivity to the pain of the bereft families came to the fore when the yeshiva's library was built and dedicated to the memory of the fallen. He insisted that the memorial niches scattered throughout the library would be equal.

Occasionally this sensitivity was demonstrated toward other fallen soldiers, who did not study in the yeshiva. R. Ya'akov Medan tells of one such incident: A short time after the death of Benny Gal, a memorial service was held for him in Reḥovot, and Rav Amital was invited to speak. When he arrived, he realized that the service was also in memory of another soldier from Reḥovot who had fallen in the war, who Rav Amital did not know. The first two speakers talked mainly about Benny Gal, who was a very special young man. The third speaker, who was supposed to speak about the other soldier, delivered a homily and only mentioned the deceased briefly. Rav Amital, with his sensitivity, discerned that one of the two fallen soldiers had been given short shrift by the speakers, and so he decided to change the speech he had intended to give, to restore balance. In the short time he had before being summoned to the dais, he sought out people who knew the other boy, collected some stories that captured his personality, and, when it was his turn to speak, devoted almost his entire speech to a boy that he did not know at all. As soon as he had finished and descended from the dais, he approached Benny Gal's father and explained why he did what he did.

That summer, Rav Amital's daughter Devora wed Shmuel Karsch, a student from the yeshiva's first class. Yeshivat Har Etzion had a student band, but Rav Amital wanted the wedding to be without music. "I'm in mourning," he explained to his daughter and her intended. Ultimately there was a band at the wedding, which played part of the time, but Rav Amital could not dance to its chords. He felt like a mourner in every way.

The High Holidays of 5735 (1974) returned Rav Amital to the events of the previous year. On the first night of *Seliḥot,* he spoke about the verse (based on Ps. 71:9) that appears in *Seliḥot*: "Do not cast us off in old age; when our strength fails, do not forsake us." "We once thought that this verse speaks about old people, not about us," he said to his students, "but now, after the events of the past year, we see how much we've grown up, how old we've gotten, and we understand that the petition of this verse speaks to us as well. We ask God not to cast us away, and to give us the strength to cope."

Shlomo Brin, later a *ram* in the yeshiva and Rav Amital's son-in-law, was then a second-year student. He knew Rav Amital a little bit as a friend of his parents, but had not really gotten to know him as Rosh Yeshiva, since he had been called up to the war for his entire first year in yeshiva. These are his recollections of Rav Amital during the period between Rosh HaShana and Yom Kippur, 5735:

> One day, Rav Amital gathered my class at his apartment in Alon Shvut. He spoke about the fact that the High Holidays have always been difficult for him. He told us about a Yom Kippur he experienced in the ghetto, perhaps also about Yom Kippur during the War of Independence, and then spoke about Yom Kippur

> of the previous year, when the war broke out. He got choked up and burst out crying – not a couple of tears, sobbing. We were very young, shocked and confused by his crying. He sensed our confusion and said, "You are my Western Wall, my Kotel. Everyone turns to me, but I also need to turn to someone." After a few more supercharged minutes, he managed to change the mood and lead the conversation in a different direction.

Two months after the war, Rav Amital's friend Meir Ḥovav began pushing him to publish the war-related discourses, speeches, and talks he gave in the yeshiva, on the front, and over the radio waves. Ḥovav, who had edited and published numerous volumes, knew his friend well enough to realize that it would not be easy to persuade him to publish his words in book form. He therefore collected his own summaries of discourses that Rav Amital gave before and after the war, edited and printed them, and waited for an opportune time. One day, when he knew that Rav Amital planned to visit him, Ḥovav spread the printed essays out on the living room sofa. When Rav Amital arrived and saw the edited material, he agreed to the book's publication. In the introduction, the explained his reasons for consenting to the book's publication – pressure from friends and students who had been on the front and wanted something written about the meaning of the war and the processes of redemption. The book, *HaMa'alot MiMa'amakim* (Steps from the Depths), was published in Shevat 5734 (1974) by Yeshivat Har Etzion. It anthologized essays dealing with the war as well as words written and spoken by Rav Amital going back to the establishment of the state. Ḥovav also included an essay that Rav Amital penned during the War of Independence – "On the Path of the Religious Soldier during the War of Independence." Later published as "*Darkeinu*" ("Our Path"), it became a sort of manifesto for all religious soldiers.

After the publication of *HaMa'alot MiMa'amakim*, Prof. Joseph Dan of the Hebrew University had this to say about it:

> This book is worthy of being read by every Jew, religious or non-religious, whether or not he agrees with the author, because of the spiritual power and personal charm that can be found in each

> and every discourse and homily. This power and charm stem from two qualities, rare in our day and age, of the author's thought and manner of speaking/writing. On one hand – boundless faith, without any reservation or objection, in the Eternal Rock of Israel; profound and boundless religious faith, nourished and reinforced by the belief that we are living at the time of redemption, and that everything going on around us, even the most bitter events, are rungs in an ever-ascending ladder. On the other hand – extreme humility, a meekness of spirit in his dealings with every Jew, religious and non-religious; those who were brought up religious and those who experienced a religious awakening in a foxhole; those who share the author's spiritual world and those who are distant from it.

* * *

Two years after the Yom Kippur War, in November 1975, Rav Amital lost two other students. Bentzi Leibowitz and Naḥum Fenigstein, members of the yeshiva's seventh class, were traveling to spend Shabbat with friends at Yeshivat HaGolan in Hispin and were killed in a terrorist attack. A month after their deaths, the yeshiva held a memorial service for the pair. As he walked into his home after the ceremony, the telephone rang with more terrible news: during a security drill held by the yeshiva after the ceremony, Yitzḥak Lavi, a member of the yeshiva's fifth class, was accidentally shot and killed. Just seven years after its founding, the yeshiva had already buried eleven students.

The deaths of his students etched themselves deep in Rav Amital's heart and affected his personality. On the thirtieth anniversary of the Yom Kippur War, speaking at a memorial service on Mount Herzl, Rav Amital described the deep impression that the fallen left on him:

> At the memorial service held for the yeshiva's fallen, I made a supreme effort to characterize each and every one of them. It wasn't simple. I labored hours upon hours to know and remember all of them. I tried, and I was more or less successful. The families can tell you. But I want to tell you: I internalized everything. It became part of my personality. They live inside me. God, Knower

> of thoughts, Examiner of hearts, knows that there are elements of my personality that I internalized from what I remembered of them. I have been passing them onward for thirty years now, and so these elements yet live. In this respect, they are my teachers. My personality has been enriched.

There is a small measure of comfort, he continued, in the fact that the fallen have become part of the personalities of those who knew them:

> Fifty years ago, I knew an old man, a Holocaust survivor, in Reḥovot. He came to me and begged me to procure a tape recorder for him. "Why do you need a tape recorder?" I asked him. He replied, "I'm the only one who remembers a certain tune for *Tefilat Tal*, the Prayer for Dew. If I pass on, nobody will know the tune." The tune is still playing. Don't take it lightly. As someone who passed through the abyss of the Holocaust, I say to you: Tens of thousands of people perished together with their memories…Those who fell in the Yom Kippur War left a book of memories that is occasionally opened. They live on within us, and we pass on everything we learned from them.

Chapter Eight

In the Abyss of the Holocaust

*There is a way to avoid confronting the Holocaust. There are those who talk about God "concealing His face," "*hester panim.*" What is* hester panim*? Is God a human being who can hide his face and not see? We cry out together with the prophet Ḥavakkuk (1:13), "You whose eyes are too pure to look upon evil, Who cannot countenance wrongdoing, why do You countenance treachery and stand idly by while the wicked devours the one more righteous than he?"*

From Rav Amital's speech at an evening held in honor of the publication of A World Built, Destroyed and Rebuilt, 5763 (2003)

Even before Germany occupied Hungary, R. Ḥayyim Yehuda Levi, Yehuda Amital's mentor, was taken to a forced labor camp. Under the influence of anti-Semitic politicians in Grosswardein, the Hungarian military authorities wished to get rid of the topmost echelon of the city's Jewish community, and throughout 1942 they rounded up and deported the cream of Jewish society to labor camps. For Yehuda, who was very close with his teacher, this was a particularly harsh blow. When Rav Levi returned to Grosswardein after a long while, Yehuda asked him what would happen to their shared dream of magnifying and glorifying Torah. Rav Levi answered his closest pupil: "The essence of all our aspirations is to do God's will. If it is God's will that we be killed in the sanctification of His name, then we will aspire to attain this goal, making peace with it and desiring to perform His will." Rav Levi's words resonated in Yehuda's soul. Willingness to die *al kiddush HaShem* suffused all of his actions for the duration of the Holocaust.

The Germans occupied Hungary in March 1944. Until then, Hungarian Jews had repressed the terrible rumors that had been reaching them from neighboring European countries regarding the extermination of the Jews. Grosswardein's secular Jews were staunch Hungarian nationalists, many of whom deluded themselves into believing that their nationalism would work to their benefit at the moment of truth, and that they would avoid the fate of Polish Jewry. Even amongst the Orthodox, many believed that the Magyar nation would not allow the Germans to harm the Jews of Hungary in the same way that they had harmed the rest of Europe's Jews.

The only place in Grosswardein where they spoke of the atrocities being committed elsewhere in Europe was the central Orthodox synagogue, where the Klein family prayed. It was to there that Jewish refugees who had escaped Poland flowed, and they told terrifying stories about what was going on in the neighboring countries. One day just before Pesaḥ in 5704 (1944), one of the refugees grabbed Yehuda Klein by the arm and said to him, "You know, they're slaughtering Jews there." The refugee's words did not surprise Yehuda. The Klein family had their eyes and ears open. Yehuda and his parents knew that unless a miracle occurred, on the day the Germans would reach Hungary, its Jews would be subject to the same fate as the Jews from the rest of Europe.

And the Germans came. On 24 Adar 5704 (March 19, 1944), Germany invaded Hungary; the Jews of Grosswardein began to confront a harsh new reality and they feared for the future. A week after the German occupation, the heads of the Orthodox and Neolog communities were summoned to Budapest, to a meeting of the Council of Hungarian Jewry, established at the request of the Germans. At the conference, German SS officers informed the community leaders that the Hungarian government had undertaken to deal with the "Jewish problem," and that the German military authorities were only there to supervise the efficient and orderly implementation of the regulations. Alexander Leitner, the head of the Grosswardein Jewish community, wrote thus in his journal on his way back from the conference: "Our fate depends – if only just partially – on the Hungarian authorities, and this is a good sign. They will not want or be so bold as to behave like the Germans." But on 7 Nisan (March 31), all illusions vanished. A group of SS doctors condemned the local Jewish hospital. Five days later, Jews were ordered to wear a patch on their clothes, and thus the last of the optimists began to realize that their situation had changed.

Many Hasidim trimmed their long beards and sidelocks to reduce the chances of German provocations. At the synagogues and other communal gathering places there was debate about what to expect and how one should act in any given scenario. Yehuda Klein was present for a particularly vigorous debate. It was *Ḥol HaMo'ed* of Pesaḥ, and the debaters were young men of Yehuda's age who had gathered in the synagogue courtyard. The discussion revolved around their fears for the town's Jews. Two opinions dominated the disagreement, one espoused by Yehoshua "Shiko" Hager, the Vizhnitzer Rebbe's nephew, and the other by Yehuda Klein. Hager, a stormy and hot-headed youth, argued forcefully that the only practical solution was to flee Hungary as soon as possible via the Romanian border. He contended that any Jew who remained in Hungary would meet the same fate as Poland's Jews.

Yehuda Klein disagreed. In his estimation, fleeing was unrealistic. "Who guarantees that Romania will be any better?" he challenged Hager. "There is no reason to flee. The Germans are pursuing us and will reach us wherever we may flee." Channeling what his *rebbi* had told him two years earlier, Yehuda said to his friends, "We have to be prepared for the worst. If we must, we will sanctify God's Name at Auschwitz." Hager viewed Yehuda's statements as defeatist, stemming from despair. He contended that sitting and waiting meant relying on the *goyim*, and other European countries had already demonstrated what fate met Jews who put their trust in *goyim*.

Yehuda viewed Hager's proposal as being excessively belligerent as well as unrealistic: fleeing to Romania not only did not guarantee rescue, it also was not a solution for the masses. Without money, passage into Romania required prior familiarity with people on the other side of the border. The court of Vizhnitz had connections in Romania: In Arad, a city on the border between Hungary and Romania, lived many Vizhnitzer Hasidim who helped smuggle Jews out of Hungary after it had been occupied by the Germans. Yehuda Klein, who like most Jews of Grosswardein was not wealthy and did not belong to the court of Vizhnitz, ruled out fleeing, taking the sober view that for people like him it constituted excessive risk. Hager did not deny that rescue was not guaranteed on the other side of the border, since the Germans ruled Romania as well. Nevertheless, he claimed that the Romanians were friendlier to the Jews than the Hungarians. He did not address Yehuda's contention that crossing into Romania required money and connections that most of the town's Jews did not have access to.

The debate between Yehoshua Hager and Yehuda Klein was very practical, but rooted in their different personalities: Yehuda's realism, bordering on pessimism, and Yehoshua's pugnacity and unwillingness to make peace with reality.

Yehoshua Hager and Yehuda Klein never reached an agreement, and each remained true to his words. Hager was soon able to cross the border into Romania, and some two months later immigrated to Palestine. Yehuda Klein remained in Grosswardein. Years later, when they met in Israel after the Holocaust, they resumed their debate.

The ghetto decree was issued on 9 Iyar (May 2). Proclamations published in town set its borders, and gave the Jews four days to leave their homes outside the new boundary. Some twenty-thousand Jews were ordered to squeeze into the limited space of the ghetto, sixteen people per room, in accordance with the instructions of the German officers.

The Kleins' home was within the ghetto, so they did not have to move, but relatives and others were relocated into the small Klein apartment. Yehuda stayed with his family in the ghetto for only a few days, of which he remembered the horrible appearance of rabbis and rabbinical court judges, shorn of their beards and sidelocks.

Another traumatic experience of those days left an indelible impression on Yehuda: the Germans forbade the Jews to bring money into the ghetto. One day, a municipal clerk came into the Klein home together with a police officer and demanded that the father, Zalman Klein, display his money. Zalman took out his wallet and began pulling coins out of it. The clerk felt uncomfortable at the whole situation and apologized to Zalman that he was forced to demand his few possessions. Touched by the clerk's humanity, Zalman burst into tears in front of his family.

After two days in the ghetto, Yehuda received a draft notice for a labor camp. His parents were satisfied with the order; they understood that it could lead to his salvation. "I have full faith that you, my son, will survive and make it to Eretz Yisrael," father said to son. Taking leave was difficult. Yehuda and his parents all realized that this was no temporary goodbye, and that the chances they would see each other again were very low. Devora Klein implored her son to take family photographs as a souvenir; who knew when they would meet again? Yehuda refused. He did not delude himself for a moment, but he saw taking the pictures as an admission that their separation was to be permanent. "We will meet again," he told his mother, even though he did not believe it in his heart. Indeed, it was the last time that Yehuda Klein saw his parents, Zalman and Devora, his brother Yoel, his sister Ḥayya Sarah, and his grandmother Dina.

The Klein family was taken to Auschwitz at the end of May. Dina, Devora and Yoel were sent to their deaths immediately upon arrival at Auschwitz. Ḥayya Sarah survived the death camps but died soon after liberation due to the suffering and hunger she had experienced. Zalman was sent to the Mauthausen labor camp in Austria. In 1945, only a few months before the end of the war, he was hospitalized and apparently killed by his doctors via an injection of benzene.

Yehuda put several sacred volumes into the rucksack that he took with him from the ghetto: the Ḥumash, the Prophets, and the Mishna. When he thought about what would give him strength during the difficult days ahead, he added to his sack the pamphlet *Mishnat HaRav*. This volume anthologized some of the writings of R. Avraham Yitzḥak Kook and was edited by R. Moshe Zvi Neriya, then a young man. Yehuda had first heard of Rav Kook, who died in 1935, as a teenager. While studying R. Ḥayyim Hirschenson's *Motza'ei Mayim*, a commentary on several Talmudic narratives, he came across several quotes from Rav Kook of Eretz Yisrael. It was night, but upon reading these words Yehuda sensed a great light. The intensity of the experience of encountering Rav Kook's words led him to seek out more of Rav Kook's writings. He found the first part of *Orot HaKodesh* in the library of a prominent community member. He discovered the small booklet *Mishnat HaRav* in the library of the Grosswardein Bnei Akiva chapter, and bartered several other books for it. Throughout the difficult period in the labor camp, he drew strength and encouragement from this little work. Rav Kook's words captured his heart and had a decisive impact on his spiritual path after the Holocaust.

The first labor camp that Yehuda was taken to was Nagy Banya in Romania. As soon as he arrived, he witnessed something that troubled him greatly. Jews with money bribed camp officers in order to obtain medical work exemptions. In his sober way of thinking, Yehuda understood that work gave him his only chance to escape death. It was hard for him to remain silent in the face of his fellow inmates' evasion of work. Despite his youth, he approached the oldest of them and reprimanded them for choosing idleness. "How can you exempt yourselves from labor?" he admonished them, "if there's a chance that we'll be saved, it will be only by virtue of our work." He did not get any good answers. To excuse their behavior, some of the dodgers pointed out rabbis in the camp who also chose the path of work exemptions.

One of those rabbis was R. Yekutiel Yehuda Halberstam, the Klausenberger Rebbe. Wearing a military hat, beardless, the rebbe yet continued to lead his Hasidim in the camp. He held a *tisch*, the experiential encounter of every rebbe with his Hasidim, there in the camp, sitting on the ground together with his followers. Out of a desire to preserve their rebbe's honor, they made sure to obtain a work exemption for him. Yehuda found it difficult to countenance a rebbe and his disciples choosing a path that could place their lives at risk in the near future.

It was not long before Yehuda's concerns were borne out. The camp's personnel were replaced, and with it the phenomenon of bribes and exemptions came to an end. All of the camp's inmates were made to stand for hours with their hands raised, stripped of their clothes and their money. Those who were ill or pretended to be ill were rounded up by the commanders and sent to Auschwitz. The Klausenberger Rebbe was taken, too. He was first sent with a labor force to evacuate the Warsaw Ghetto, but afterwards he, too, was taken to Auschwitz and suffered terribly. By a roundabout means, he somehow survived and managed to get to Israel.

From the day that the personnel changed, the inmates' workload increased. Yehuda, who never possessed great physical strength, worked carrying bags of cement. As he climbed to the top of a four-story building while burdened by the heavy sacks, he was close to collapse. Yet even at those difficult moments he remembered to thank God that he was numbered among the workers and not among those transported to the death camps.

After about a month, Yehuda and the other inmates were returned to the Grosswardein ghetto. The sight that greeted them was unbearable. The ghetto was empty. All of its residents had been taken to Auschwitz. Yehuda returned to the neighborhood where he grew up, which had been a vibrant Jewish neighborhood and was now desolate and devoid of people. No less difficult was the knowledge of what had befallen all of those Jews, including his entire family and his beloved *rebbe*. And if that was not enough, the work given to him and the other prisoners at that time was to gather and sort all of the objects left behind by the townspeople. One of the homes to which Yehuda was sent belonged to R. Zalman Fuchs, a prominent member of the community.

The Fuchs home was well known to Yehuda. During the first days of the ghetto, the family of R. Ḥayyim Yehuda Levi, Yehuda's *rebbe*, moved into the Fuchs house. Rav Levi, his wife, and his three daughters were taken with the Fuchs family to Auschwitz on Shavuot of that year. When Yehuda came to the house several weeks later, he discovered his *rebbe*'s writings scattered on the floor of the empty apartment. In addition to his comments on Tractate *Gittin*, there were also letters of recommendation and appreciation from R. Ḥayyim Ozer Grodzinsky of

Vilna, Rav Finkel of Mir, and other great Lithuanian rabbis. To his great chagrin, Yehuda could not take all of the papers he found. Inmates were warned by the commanders not to take anything for themselves. Nevertheless, thinking and hoping that his mentor would need the letters of recommendation after the war, Yehuda took them. Unfortunately, Rav Levi did not survive the death camps. He was taken to his death at Auschwitz together with his wife and young daughters. The letters of recommendation did not survive, either – Yehuda lost them at some point during that period.

The sight of trains loaded with Jews leaving from Grosswardein to Auschwitz sharpened Yehuda's sense of a complete lack of understanding of events. The military front against the Soviets had already collapsed, and yet the German authorities still preferred to leave entire brigades at the home front in order to free up trains that would send Jews to their deaths. Military need was superseded in favor of the "final solution," and thousands of German soldiers sat idly next to the train tracks as trains filled with Jews rolled past. In Yehuda's view, this insane scene was so illogical that he could only see it as Divine intervention. "I saw God's hand in it," he described many years later, "I simply did not understand its meaning. He spoke to me, and I didn't understand a word."

By that stage, everyone had already realized that hard work could save one from death. But another illusion took root amongst some Jews: there was a rumor that conversion to Christianity could save one from the trains to Auschwitz. Not only that, it could bring one's family back to the city. This belief was reinforced somewhat by the fact that Christianized Jews wore a different mark than other Jews. Whereas all Jews in the work camp wore, aside from the yellow patch, a yellow ribbon, Jews who had converted to Christianity were required to wear a white ribbon. Sober Yehuda ridiculed the delusion of conversion to Christianity. One such apostate was a camp commander. However, after encouraging others to act as he did, he began to have qualms. His regret over his earlier actions caused him to sink into a deep depression, and many Jewish prisoners showed him compassion. Yehuda did not join those who identified with this man, and once even rebuked the commander, who was thirty years older than him: "I do not go along with those who show you mercy now. You brought this on yourself, so bear the consequences. The Torah says, 'You shall be whole with the Lord your God.' Only when you're with the Lord your God can you feel whole and complete with yourself. But if you're not with God, it's better that you suffer from this lack of tranquility."

Keeping mitzvot in the camp was not a simple task. Yehuda managed to keep kosher – he left over the meat that was provided for the inmates and subsisted on dry bread and onions. He also managed to put on *tefillin* every day, but he was forced to violate Shabbat in order to work. Nevertheless, he tried to mark the beginning of Shabbat in various ways, depending on his situation. One Friday, he put a clean shirt in his pocket. When Shabbat began, he quickly, while working, took off his sweaty shirt and put on the laundered shirt in honor of Shabbat. When he finished changing shirts, he quietly declared "*Shabbes*!" and was filled with the satisfaction of successfully marking the transition from profane to sacred, even while working.

The difficulty of keeping mitzvot at the camp in Grosswardein led Yehuda to jump at the opportunity that presented itself a few months later, to go out with a group of young men, all of whom were observant of the Torah and mitzvot, to work at a local village. Also in this group was Wolf Weiss, a cousin of Yehuda's father, whose wife and children had already been sent to Auschwitz. He was sent with Yehuda to a labor camp.

The fifteen group members managed to reach an agreement with the two Hungarian officers in charge of them: instead of working on Shabbat, they would work extra hours during the week. They also found a solution for kosher food: the butcher attached to the group was discovered to be a Jew. The officers supplied him with kosher foods to cook, mainly potatoes, and for those few weeks the prisoners could enjoy kosher cooked food. Additionally, the religious group had a small Torah scroll and a small shofar that they managed to smuggle out of the abandoned ghetto in Grosswardein.

The period that they worked in the village, which was the easiest part of a difficult half year of the Holocaust that Yehuda experienced, came to an end on the day before Yom Kippur, 5705 (1944). On Rosh HaShana, Yehuda and his friends were still able to enjoy their agreement with their commanders; they recited the special prayer liturgy, blew the shofar, and did not work. Two days before Yom Kippur, as they were in the midst of reciting *Seliḥot* for the Ten Days of Repentance, the group received an order to return to camp at Grosswardein, where the Hungarian army was preparing for the invasion of the Soviets. The group marched all night in heavy rain, drawing strength from the Torah scroll that they carried. All night, they passed the scroll amongst themselves. When Yehuda's turn came to carry the Torah, he felt that it was pouring strength into him and encouraging him as he walked toward the unknown.

The group reached Grosswardein on the day before Yom Kippur. One of the two commanders left them at the train station as he went to clarify who they should join up with. The group members decided to take the opportunity to flee. Yehuda, as usual, did not believe in fleeing, but since all the members of the group had scattered, he fled as well and hid with several other boys in the vineyards, not far from the city. Most members of the group were discovered quite quickly by the gentile residents of the city and held for the irate commander, who threatened them with death. The prisoners tried to bribe their commander to release them and exempt them from punishment, but he refused and led them toward the battalion headquarters. At that exact moment, the retort of combat weapons was heard. The commanders, who realized that the Soviets had arrived, abandoned the prisoners and fled in confusion.

Yehuda and his friends were left alone, without commanders. For the first time in several months, they felt freedom, even though uncertainty about their fate dampened that feeling as well. Yehuda and his cousin decided to stay at the family's home in the destroyed ghetto until the Soviet occupation. The community-owned building where the Kleins had lived had a cellar for storing wine. Yehuda and Wolf chose to hide there for the duration of the holy day. They got there a few hours before the beginning of the fast. Their only food was a slice of bread. They shared part of it for their pre-fast meal, and saved the rest for after the fast. They found other Jews and thus were able to pray with a *minyan* in the dank cellar. They had one *maḥzor* from which one of the worshippers would read aloud, with the rest listening and responding. Among the worshippers were Jews who had lost parents, children, spouses, and siblings. Yehuda was gripped by a powerful storm of emotions during those prayers: he began to realize the impossibility of basing one's service of God solely on the recognition of God's goodness and kindness. It became clear to him that a Jew who lost his wife and children is unable to base his worship of God on gratitude alone. "For the generation that experienced the greatest destruction in Jewish history," he would later explain to his students, "love of God could be based only on faith that stands strong even during a time of *hester panim*. As Job said (13:15): 'Though He may slay me, in Him I trust.'"

Another insight that coalesced in Yehuda's mind during his prayers in the midst of the Holocaust related to reciting the blessing "*she-lo asani goy*" ("Who has not made me a gentile") during the daily morning prayers. He never recited "*she-lo asani goy*" with fervor like he did at that time. Despite all the suffering he experienced during that period, Yehuda was proud to belong to the murdered and not the murderers; to the persecuted and not the persecutors.

Yom Kippur ended and the leftover bread failed to alleviate the hunger of Yehuda and Wolf. The next morning, they were forced to leave their cellar in search of food. They went through the apartments in the building. In Yehuda's parents' apartment, they found a piece of bread covered in a layer of green mold and rejoiced as if they had found a treasure. They brushed off the mold, divided the bread, recited the blessings, and ate. Years later, every time Yehuda would notice bread left over at the end of a meal, he would immediately begin calculating how many days it is possible to survive on such a quantity of bread.

But before they could finish eating the moldy slice, they heard the gate burst open and shouts ascending from the street. The shouts were addressed to them; they were being called to exit the building. As at other moments of danger, Yehuda did not believe in running away this time, either. He intended to hand himself over to them. "We have no reason to stay here," he told Wolf. But Wolf vehemently opposed giving themselves up, and Yehuda acceded. They hid in one of the rooms of the apartment. Yehuda the pessimist began saying his deathbed confessions. Wolf, hoping to be saved, recited chapters of Psalms. The Hungarian police officers broke down the door to the apartment and entered. They passed through the foyer, surveyed the kitchen and two other rooms, and left the way they came. Wolf and Yehuda breathed sighs of relief. Later they learned that the danger was not a great as they thought. Due to a temporary retreat of Soviet forces, the Hungarian commanders decided to reinstate the work of Jewish prisoners, and to that end they combed the streets of the ghetto in search of laborers. True to his approach that work would stave off death, Yehuda returned with his cousin to the labor camp. Together with one hundred and fifty other prisoners, they were put to work digging defensive trenches in anticipation of the Soviet invasion.

Sukkot presented Yehuda with a new challenge in his attempt to uphold a life of Torah and mitzvot under adverse conditions. In one of the courtyards he found a window with a large shutter, and he began planning to build a *sukka*. He opened the shutter in such a way that it would form a third wall, in addition to two walls of the building. Small beams that he had collected served as *sekhakh*. So that the *sukka* would not attract the attention of the Hungarian guards, he "decorated" by hanging his laundry out in it. Just before the sunset as the holiday began, Yehuda alerted his friends to existence of his improvised *sukka*. One after another the Jewish prisoners entered the tiny *sukka*, ate a *k'zayit* of bread, and recited the blessing on sitting in the *sukka* with great feeling. At some point during the holiday, the guards discovered the *sukka* and demolished it. To the great joy of Yehuda and his compatriots, heavy rains fell for the entire holiday, thereby exempting them from having to fulfill the mitzva.

By Simḥat Torah of the year 5705, the Jewish prisoners no longer went to work. The Soviet forces were so close to the city that it was impossible to leave. Yehuda and his companions managed to hold a festive holiday prayer service and dance with the Torah scroll that they had with them. After the Musaf service, the Hungarian commander of the labor regiment came and announced to his prisoners, "You're free." As the one who had protected them from Auschwitz, he added in an undertone, "Until now I safeguarded you. Now – you protect me."

Yehuda went out to the street and witnessed the declaration of liberation with his own eyes. Thousands of Russian soldiers marched through the streets of Grosswardein. He was completely overcome with emotion as he stood and shouted to the soldiers in Yiddish: "Jews! Jews!" Perhaps, he hoped, there were Jewish soldiers in the Soviet army who could help him survive the next days. A few minutes later, a soldier from the convoy shouted to Yehuda, with no less excitement, "Jew! We had a *minyan* of soldiers for Rosh HaShana!" – and continued on his way.

Yehuda and his companions, freshly liberated, still did not feel safe. They still did not know how the Russian soldiers would treat them. Within a few hours, the group had found two Soviet officers who agreed to protect them in exchange for Yehuda and his friends obtaining food for the officers. But the agreement did not last more than twenty-four hours. The next day, one of the officers came to the group's hiding place, injured and with his head bandaged. He told them that he was hit by the ricochet when he fired his weapon at a wall. When his condition deteriorated, he began screaming, "Oh, God! Oh, God!" Yehuda understood that when a Marxist Communist calls for God, his condition is indeed critical Together with Wolf, he tried to lobby the other officer to evacuate his friend to the hospital. The officer eventually agreed to take his wounded comrade to the hospital in a horse-drawn wagon. But when he returned, he told Yehuda that he left the other officer in the hospital courtyard since they would not admit him. "How is he?" asked Yehuda. The officer replied, "Kaput." When Wolf and Yehuda saw how the officer treated his comrade, they immediately understood that it would not be worth it for them to place their trust in him, and they began searching for an alternative hiding place.

Thus they reached the home of a gentile widow who agreed to host them on condition that they protect her from the Russian soldiers. The latter indeed arrived one night. They banged on the metal door until Yehuda opened it for them. The soldiers grabbed hold of him and pressed a gun against his chest. He begged them for his life. After a few nerve-wracking moments, the Russians calmed down a bit, but demanded that the two Jews play cards with them. The group went into the room and began to play. A bottle of vodka was opened and the Russian soldiers drank themselves to intoxication. At one point, one of them felt bad and lay down on the floor. The terrible attitude that Yehuda and Wolf had seen with the two officers repeated itself: one soldier went over to his sick compatriot, took his pulse, and said: "You're going to die, so don't interrupt our card game."

A few days later, Yehuda decided to go with some fellow Jews, on foot, to the Romanian city of Arad. In contrast to the Hungarian communities, the Jewish communities of Romania remained intact and functioned routinely even then. Yehuda hoped that he might be able to reach Palestine from there – a somewhat delusional hope according to many fellow refugees. Despite all they had suffered, only a very few refugees spoke about immigrating to Eretz Yisrael.

After walking a few miles, they were arrested by Soviet soldiers, returned to Grosswardein, and interred in a large courtyard together with other Jews and Hungarian gentiles. A sense of uncertainty and fear again hung in the air. A rumor began to spread among the inmates that they were going to be sent to Siberia. One after another the inmates were called in for interrogation by a Soviet officer. One of the inmates was a Hasidic Jew. When he was brought into the interrogation room and told to empty his sack, his *tallit* and *tefillin* fell out. The officer asked the Hasid about the nature of these objects. The Hasid guessed, for whatever reason, that the officer was a Jew, and he began cursing him in Yiddish: "How dare you ask me what these are! Shame on you for not knowing about these objects!" The gamble paid off. The officer smiled and eventually freed all of the inmates in the yard.

Wolf, Yehuda's cousin, decided to remain in Grosswardein and do business with the Soviet forces in the city. Eventually he reached Paris, remarried, started a family, and became wealthy. Yehuda, determined to reach Eretz Yisrael, decided to try again to reach Arad, and was successful. There, for the first time in seven months, he saw Jewish women and children.

Yehuda and his companions reached Arad late at night and immediately sought the main synagogue in town. Happily, they found it open and all lit up. Yehuda finally felt some relief. An open, illuminated *shul* full of books injected him, for the first time in months, with a feeling of mild serenity. At four o'clock on Friday morning, Yehuda and the other refugees he had arrived with began looking for the synagogue's *mikveh*. The Jewish refugees wished to immerse themselves before Shabbat. When they found it, they met a Jewish officer from the Soviet army. "Get out of here fast," he urged them, "the Russians are terrible anti-Semites. I wish I could run away."

The officer's advice suited Yehuda's plans. Right after that Shabbat, he hurried to the Communist party headquarters in town to procure a permit to travel by train to Bucharest, the Romanian capital. He had to debate with the Communist clerks whether Jews constitute a nationality in order to obtain the permit. The train was so crowded that he could not reach the restrooms. For that reason, he did not put on *tefillin* that day.

When he arrived in Bucharest, he found many Jewish refugees, including a family from his hometown of Grosswardein who offered him lodging. His primary concern at the time was to find the quickest possible way to immigrate to Palestine. Tzipora Hager, the daughter of the Vizhnitzer Rebbe, who was then in Bucharest, remembers the pain that Yehuda projected as a result of his stay in Romania: "I can't breathe the air here anymore," he told her, "I'm simply suffocating."

Just before Ḥanukka, 5705 (1944), a path to Eretz Yisrael opened. He sailed from Bucharest, via the Black Sea, to Istanbul, Turkey. He obtained a certificate there and traveled by train, via Syria and Lebanon, to Palestine. He lit the first Ḥanukka candle in his rail car on Syrian soil, but lit the second candle in Eretz Yisrael already. After long months of suffering and travail, he reached Eretz Yisrael on 26 Kislev, 5705.

Until he reached Eretz Yisrael, he did not see his rescue as a complete salvation. The dangers he faced even after his liberation from the labor camp showed him that only *aliya* to Eretz Yisrael would constitute a true rescue. Even after he started a family and decided to commemorate his survival each year with a family thanksgiving meal, he chose not to commemorate the day that Hungary was liberated from the Germans, and not the day that he escaped its soil, but the day he arrived in Palestine.

But there was another reason that he refrained from marking the date of his rescue: he was always bothered by the question of why he survived. "Was I saved because God selected me and rescued me from the Holocaust," he wondered in his students' presence, "or was it a time of *hester panim*, during which – according to the Ramban – God leaves His people to random chance, and I was saved by chance?" These questions never stopped bothering him. Therefore, he did not declare a personal holiday to mark his rescue, but rather celebrated his salvation together with his arrival in Eretz Yisrael.

The fact that he survived infused Yehuda with a sense of responsibility. He felt that he was obligated to redouble his efforts to replace those who were not fortunate enough to survive. He claimed that his survival gave him the courage to do things that would naturally have been beyond his individual ability.

Chapter Nine

A Survivor in Yeshiva

Those days, when I was studying at Yeshivat Ḥevron, yeshivot were viewed as outdated, even in religious circles. That a girl would agree to go out with a yeshiva boy? God forbid! I remember than after I got engaged, my fiancée – now my wife – introduced me to some of her neighbors. They asked what my occupation is. When I told them that I'm a yeshiva bakhur, *they looked at her with pity.*

Speech at Yeshivat Har Etzion,
5756 (December 1995)

On Tuesday, 26 Kislev, 5705 (December 12, 1944), Yehuda Klein arrived in Palestine with other Holocaust survivors, and was immediately taken to the Atlit Detention Camp. The camp had been set up as a military prison by the British in the nineteen-thirties and later converted to a detention camp for illegal Jewish immigrants. The refugees were overcome with excitement when served a supper that included butter and cream. Later they learned that the butter was in fact margarine and that the cream was in fact *leben*, but this discovery did not diminish their excitement about the welcome they had received.

Twice during the Holocaust, when his life appeared to be in danger, Yehuda vowed to himself that if he managed to survive and reach Eretz Yisrael, he would head for a yeshiva in Jerusalem to continue immersing himself in the world of Torah. Equipped with a miniscule sum of money, Yehuda left Atlit intending to fulfill his promise. Living in Jerusalem at that time were his grandparents and his father's two brothers, Gedalya and Eliezer, both carpenters. It would have been natural at that time to expect a penniless refugee to go to work and earn himself a living. When he arrived in Jerusalem, the uncles lobbied Yehuda to join them in their carpentry shop, but to no avail. Even a more honorable job, as beadle at the Yeshurun synagogue, which one of the uncles later arranged, did not succeed in winning him over. Yehuda was determined to immerse himself in the world of Torah, and so he sought out a yeshiva.

Enraptured by the writings of Rav Kook, he first went to Merkaz HaRav, the yeshiva founded by Rav Kook in Jerusalem. When he arrived, he was disappointed to find only a few students studying diligently – along with many others who studied there far more irregularly. As a budding scholar, he sought a yeshiva with a serious and erudite atmosphere, full of intellectual ferment.

The next option was Yeshivat Ḥevron, which had been founded in the city of Ḥevron in 1924 but moved to Jerusalem in the wake of the 1929 riots. Yeshivat Ḥevron in 1945 was modern and somewhat Zionistic for its time. Its students were primarily from the new Yishuv. For lack of other serious options, boys who belonged to the "*Mizraḥi*" community – what would later be known as the religious-Zionist community – attended the yeshiva as well. Out of approximately two-hundred students in Ḥevron, at least ten were "Mizraḥnikim" or "Kooknikim," as religious-Zionist followers of Rav Kook were called by their peers in the *beit midrash*.

Ḥevron's Rashei Yeshiva at the time were R. Yeḥezkel Sarna, R. Aharon Cohen, and R. Moshe Ḥevroni – the three sons-in-law of the prior Rosh Yeshiva, R. Moshe Mordekhai Epstein, who had moved the yeshiva from Lithuania to Palestine.

The "identity card" that Yehuda Klein presented to the Rashei

Yeshiva was the booklet *Mishnat HaRav*, that same small work that he had in the labor camps, that had given him strength at the most difficult moments. By presenting the booklet, Yehuda wished to make it clear to Rav Cohen who his spiritual mentors were, and with which religious approach he identified. Yehuda also used the booklet to answer the question of many in the yeshiva: how did he remain spiritually strong after his experiences in the forced labor camps? Not many Holocaust survivors made their way to yeshiva. Yehuda, who was often asked how – despite all the hardships he suffered – he had remained a *yeshiva bakhur*, used to present *Mishnat HaRav* as an answer.

Then as now, Rav Kook's teachings were not accepted in Yeshivat Ḥevron. Yehuda's public identification with Rav Kook was considered bold. It was a few more months before Rav Cohen appreciated Yehuda's erudition, at which point he began teasing Yehuda about his identification with Rav Kook: "Rav Kook's teachings are for the masses," Rav Cohen said, "not for a *bakhur* like you." Yehuda reacted angrily and enthusiastically defended his *rebbe*'s honor. Later, regretting that he spoke disrespectfully to the Rosh Yeshiva, he sought to appease him, but before he got the chance, Rav Cohen approached Yehuda to apologize for his words.

In any event, Yehuda Klein-Amital remained committed to the teachings of Rav Kook. More than a decade later, in the late 1950s, he published three articles about Rav Kook's thought – important and novel essays that garnered much attention. The first article appeared in the periodical *Sheluḥot* in 1958, and dealt with the concept of Israel's uniqueness in Rav Kook's thought. The second essay, "The Spiritual Confusion of the Generation in the View of Rav Kook," was published in 1960 in *Halikhot* and in the collection *Shana BeShana* published by Heikhal Shlomo. In this article, Rav Kook demonstrated his impressive mastery of Rav Kook's writings, which were not as readily available and accessible as they are now. Rav Amital concluded the essay:

> Although Rav Kook passed away twenty-five years ago, his analysis of the nation's spiritual condition remains valid. Anyone whose faith is precious to him cannot absolve himself from the

> responsibility that presently devolves upon him. The order of the day is to increase knowledge and light, and thereby to exalt, refine, and purify faith. This obligation pertains to everyone – the obligation to sanctify God's name, concern for the victory of sanctity, morality, and justice that shall become realized in life.

The third essay, entitled "Rav Kook for Our Time," was also published in *Sheluḥot*, in 1961. Rav Amital described the confusion of the believing individual who witnessed both the divine revelation manifested in the establishment and continued existence of the state, as well as the negative moral and religious phenomena in that very state. "Is this what the longed-for first flowering of our redemption looks like?" Rav Amital asked. He proposed seeking the answer in Rav Kook's writings: "All of these phenomena, those that existed in [Rav Kook's] time and those that appeared during the twenty-five years since his death, have their explanation in, and are compatible with, his profound teachings," he wrote. Twenty-five years later, however, Rav Amital was saying things that were completely different.

Rav Amital's answer in 1961 was that the State of Israel was indeed the first flowering of our redemption, but that it was accompanied by the processes of spiritual rebellion that Rav Kook foresaw sixty years earlier. He concluded the essay with a word of caution against delving into Rav Kook's writings without a great deal of faith: "for those of little faith, who believe halfway or a third, these gates remain closed."

In retrospect, the interesting point about this essay by Rav Amital is its complete disregard of the Holocaust. Twenty-five years after writing that article, Rav Amital wondered aloud about the students of R. Zvi Yehuda Kook and how they could implement the teachings of Rav Kook senior, speaking with certainty of the State of Israel as the first flowering of redemption, when in the meantime, between Rav Kook's articulation of his vision and the establishment of the state, the greatest destruction of the Jewish people took place.

* * *

Among the students at Yeshivat Ḥevron at that time was someone who would later gain renown and win the Israel Prize for his work on the

Masoretic text of the Torah: R. Mordekhai Breuer. Breuer, the scion of a notable German rabbinic dynasty and the great-grandson of R. Samson Raphael Hirsch, immigrated to Palestine in 1934, at the age of thirteen. After studying at Jerusalem's Ḥorev school and Yeshivat Kol Torah, he began studying at Yeshivat Ḥevron. This is how he described Yehuda Klein's arrival in the *beit midrash*: "A young *bakhur* with no glory or grandiosity, without any status or appellation, straight from the death camps to the house of Torah. Yesterday there was a knife at his throat and today he is entirely focused on studying Torah. Thus he seated himself on the bench of the *beit midrash*, like one of the fellows, beloved by all but not standing out amongst them."

Nevertheless, though he did not stand out, many sensed his unique qualities. One trait that caught the attention of his peers was his sincerity: "He's an interesting fellow," one of the *bachurim* stated with Breuer in earshot, "He acts so openly and simply, one gets the sense that he has nothing to hide." Another trait noted by his compatriots was his modesty. A student who knew him from childhood said of him, "He had some kind of mental developmental disorder that has persisted since childhood. From the day he learned to speak, there's one word, central for any normal person, that he has not been able to incorporate into his vocabulary: the word 'I.'"

For Breuer himself, Yehuda's arrival at Yeshivat Ḥevron had a decisive impact. At the time he was undergoing a crisis in his own studies; he had trouble digesting the yeshiva's Lithuanian style of learning. He later described Yehuda Klein's appearance as no less than meteoric: "He was my guiding star." For Breuer, Yehuda's most impressive attribute was his incredible integration of a brilliant intellect and a powerful faith.

> On the one hand, his faith was amazing in its simplicity. It was not dogmatic, forced, contrived, or artificial. It was not because the Torah or the Sages said such-and-such, but because the heart says such-and-such, and no man can deny the faith that emerges from the depth of the believing heart. On the other hand, he was an extreme rationalist, a clear thinker. He possessed a healthy, straightforward logic, profound understanding, and the sharp analytic skills of both a scientist and a Torah scholar. And these

> traits coexisted in complete peace and harmony: his intellect was not hurt by his faith, and his faith was not damaged by his intellect.

Yehuda Klein and Mordekhai Breuer developed an intimate friendship that would last a lifetime.

Outside the *beit midrash*, the *zeitgeist* grew ever more turbulent. The Jewish Underground had begun to operate in earnest, the struggle against the British was in full force, and the nationalist atmosphere influenced the group of *Mizraḥnik* students at Ḥevron. Most of them were active in the Hagana, and a few in the Irgun and the Stern Gang. These latter groups tried recruiting Yehuda into their organizations, but he chose the Hagana, the organization identified with the establishment. Meir Ḥovav, who enrolled in the yeshiva for the 1945–46 year after graduating from Moriah High School in Tel Aviv, remembers Yehuda Klein as someone so temperamental that he often suspected him of involvement with the Underground. But Yehuda's turbulent soul never expressed itself through extreme action. As during the Holocaust and later periods of his life, when the issue was taking action to change reality, Yehuda Klein always chose to work within the establishment and not to disturb equilibrium or breach boundaries.

Nevertheless, when it came to ideas and opinions, Yehuda's courage and stubborn insistence on his path came to the fore. Just as he was not afraid to present his divergent worldview to R. Aharon Cohen in their first meeting, he also did not attempt to conceal the singular relationship that he forged – while still a student at Yeshivat Ḥevron – with R. Ya'akov Moshe Ḥarlap. Rav Ḥarlap, a disciple of Rav Kook, was then Rosh Yeshiva of Merkaz HaRav. Late on Shabbat afternoon, a time considered propitious for discussing deeper aspects of Torah and theology, many students, among them Yehuda Klein, would visit Rav Ḥarlap at home to hear him speak. Yehuda was impressed with Rav Ḥarlap's righteousness, piety, and spiritual notions. Rav Ḥarlap's words about the sanctity of the Jewish people reconnected Yehuda with Rav Kook's ideas. Rav Ḥarlap's discourses provided what Yehuda could not get from his teachers at Yeshivat Ḥevron. Yehuda even felt that Rav Ḥarlap was almost telepathic, for on numerous occasions he spoke about precisely those issues that were at that moment bothering Yehuda. For his part,

Rav Ḥarlap admired the young man who visited his home on Shabbat and holidays. Yehuda also had opportunities to discuss matters with Rav Ḥarlap privately, deepening their relationship. It is possible to get an impression of the degree of esteem in which Rav Ḥarlap held Yehuda from a letter he sent him in response to a question. The letter opens: "The honorable young man, the superb and excellent, full of God's blessing, our master and teacher R. Yehuda Klein," and concludes: "Your friend, who wishes you all manner of goodness and sweetness, signed with anticipation for a speedy salvation, Ya'akov Moshe Ḥarlap."

R. Yeḥezkel Sarna did not look kindly upon Yehuda's visits to Rav Ḥarlap, and he criticized him for it. Yehuda replied to Rav Sarna that in his opinion, it is an honor for the yeshiva that its students seek out Torah elsewhere as well.

* * *

Once, Yehuda wished to stroll through the Judean Hills and visit the religious kibbutz Kfar Etzion that had been founded two years earlier, in April 1943. Together with a friend from yeshiva, they traveled on an Arab bus from Jerusalem, headed in the direction of the city of Ḥevron. When they neared Kfar Etzion, the pair disembarked and walked toward the new settlement on foot. On the way, they met a group of boys from the kibbutz clearing stones from the soil. Yehuda was surprised to find his old disputant from Grosswardein, Yehoshua Hager, among the stone-clearers. Hager had joined the Kfar Etzion pioneers soon after arriving in Eretz Yisrael. He was just as surprised to see Yehuda. At the moment of their meeting, they both remembered the debate that they had at the *shul* in Grosswardein on *Ḥol HaMo'ed* Pesaḥ. "Yehuda, is that you? A wicked one such as you survived?" he attacked, "You, who insisted that we prepare to die in the sanctification of God's name? According to your own words, you should have gone to Auschwitz! I'm amazed that you're alive!" In his heart, Yehuda answered Yehoshua, "What gall! You, the only one who fled, are calling me wicked..." Out loud, however, he merely said, "Thank God, I survived." But Yehoshua refused to let up: "Do you still believe? Did you remain religious?" Yehuda answered, "Had I lost my faith, would I have answers? Would the phenomenon be more understandable, clearer?" Rav Amital repeated this answer many times over the years when speaking about how a believing person deals with the Holocaust. "I saw God's hand in the Holocaust, but I did not understand what it meant," he told his students. His questions remained without answers, yet his strong faith never wavered.

Yehuda's vociferous opposition to attempts to rationalize the Holocaust found expression in another encounter with his past that he experienced at that time. In his hometown of Grosswardein was a small community of Satmar Hasidim. Already in his youth, Yehuda was revolted by the radical path of these Hasidim and the belligerent leadership of their rebbe, R. Yoel Teitelbaum. Rav Teitelbaum's rabbinate was in Satmar (Satu Mare), Transylvania, but his influence penetrated many Jewish communities in the region, including Grosswardein. When the Nazis occupied Hungary, Rav Teitelbaum was forced to flee to Klausenberg (Cluj), still under Romanian control, where he was arrested and brought to the ghetto. He ultimately escaped Nazi-controlled Europe aboard the Kasztner train and was severely criticized for abandoning many of his Hasidim in Hungary, where they were murdered. He immigrated to Palestine in 1945 and then moved to the United States a year later. During the year he was in Eretz Yisrael, he learned of the refugee from Grosswardein who was studying at Yeshivat Ḥevron, Yehuda Klein, and wished to meet with him. R. Aharon Cohen told Yehuda that the Satmar Rebbe wanted to see him, but Yehuda adamantly refused. "He knows my address," he told the Rosh Yeshiva. When Yehuda saw that Rav Cohen was taken aback by his audacious response, he explained: "In Transylvania they tormented anyone who didn't agree to accept his authority."

Yehuda's anger at the Satmar Rebbe's extremist behavior was compounded over the years by rage at the rebbe's attitude toward the Holocaust. Rav Teitelbaum, one of Zionism's staunchest opponents, claimed in his book *Va-yo'el Moshe*, published in 1960, that Zionism was the direct or indirect cause of the Holocaust. According to him, the Holocaust was both the result of and the punishment for Zionism. Yehuda Klein, by then Rav Yehuda Amital, was shocked by this teaching of the Satmar Rebbe – not just because of its anti-Zionist substance, but also because of its very attempt to justify the Holocaust. "A million children were murdered in the Holocaust," he railed, "The worst kind of paganism doesn't deserve a punishment like that! Nothing in the world can justify the murder and incineration of hundreds of thousands of Jews! There can be no answer to this question."

The time spent in Yeshivat Ḥevron did not bring Yehuda closer to the *ḥaredi* community with which the yeshiva was associated. Aside from differences in worldview, its gloomy lifestyle did not speak to him. He later explained that he never found any motifs of beauty, aesthetics, or warmth in the Ḥevron orbit. Ethics, Torah, and fear of Heaven were in abundance at the yeshiva, but he missed the warm and welcoming face of Torah. He sensed that a dark cloud hovered over the yeshiva students. "They acted as though they were constantly taking a defensive position against an attacker," he later described.

During Pesaḥ vacation of 5706 (1946), Yehuda wished to avail himself of some opportunities to work, in order to fund his continued enrollment in the yeshiva. Dov Schwartzeman, a fellow yeshiva student (and later the Rosh Yeshiva of Beit HaTalmud), told him that there was work to be found in the orchards of Pardes Ḥana. Yehuda and his friend Mordekhai Breuer decided to try their luck, and off they went. At that time in Pardes Ḥana, there was an attempt underway to rebuild Yeshivat Kletzk, which had been active in Poland until 1925, with students from Yeshivat Ḥevron.

The Rosh Yeshiva of Kletzk back in Europe had been R. Isser Zalman Meltzer, a disciple of R. Natan Zvi Finkel, the *Alter* of Slabodka. When Rav Meltzer made *aliya*, he was appointed Rosh Yeshiva of the Old Yishuv's Yeshivat Etz Ḥayyim. Rav Meltzer, considered a leading figure among the *ḥaredim*, was affiliated with the Agudat Yisrael party, and toward the end of his life even headed the Agudah's Council of Torah Sages.

The rebuilder of Yeshivat Kletzk in Eretz Yisrael was his son, R. Zvi Yehuda Meltzer, the rabbi of Pardes Ḥana. Rav Zvi Yehuda was fascinating in his own right. Even though his father, Rav Isser Zalman, sympathized with Zionism, he was considered *ḥaredi* since he served as Rosh Yeshiva of an Old Yishuv institution. His son, on the other hand, affiliated with the Zionist movement and belonged to the HaPo'el Mizraḥi party. The younger Rav Meltzer was a maverick in many ways. As an adherent of the Novardok school of self-improvement, he espoused irregular habits, did not submit to convention, and never paid attention to what was said about him on the street. For example, he wore a straw hat, not a black hat as was accepted in those times. He would often hitch rides on a horse-drawn wagon, not caring about his honored position as rabbi. When he was appointed rabbi of Pardes Ḥana, he moved there with his wife and three children. At the time there were very few religious families in the town, and its only school was the secular public school. Rav Meltzer debated whether to open a new religious school or to strengthen the existing public school by adding two Tanakh teachers. He discussed the matter with the Ḥazon Ish (R. Avraham Yeshaya Karelitz), who told him: "That's a difficult question. You are the rabbi of the locale, and therefore you have God's assistance (*siyata deShemaya*). I leave the decision to you." Rav Meltzer decided not to open the religious school and instead to strengthen the existing school. His own children even attended the town's secular public school.

When Yehuda Klein and Mordekhai Breuer arrived in Pardes Ḥana, they discovered, to their chagrin, that there was no work. In the meantime, they parked themselves in the *beit midrash* of Yeshivat Kletzk. When they first met the Rosh Yeshiva, Rav Z. Yehuda Meltzer, Yehuda had no idea that this meeting would have such a far-reaching effect on his life.

Rav Meltzer was very impressed with this unknown student's learning skills. After learning that the young man was a refugee who survived the Hungarian labor camps, Rav Meltzer began talking to him about his spiritual attitude toward the Holocaust. He saw that Yehuda refrained from interpreting events, so he tried to offer his own explanations for the Holocaust of European Jewry. Yehuda adamantly refused to accept his statements. Rav Meltzer began quoting a certain midrash, by means of which he wished to explain the Holocaust, but Yehuda remained insistent: "The Rock – His deeds are perfect," he would say, quoting Deuteronomy 32:4, "I am not prepared to listen to any explanation." Yehuda's complete and firm faith captivated Rav Meltzer. He was so impressed with this boy that he decided to offer his daughter's hand in marriage. Yehuda, flabbergasted, only wanted to know one thing about Rav Meltzer's daughter: "Does she have a good heart?"

Rav Meltzer's selection of Yehuda, the unknown yeshiva student, the refugee with no family, was highly characteristic of his personality. He ignored the consensus that as a Rosh Yeshiva and as the son of a Torah giant he had to marry his daughter off to a young man with family pedigree. He chose to give precedence to his own inclinations and personal impressions over accepted principles. He nevertheless wished to hear the opinion of Rav Ḥarlap about the boy he chose for his daughter. Rav Ḥarlap said about his student Yehuda: "He gets to the root of the matter."

Miriam Meltzer was the oldest daughter of Rav Zvi Yehuda and Sonia Meltzer. She was born when the family still lived in Jerusalem and was ten years old when the family moved to Pardes Ḥana. After completing her studies at the local secular public elementary school, she went to the Efrata Seminary in Jerusalem, then known as the "Mizraḥi Seminary," for high school. The final two years of high school included the study of pedagogy, and after five years students graduated with matriculation certificates as well as teaching certificates. In the middle of her final year of high school, Miriam was summoned to teach at the school administered by her uncle in Kfar Ata (now Kiryat Ata). As the granddaughter of R. Isser Zalman Meltzer and the daughter of R. Zvi Yehuda Meltzer, Miriam was considered a desirable match in the yeshiva world. When she came of age, the best *bachurim* from Yeshivat Ḥevron were suggested to her. Miriam met several of them, but did not find what she wanted.

After her father decided to offer her hand to Yehuda, he wanted to hear her opinion as well. One evening her mother called her to the kitchen. "Father is sitting with two boys from the yeshiva," she told her, "Go see if you like one of them." Miriam entered the room where her father was sitting with Yehuda Klein and another boy. They had come to Rav Meltzer to wish him a happy Pesaḥ and to ask him for some money that they needed to get back to Jerusalem. The second boy began conversing with Miriam. Yehuda was silent. Miriam glanced over at him – and was enraptured. She noticed a great intensity in his eyes. "That's the boy I want to marry," she told her parents that evening, "I saw his eyes, and that was enough for me." In Yehuda Klein's eyes she saw the intensity that she knew well from her father.

Yehuda and Miriam met three times, "unnecessarily," in Miriam's words, and decided to get married. "I didn't find work in Pardes Ḥana," Yehuda used to say, "but I found a wife."

The match greatly surprised the yeshiva world. The granddaughter of R. Isser Zalman Meltzer was going to marry an orphaned Holocaust survivor with no pedigree. Some members of Miriam's extended family even reacted with surprise. Her grandfather, Rav Isser Zalman, and his wife Beila Hinda, accepted Yehuda happily. Even before their engagement, Rav Zvi Yehuda took Yehuda to meet his father. Without prior warning, he asked Yehuda to say some words of Torah. Yehuda was embarrassingly unprepared, but managed to say some things that apparently impressed his future grandfather-in-law. Miriam's grandmother was particularly impressed with the joy he radiated. "A survivor, and yet so full of joy?" she asked in amazement.

Immediately after his engagement to Miriam in the summer of 1946, Yehuda returned to his studies at Yeshivat Ḥevron, but one sentence spoken to him by one of the Rashei Yeshiva caused him to leave. One evening during Elul, Yehuda was escorting R. Yeḥezkel Sarna home after they had visited R. Isser Zalman Meltzer. Rav Sarna began to discuss something that had been said in a discourse at the yeshiva, and Yehuda apologized that he had not been present since he was with Rav Ḥarlap at the time. Rav Sarna reacted angrily and spat, "You are not my students," referring to all of the students who regularly visited the home of Rav Ḥarlap. At that moment, Yehuda decided that his time at Yeshivat Ḥevron had come to an end. As a man of truth, he could not bear to study in a yeshiva where one of the Rashei Yeshiva had a grievance against him. He switched to his future father-in-law's Yeshivat Kletzk in Pardes Ḥana.

Around that time, R. Zvi Yehuda Meltzer decided to establish a yeshiva high school in Pardes Ḥana. The concept of a "yeshiva high school," having a full dual curriculum and engaging in serious Torah study, while preparing students for matriculation, did not yet exist. The yeshiva at Kfar HaRo'eh, established by R. Moshe Zvi Neriya in the early 1940s, still did not incorporate matriculation studies at the time, since Rav Neriya opposed it. Rav Meltzer recruited Yisrael Sadan, Michael Tzur, and R. Yehoshua Yogel and allocated them land next to Yeshivat Kletzk for them to establish their school, Midrashiyat Noam. Rav Yogel occasionally invited Yehuda to speak to the Midrashiya students, and it was there that he had his first experiences as a rabbi and teacher. At one of those speeches, a student asked what he thought about the debate raging in the world of biblical criticism about whether *Yeshayahu* had one author or two. To the students' surprise, Yehuda answered that he did not know. Rav Yogel, who occasionally would occasionally listen to Yehuda's discourses from behind the door, later approached Yehuda to express his dissatisfaction with the response. "How could you say that you don't know the answer?" he wondered. Every *yeshiva bakhur* was supposed to vehemently deny any uncertainty about the unity of one of the books of the prophets. Yehuda's imaginative response to Rav Yogel is instructive about the educational perspective that Yehuda had adopted even then: "This *shmendrik* is not really bothered by the integrity of the book of Isaiah. He's looking for an excuse to stop wearing *tefillin* and keeping the mitzvot. In my answer, I wanted to show that I, despite not knowing how to answer every question, continue to put on *tefillin*." The educational message that not every question has an answer, but that doubt should not undermine intense faith, characterized Yehuda Klein as a believer and as a teacher. Wherever he taught, he tried to impart to his students that intense faith that should not be shaken by questioning and pondering.

* * *

Years later, when Rav Amital was a *ram* and spiritual supervisor at Yeshivat HaDarom, he taught alongside his friend R. Mordekhai Breuer, who chose to use his *shiurim* to address biblical criticism directly and consistently.

In those years that he taught at Yeshivat HaDarom, Rav Breuer developed a method of biblical interpretation that later became known as the "theory of multiple perspectives," or *shitat habeḥinot*.

According to the book *Shitat HaBeḥinot*, published by Herzog College, Rav Amital played a decisive role in the birth of this method. The two of them were once discussing the verse in Genesis that describes Avraham's war against the four kings, saying (Gen. 14:14): "and he pursued them until Dan." Rav Breuer said that he had a hard time explaining this verse since the city of Dan had not yet been built in Moshe's time, and if so, it is unclear why it would be mentioned in the Torah given to Moshe at Mt. Sinai. Rav Amital, puzzled, answered his friend: "God couldn't know where Dan was even before its founding?" "His answer astounded me and affected a real transformation in my thought," Rav Breuer described, "I learned from him that the doctrine that Torah is from Heaven does not attribute the Torah to Moshe, writing under prophetic inspiration, but rather to God Himself, Who dictated the Torah to Moshe at Mt. Sinai." Consequently, Rav Breuer began to investigate the claims of Bible critics. He read their commentaries and developed a consistent methodology to deal with the biblical contradictions that their works present. This methodology came to be known as the "theory of multiple perspectives" since it treats the text of the Torah as being comprised of multiple aspects of the divine truth, aspects that originate in the hidden dimensions of Torah. According to Rav Breuer, God first wrote the sources of the Torah such that each of them expressed one aspect of the truth, and then combined the aspects into a single book that expresses the full divine truth. In *shiurim* that he taught his students, Rav Breuer repeated the questions asked by Bible critics, without informing his students of the source of his questions, and then resolved the questions using his theory of multiple perspectives.

At some point, a member of the editorial board at *De'ot* became aware of Rav Breuer's method, and the board asked him to write an article on the topic. Rav Amital read the essay and told his friend, "This essay is of historical significance." And indeed, it was a historic article. It was published in early 1960 and aroused a furor in the religious community. Many had a hard time digesting Rav Breuer's claims that the scientific conclusions of biblical criticism are important and even necessary for anyone who studies Torah for its own sake. A special conference, attended by numerous academics, was called to discuss Rav Breuer's article, and all of the speakers attacked his methods harshly. Many years later, Rav Breuer described with frustration what he felt like after the conference:

> Of everyone who read my article, there was barely anyone who understood that I accepted from the Bible critics only the discovery that the Torah has multiple sources, which can be proven scientifically. At the same time, I do not accept their opinion that these sources were written by multiple authors. Rather, I instead offer the Jewish belief that they were indeed authored by God,

> for this question depends solely on faith; science can offer no opinion on this. This distinction, which is rooted in the philosophy of Kant, was understood only by Rav Amital, who grasped it as soon as he read the essay. I found that to be amazing; after all, Rav Amital's formal schooling consisted of four years of elementary school, followed by study in various yeshivot, whereas the rest of the participants in the conference – all academics and professors who spent their best years in universities and temples of learning – could not understand what a Torah scholar of Rav Amital's stature understood immediately and without difficulty.

Some ten years later, Rav Amital invited Rav Breuer to teach Tanakh in accordance with his methods at Yeshivat Har Etzion. Rav Breuer taught at the yeshiva for thirty-five years, until his passing in 2007. At his funeral, Rav Amital eulogized him by saying that he foresees a time when the theory of multiple perspectives would be the sole method used to teach Tanakh.

* * *

The Meltzer-Klein family moved to Reḥovot – the city where they lived for nearly twenty years, founded Yeshivat HaDarom, and where Yehuda Klein's educational career began in earnest – as the result of family connections. Sonia Meltzer, Rav Zvi Yehuda's wife, was the daughter of R. Zvi Steinman, the chief rabbi of Reḥovot. Rav Steinman passed away in Shevat, 5707 (February 1947), and the people of Reḥovot urged his son-in-law, Rav Meltzer, to inherit his office. Rav Meltzer acceded to their request and began serving as Reḥovot's chief rabbi in 1947. The Meltzer family moved from Pardes Ḥana to Reḥovot, and with them Yeshivat Kletzk also migrated southward. R. Elimelekh Bar-Shaul, who had left Ḥevron to join the faculty of Yeshivat Kletzk in Pardes Ḥana, moved to Reḥovot with the yeshiva and served as its spiritual director. Alongside the yeshiva – and as a sort of branch of it – Yeshivat HaKibbutz HaDati began operating in 1948, and Yehuda was appointed to give a *shiur* there. At that time, a very close relationship developed between the Religious Kibbutz Movement and the faculty of Yeshivat Kletzk. An especially close relationship developed between R. Zvi Yehuda Meltzer and the members of Kibbutz Be'erot Yitzḥak, which was then located in the Negev. The kibbutz members' familiarity with Rav Meltzer began earlier, when the kibbutzniks lived in a temporary encampment for seven years in Pardes Ḥana, while Rav Meltzer was its rabbi. In 1943, they founded their permanent settlement near Gaza. The relationship was renewed when Rav Meltzer moved to Reḥovot. Rav Meltzer would officiate at weddings in Be'erot Yitzḥak, and his wife forged relationships with the women of the kibbutz. In the summer of 1947, as the wedding of Yehuda and Miriam neared, the kibbutz members offered to hold the wedding on their kibbutz. Since Rav Meltzer never accepted payment for officiating at weddings of kibbutz members, they saw his daughter's wedding as an opportunity to repay him.

On the night of 12 Av, 5707 (July 28, 1947), Yehuda Klein and Miriam Meltzer were wed at Kibbutz Be'erot Yitzḥak in the Negev. The night before the wedding, the British authorities declared a curfew on the Jewish Yishuv, in the wake of the kidnapping of two British soldiers by the Stern Gang, who held them hostage, demanding the release of their imprisoned personnel. Wedding guests were delayed by makeshift British checkpoints as they traveled south to the wedding. Only one bus made it from Reḥovot, and a single cab from Jerusalem – containing Yehuda, his grandparents Zvi and Esther Klein, R. Isser Zalman Meltzer, and his wife, Beila Hinda. Yehuda invited Rav Ḥarlap to the wedding, but the elderly sage responded, "Who has the strength to absorb all the [holy] light of the new settlements in the Negev?"

The wedding started earlier than the time called for by the invitation since they realized that no more guests would be arriving. The two grandmothers escorted Yehuda and Miriam to the *ḥuppa*, which stood between two haystacks. Rav Isser Zalman officiated. The wedding banquet, a mixed-seating affair, took place in the kibbutz dining hall. Members of two religious kibbutzim, Be'erot Yitzḥak and Sa'ad, sang and danced, bringing joy to the newlyweds. One of the songs sung by the kibbutzniks was "*Zemer Zemer Lakh*." The Amitals' descendants would sing this Israeli folk classic for the couple every year on their wedding anniversary.

Chapter Ten

Go Shave – It Is a Holiday

How can we not thank the Almighty for all the kindness that He has showered upon us? First and foremost, the State of Israel serves as a safe haven for millions of Jews. After the nightmare of the Holocaust, hundreds of thousands of Jewish refugees wandered around the globe, finding a home and refuge only in Israel. The state has contributed an incalculable amount to the restoration of Jewish pride after the devastating ḥillul HaShem *(desecration of God's Name) caused by the Holocaust. Today, too, the state plays an enormous role in the Jewish identity of our brethren throughout the world. For so many of them, the emotional attachment to the State remains the final thread connecting them to the Jewish people and to the God of Israel.*

From a discourse at Yeshivat Har Etzion,
Ḥanukka 5757 (1996)

Go Shave – It Is a Holiday

After their wedding, Yehuda and Miriam lived in Reḥovot. Yehuda continued teaching the religious kibbutz boys in the yeshiva, and Miriam found work as a teacher. Each Shabbat, they would travel to Kibbutz Be'erot Yitzḥak, where Yehuda would give *shiurim* to the kibbutz members. The young Torah scholar won the kibbutzniks over, and they tried to convince him to serve as their rabbi; he was in no rush to give them an answer. Ultimately, current events at that time rendered the question moot.

On Saturday night, 17 Kislev, 5708 (November 29, 1947), the UN voted to recommend the partition of Palestine, heralding the birth of a Jewish state. Yehuda and Miriam had spent Shabbat on the kibbutz, and gathered with everyone else in the dining room on Saturday night to listen to a radio broadcast of the dramatic vote. When the voting was completed, rejoicing broke out. The tables were covered in white tablecloths, the kitchen staff brought out wine and pastries, and Yehuda raised his glass and recited the blessing of "*Sheheḥeyanu*."

In the wake of the declaration, there were increased warnings about Arab attempts to attack Jews traveling on local roads. The kibbutz members urged Yehuda and Miriam to remain on the kibbutz, but due to Miriam's work schedule the couple refused to stay. The bus they took to Reḥovot the next day was the last to leave the Negev. It sustained hits from rocks in a Gaza side street, but arrived safely at its destination. From that day on, travel to Be'erot Yitzḥak in the Negev could only be done in armored vehicles. That Shabbat turned out to be the couple's final visit to Be'erot Yitzḥak in the Negev; the kibbutz was forced to evacuate during the war that ensued, and was re-established near Petaḥ Tikva.

The situation at that time caused Yehuda to want to enlist. His students, however, urged him to remain, telling him that if he left the yeshiva, they would, too. Since he did not want to dismantle the yeshiva, he decided to hold off his enlistment temporarily, but he never stopped thinking about it. Rav Bar-Shaul expressed opposition to the enlistment of yeshiva students; he feared that if the yeshivot were to close because their students enlisted, they would never reopen.

Rav Meltzer made sure to get himself a personal weapon. As mentioned above, his positive attitude toward the participation of Torah scholars in the defense of communities later led him to create, with the encouragement of his son-in-law Yehuda, a track combining military service and yeshiva study.

Yehuda's indecision about whether or not to enlist came to an end with the declaration of statehood on Friday, 5 Iyar, 5708 (May 14, 1948). The Kletzk Yeshiva students gathered at a small eatery on Herzl Street in Reḥovot to hear David Ben Gurion declare the establishment of the State of Israel. It was the middle of the *Omer* period, and so the boys all had gone unshaven for several weeks as a customary sign of mourning. Suddenly, Yehuda showed up wearing a white shirt. "Go shave," he told them, "What's with you? Next year, this day will be a holiday. Now, as the holiday comes into existence, you're not going to shave?"

That Friday night, Yehuda and Miriam were paid a visit by Yehuda's old friend from Yeshivat Ḥevron, Meir Ḥovav, who later would join the faculty of the yeshiva in Reḥovot. "I have decided to enlist," he announced to them. "The Chief Rabbinate permitted traveling on Shabbat to the assembly point at Tel HaShomer; I'm going tomorrow morning." Yehuda looked at his friend and smiled his broad smile. He pointed to a corner of the room, where his own rucksack sat, packed and ready. The enlistment of Yehuda and Meir on Shabbat – particularly Yehuda as a teacher in the yeshiva and a newlywed – made a strong impression on the yeshiva boys, and the news spread to other yeshivot as well.

That Shabbat morning, Miriam escorted Yehuda, with a heavy heart, to the bus that awaited the enlistees. The bus went from Reḥovot to Nes Ziona to collect more enlistees. When they got to Nes Ziona, Meir wished to get off the bus to watch the enlistees take leave of their families, but Yehuda instructed him to remain seated on the bus: "We have left our *teḥum Shabbat*," Yehuda explained, reviewing the laws of Shabbat boundaries. From Nes Ziona, the bus made its way to the assembly point at Tel HaShomer. There, Yehuda and Meir went their separate ways. Yehuda was sent to a military camp at Kibbutz Ḥulda, where the Seventh Armored Brigade was then being formed, and which served as a base for forces attacking Latrun.

When Yehuda reached Ḥulda, one of the officers called him over. "I don't know you," he said, "but according to the data I have, you were in the Hagana and have handled weapons before. You'll receive a division of immigrants who arrived yesterday from Cyprus, and you will command it." Yehuda refused to accept the assignment. "I don't have the training to command a division," he explained to the officer. Years later, Rav Amital loved to return to that moment and contemplate its fateful significance with a smile. Had he accepted the assignment, it could have been the beginning of a stellar military career...

Rav Amital ultimately enlisted as an ordinary soldier in the Seventy-Second Battalion of the Seventh Brigade. On 12 Iyar (May 21), the brigade set out to conquer the Latrun region. Yehuda's battalion was given the task of conquering the village of Beit Jiz and the hills between it and Deir Ayoub. Yehuda's battalion did not participate in the battles themselves; rather they set ambushes in Beit Jiz after its conquest. The performance of Yehuda's battalion commander disappointed him, causing him to rethink his refusal to accept the assignment. The inexperienced commander spoke to his soldiers mostly about how to retreat and recommended that they recite chapters of Psalms. When they returned to headquarters, Yehuda decided to report the behavior of the battalion commander to the brigade commander, Ḥayyim Laskov. Completely lacking in military discipline, Yehuda naively went directly to Laskov, but was rebuffed. Laskov gestured with his hands for Yehuda to go away, refusing to be addressed directly by a simple soldier. Yehuda decided to forget about it.

On 4 Sivan (June 11), the first ceasefire came into effect and the military used the opportunity to rebuild the battalions of the Seventh Brigade that had sustained severe losses in the battles for Latrun. Meir Ḥovav and Yehuda, who met up again during the temporary truce, joined the Seventy-Third Battalion, which later became the Seventy-Ninth Battalion.

Many soldiers in the battalion were new immigrants, mainly Yiddish-speaking. Headquarters called for Hebrew-speakers in the battalion to help it with the large amount of writing that accompanied its work. Yehuda, who wanted to fight on the front lines, did not respond to headquarters' request. His evasion did not work out, though. During a more thorough search for Hebrew speakers, the commanders found Yehuda. "You don't speak Hebrew?" they reprimanded him as they conscripted him, to his chagrin, into the battalion's signal office. Meir Ḥovav claimed that Yehuda was taken to headquarters for a different reason: "The battalion commander sensed something special in him and wanted him by his side at headquarters." According to Ḥovav, Yehuda broke a lot of social tension within the battalion. The battalion had been absorbing new immigrants from different countries, and there were frequent tensions between Moroccan immigrants and Ashkenazic immigrants. Yehuda shared a tent with nine Moroccans, and in contrast to many of his peers managed to find a common language and form friendships with them.

In addition to Yehuda and Meir, there were several other yeshiva students in the battalion. One of them, Yosef Haglili, had a penchant for organizing. He made sure that a synagogue was build and outfitted with armchairs. From that moment, the battalion synagogue became a significant meeting place for the yeshiva boys in the battalion. The group got together in the synagogue not just for prayers, but also for study and camaraderie. Religious soldiers undertook to pray in the synagogue even if it had to be without a *minyan*. Instead of going to the canteen during free time, they went to *shul*. The goal was to present a Torah-centered cultural alternative to the leisure culture that had developed within the camp.

Given their disappointment with the fact that the atmosphere of the battalion's dining hall was not conducive to Shabbat, the group decided to transfer their Shabbat meals to the new synagogue. They sanctified and honored the Sabbath with songs and words of Torah, at tables bedecked in white, and with lit candles. At those moments, they felt like soldiers in the army of the biblical Joshua, the first army of Israel in the land of Israel. When they learned that the Shabbat meals in the synagogue had begun attracting many soldiers, the battalion commanders recognized that they must mark Shabbat with special meals, and an order was issued to company commanders to hold festive meals on Friday nights.

Although Yehuda Klein was ordained as a rabbi only after the war, he was made the unofficial rabbi of the group during the war because his knowledge of Torah was obvious to all. The military rabbinate was just then being organized, so Yehuda – who was sought out on many halakhic issues, primarily *kashrut*-related – occasionally issued rulings himself and other times consulted with rabbis outside the army. Initially he took a relatively stringent stance, until a particular event caused him to change his approach, at least when it came to *kashrut*: one day, he saw a young man of Sephardic extraction, who he knew as a religious person, violating Shabbat. Yehuda approached him and asked why he had stopped keeping Shabbat. The young man replied, "I don't keep kosher anyway; after all, everyone's always saying that the kitchen here is not kosher…" At that moment, Yehuda realized the dangers of excessive stringency when issuing decisions for the public. Presenting the kitchen as *treyf* caused this young man to neglect other *halakhot* as well. From that moment on, Yehuda was especially careful not to declare the battalion kitchen non-kosher. Even when he had doubts that caused him to refrain from eating the food himself, he never announced his doubts publicly. He also made sure that nobody realized that he refrained from eating, lest they announce that the *kashrut* of the kitchen is unreliable. This cautious approach to questions of *kashrut* stayed with him many years later, when he sent students to the army and had to answer their halakhic questions.

When it came to Shabbat observance, he found less room to be lenient. As a soldier in a signal unit, he was often expected to write on Shabbat. When he was once asked to write something down on Shabbat that could have been postponed until after Shabbat, he asked to be transferred to a different job, where such things would not be expected of him.

At some point, all soldiers obtained a personal identification number and were asked to sign an oath of loyalty to the IDF. As part of the oath, the soldiers undertook to fulfill all commands issued by their commanders. Yehuda refused. He did not want to commit to fulfill any order issued to him. In the short time he had been serving, he had already become quite familiar with superfluous and purposeless orders. Even after they tried to reassure him that the oath was not really binding and was merely a formal procedure, Yehuda explained that for him and oath is an oath, and that he was not prepared to sign. After a discussion with his commander, he found a unique halakhic solution: he drew a period in the middle of the text. In this way, he accepted only the first part of the oath: to maintain loyalty. The rest – to uphold any order – he did not accept upon himself.

One day during the month of Sivan, while the battalion was stationed at Ein Shemer, near Pardes Ḥana, Meir Ḥovav looked for Yehuda all over the camp but could not find him. He eventually found him in Haifa, at Yeshivat Tiferet Yisrael, sitting and studying Talmud. Yehuda told his friend that he was observing the anniversary of the death of his family members who were killed in the Holocaust. He left for Haifa in the morning, entered the yeshiva through an open window, and learned close to sixty folios of Gemara over the course of the day. For decades Rav Amital observed the *yahrzeit* of his father, mother, brother, and sister on 16 Sivan. He presumed that they were taken to be killed immediately on their arrival at Auschwitz, in Sivan 5704 (June 1944). Decades later, one of Rav Amital's students found a death certificate for Zalman Klein, and it thus became clear to Rav Amital that his father had been sent to a labor camp and was killed in the infirmary at Mauthausen, Austria, on Rosh Ḥodesh Shevat, 5705 (January 15, 1945).

As the High Holidays approached in 1948, Yehuda worked to make sure that as many religious soldiers as possible remained with the battalion for Rosh HaShana and Yom Kippur, in order to enhance the spiritual atmosphere in the camp. On the eve of Yom Kippur, Kol Nidrei night, some of the soldiers were out on a military operation, but most of the battalion remained in the camp. Hundreds of them gathered in and around the small synagogue. After the prayer service, the religious soldiers asked Yehuda to say a few words about the holiday. He began with the well-known Hasidic tale, told in the name of the Ba'al Shem Tov, about a youth who came to the synagogue for the first time on Yom Kippur and wanted to participate, but did not know how to read. The youth stood up and said: "Master of the World, I never learned to pray, but I know the letters of the alphabet. I will recite the letters, and You can combine them to form prayers." The original story ends there, but Yehuda Klein continued, adding: "Here we stand on the first Yom Kippur of the State of Israel. We hold the old *maḥzor* with its old prayers, yet our hearts are filled with new prayers. Like the boy in the story, we will say the prayers in the *maḥzor*, and God will recombine them into the new prayers that are in our hearts: that we may return to our families, whole and healthy, from the battles that still await us, that the State of Israel be firmly established and stand up to its enemies; and that peace prevail in the land." These simple words penetrated the hearts of the audience. Meir Ḥovav recounted that emotions ran so high that many of those present, including the battalion commander and the officers, shed tears.

Despite the soldiers' emotional reactions, Yehuda was restless. Several days later, he told his friend Mordekhai Breuer, who was not in attendance that evening, "It's lucky that I gave my *derasha* after the silent *amida* and not, as is customary, after Kol Nidrei. Had I spoken after Kol Nidrei, I would not have been able to properly pray the *amida* afterward." Years later, Rav Breuer explained this puzzling statement to his students: "You know Rav Amital. On such occasions he cannot control his emotions; there was apparently a real struggle between his vocal cords and his tear ducts." When the soldiers could not find the words to express their feelings about his speech, Yehuda reacted happily: "Really? It was not a *ḥillul HaShem*? Thank God." He was not concerned about his personal failure, but that he would cause a desecration of God's Name. That is what disturbed him. He was therefore happy that he spoke at the end of the prayers, not at the beginning.

Several months after the holidays, the religious soldiers in the battalion decided to publish a journal under the auspices of their synagogue. At first they discussed a battalion journal, but Yehuda urged that it be defined as the publication of the synagogue, not the battalion. He wished to demonstrate to religious soldiers in other battalions that a synagogue could become an active center of Torah and culture, not just a place to pray. And in fact, the leaflet was ultimately conceived as a publication of the synagogue of the Seventy-Ninth Battalion, appearing under the title *Moreshet*. The group decided that everyone would contribute something to the new journal, and Meir Ḥovav was tasked with collecting and editing the materials. It was never easy for Yehuda to write. He only agreed to contribute an essay after friends pressured him. His essay was called *Darkeinu*, and in it he first articulated his vision for being a religious soldier in the new army of Israel.

"Our path is not through the storm; we have not walked through the whirlwind. The paths along which we have marched are modest and calm, but we marched courageously, for indeed we envisioned great things." Yehuda began his article with these words and went on to describe the vision of the group to which he belonged: to be considered amongst the architects of the image of the Jewish army. He described four objectives: to participate, as religious soldiers, in establishing military tradition; to imprint the Torah's mark on military life; to enhance the value of military service in the view of the religious soldier; and finally, the most important objective in Yehuda's eyes, to publicly sanctify the Name of God.

Later in the essay, Yehuda distinguished between religion and Torah. He defined religion as "the manifestation of individual or public worship of God" and claimed that it does not come close to encompassing man's entire inner life. He described Torah, on the other hand, as a broad concept that expresses the fullness of spiritual life. Yehuda asserted that it is a crime to conflate these two concepts, and called for replacing the life of religion, which is "an exilic and desiccated substitute," with the life of Torah, which is better suited to the era of the "first flowering of the Jewish kingdom."

He specified how, in his opinion, the Torah could be imprinted upon the military. With regard to *kashrut,* the position of the religious soldier must be "characterized by a realistic and practical understanding on the one hand, and faith and dedication on the other." He addressed the issue of creating a Shabbat environment at length. He proposed establishing a special schedule: late wake-up, no strenuous exercises, and festive meals.

Further on in the essay, Yehuda made an emotional appeal to the upper command echelons and to the great Torah sages alike. "You should know," he addressed the Torah giants, "that the religious soldier suffers from the disgrace of hunger – not hunger for bread or thirst for water, but to hear the word of God. Give us the word of God!" To the commanders he wrote that religious soldiers refrain from taking on command positions due to concern for dealing with difficult halakhic problems, sometimes involving life and death. He asserted that efforts should be made to personally identify corpses and to insist, even in a case of doubt, on proper burial. He called for devoted treatment of enemy corpses as well.

The essay concludes with two sentences that very much illustrate Yehuda Klein's worldview. One sentence called for recognizing the value of the individual Jew: "Recognition of the value of the individual within the military is in great danger if the erroneous notion that each soldier is only a number, and therefore expendable, has taken root." In the second sentence, which ends the essay, Yehuda Klein called for his group to engage in soul-searching: "We do not pretend that everything is okay with us, and far be it from us to ignore our own faults." This call for constant soul-searching and introspection became one of the lessons most closely identified with the author of the essay.

"*Darkeinu*," also known by its full name, "On the Path of the Religious Soldier during the War of Independence" ("*LeDarko shel HeḤayal HaDati BeMilḥemet HaKomemiyut*"), became a manifesto. It was the first programmatic-halakhic essay to examine the IDF as a Jewish army, and it made a huge impression on the yeshiva world and religious community at the time. Most instructive in this regard is a single reaction, that of R. Isser Zalman Meltzer, who wept when he read it. When his confidants asked him why he was crying, he pointed to the article and said, "Until now, we have had *Oraḥ Ḥayyim* for the *halakhot* of daily life, and the Laws of Kings for the messianic era. Then our Yudl comes along and tells us that the Laws of Kings have now also become part of *Oraḥ Ḥayyim*!" These words were spoken by the Rosh Yeshiva of Etz Ḥayyim, a leading sage of the *ḥaredi* community at the time.

R. Zvi Yehuda Kook, the son of R. Avraham Yitzḥak Kook, also sent a letter to Yehuda praising him on the essay: "*Yasher Ko'aḥ*, my esteemed friend, on your brilliant and comprehensive essay, sophisticated in its structure and style. Just as it expresses an ideology and provides direction regarding the way of a Jewish army, it also serves as an inspiration and a paradigm for like-minded peers. Take strength and courage from your role in this public service." Later in the letter, Rav Kook expressed reservations about Yehuda's distinction between religion and Torah. He agreed that there are differences between religion and Torah, but refused to accept the complete invalidation of religion in favor of Torah. He signed off with the hope that Yehuda would readily accept his comments and with the expectation of "news about your wellbeing, activities, and successes." Yehuda did not respond to Rav Zvi Yehuda's letter.

Prior to the publication of the journal, the writers decided, following the *zeitgeist*, to adopt Hebrew surnames with which they would sign their work. Yehuda chose to change the name Klein to "Amital." He drew the inspiration for the new name from a verse in the book of Micah (5:6): "The remnant of Ya'akov shall be among the nations, in the midst of the many peoples (*amim*), like dew (*tal*) from God, like droplets on grass – which do not look to any man nor place their hope in humans." In this verse, the prophet compares the people of Israel to dew. The medieval exegete R. David Kimḥi, Radak, explains in his commentary that the prophet is addressing Israelite refugees who will survive a difficult purge. Radak goes on to explain why the prophet allegorizes the refugees as dew: Just as dew comes from God, and one who hopes for dew prays to God that it descend, so too those refugees will be able to rely solely on God's salvation "for they will be a nation small in number, and the nations that gather against them will be numerous; who but He will be able to rescue them?" By choosing the name Amital, Yehuda wished to enshrine the fact that he was a survivor, an ember rescued from the fire. His name also expressed the isolation of the nation of Israel in the world, and the harsh reality disclosed by the Holocaust – that the people of Israel have none to rely upon but God.

Twenty-five years later, he used a verse from the same chapter as the title for a eulogy he delivered for his eight students who perished in the Yom Kippur War.

Yehuda was a bit afraid of the reaction of R. Isser Zalman Meltzer to the Hebraization of his name. The fad of Hebraizing names was limited mainly to the secular population; it was not well received at all within the *ḥaredi* community. Yehuda showed Rav Isser Zalman the verses in *Mikha* with the Radak's comments and told him that these verses made such a profound impression on him that he decided to change his surname to Amital. Rav Isser Zalman nodded – he understood the mind of his young grandson-in-law, and accepted his decision.

Thus, from the first day of the IDF's existence, Yehuda Klein-Amital was involved in carving out a place for Torah-oriented soldiers within it, a role that he took up again twenty-five years later.

Chapter Eleven

A Rabbi in Fatigues

Some words speak; others send a message. One must be sensitive enough to hear what lies behind the words. Rav Moshe of Kobrin once arrived on Friday afternoon in the town of Rav Yisrael of Apta, and he went to see how Rav Yisrael would prepare himself for Shabbat. When everything was ready, Rav Yisrael went into the beit midrash *and began to read aloud* Shir HaShirim *with great concentration and intensity. Rav Moshe was beside himself with elation, greatly impressed by what he saw. All of a sudden, the door opened, and a barnyard stench permeated the* beit midrash. *A Jewish cowherd approached Rav Yisrael and cried out: "Rebbe, my cow, my cow!" Rav Yisrael interrupted his reading of* Shir HaShirim, *and asked what was wrong. The cowherd explained that his cow, which was ready to calve, was experiencing difficulties in the birthing process, and were the cow to die, he would lose his livelihood. The Rebbe calmed him down, sent him to a veterinarian, and even gave the cow a blessing of health. Rav Moshe of Kobrin, who witnessed the entire incident, was very troubled by what he had seen. Of course simple-minded Jews must be brought near to religion, but Rabbi Akiva teaches* (Yadayim 3:5)*, "while all books of the Bible are holy,* Shir HaShirim *is holy of holies!" How could Rav Yisrael interrupt his recitation of* Shir HaShirim *for a cow? The Rebbe asked him: "Did you hear the Jew's cry?" "Certainly," responded Rav Moshe, "he cried out, 'My cow, my cow!'" The Rebbe said to him: "You weren't listening well. The Jew was crying: 'Rebbe, I am nothing; please draw me close to you!'" The simple Jew sought the Rebbe's closeness, but what could he talk to him about? Only his everyday needs. But his words sent out a message that went far beyond what was actually stated.*[1]

During the Yom Kippur War and its immediate aftermath, Rav Amital would travel, as mentioned, from base to base, visiting his students. Not infrequently he could only get onto the base by means of a clever ruse. One was a picture that he kept in his wallet. The picture appeared in the newspaper *Haaretz* soon after the yeshiva moved to Alon Shvut. It shows Rav Amital sitting in a *sukka*, flanked by Defense Minister Moshe Dayan and Central Military District Commander Reḥavam "Gandhi" Ze'evi. On one of Rav Amital's visits to Sinai after the war, soldiers stopped him at a checkpoint and informed him that the area had been closed to visitors under the general's orders. Rav Amital took the checkpoint commander aside and showed him the picture. Dayan was still serving as Defense Minister, and Ze'evi was the head of the General Staff Directorate and Special Assistant to the Chief of Staff. "As you can see," Rav Amital said to the officer, "I would have no problem getting

1. Rabbi Yehuda Amital, *Commitment and Complexity* (Jersey City, NJ: KTAV Publishing House, 2008), pp. 54–55.

A rabbi in fatigues: With students from the yeshiva's second class at the conclusion of a paratrooper training course.

Visiting his students in the army after the Yom Kippur War. Sitting next to Rav Amital is Yehuda Schwartz. The soldier on the far left is Shlomo Brin, later to become Rav Amital's son-in-law.

Visiting students with Rav Lichtenstein and Dr. Meyer Brayer.

approval to pass through." The officer was convinced, and he allowed Rav Amital and his escorts to continue on their way.

His frequent visits brought him into close contact with senior IDF commanders, and soon after the war he was asked by the upper command echelons of the IDF to be the rabbinic liaison between the army and the *hesder yeshivot*. The military even awarded him a brevet rank and unfettered entry, in uniform, into IDF camps. In the context of this role, Rav Amital often met with General Staff officers, especially the heads of the Manpower Directorate, whose role included responsibility for the military service of *hesder* students. With nearly all of them, Rav Amital developed warm relationships that continued even after he concluded his tenure in the mid-1980s.

After the Yom Kippur War, the IDF viewed *hesder* students as a significant pool from which to replenish the battalions depleted by the war. The many *hesder* students who took part in combat made a very positive impression on the chain of command, and the army began pressuring them to extend their military service and to become commanders and officers, an option that until then had not been available to *hesder* students. In that vein, the military brass agreed to open an officers' course, shorter than the regular officers' course, especially for *hesder* students.

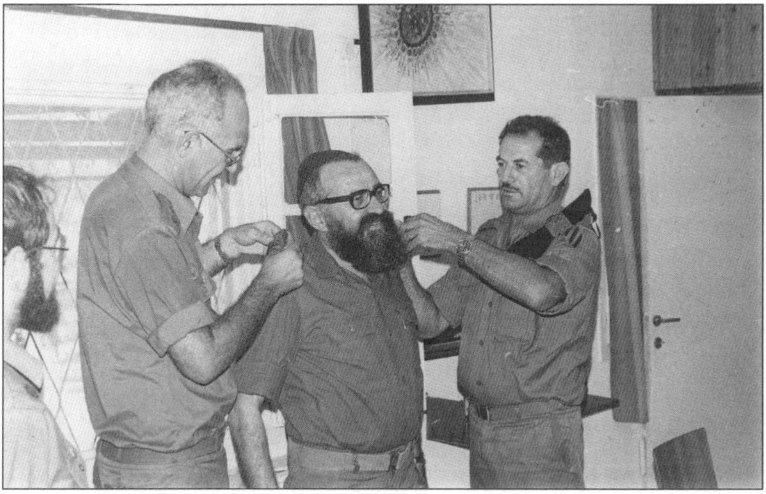

Receiving his brevet rank. To the right: Armored Corps Commander Brigadier General Moshe (Musa) Peled. To the left: Colonel Albert Shaulov.

With Major General Ori Orr.

Rav Amital was instrumental in creating the special course for yeshiva boys. During his military service, R. Yehoshua Ben-Meir, founder and

With his granddaughters Anat and Adi, upon receiving brevet rank.

Rosh Yeshiva of the Shvut Yisrael *hesder* yeshiva in Efrat, got to know the commander of the IDF Armored Corps, General Moshe "Musa" Peled. Rav Ben-Meir described how Peled got angry with him for introducing him first to rabbis who opposed opening the officers' course for *hesder* students and not immediately to Rav Amital, whom he discovered to be "an amazing Jew." "I sat down with him," Peled recalls, "and within an hour and a half we had come up with an excellent course." Over the years, Peled and Rav Amital developed a deep and meaningful relationship. In December 1978, the day before completing his task as the commander of the Armored Corps, he wrote to Rav Amital: "I received a lot of help from you – more than you can imagine: spirit, faith, tenacity, friendship, and love of the people and the land..."

Brigadier General (Res.) Maxie Ben-Ner then served as the head of the Manpower Planning Division of the IDF's Manpower Directorate. He recalls that Rav Amital did more than coordinate the yeshiva students' officers' course with the army; he obtained consent for the creation of the course from other Rashei Yeshiva:

> We convened the Rashei Yeshiva to discuss the issue. Defense Minister Shimon Peres participated as well. At the beginning of

> the discussion, Peres asked me to present the issue, but I asked Rav Amital to do it. He said, 'We met with the Manpower Planning Division, listened to their needs, deliberated, and decided that we could not remain apathetic and that we must step up. We express our consent for the expansion of this course and for enabling our students to become officers and commanders.' At the time, the course was defined as a temporary measure due to extenuating circumstances, but it took root and continues to this day.

Among the first officers to come out of Yeshivat Har Etzion were General Gershon Hacohen, the son of Rav Amital's friend Yedaya Hacohen; his brother, Rav Re'em Hacohen, who now heads the *hesder* yeshiva in Otniel; and Rav Yuval Cherlow, now head of the *hesder* yeshiva in Petaḥ Tikva. Cherlow and Re'em Hacohen both belonged to the eighth class of the yeshiva, which began its studies during the 1974–75 academic year – the year after the Yom Kippur War. The following class produced more officers than any other: half of the students in the class served as officers. Col. (Res.) Bentzi Gruber, later commander of an armored division in the reserves, belonged to that ninth class, and he describes the strong sense of mission that Rav Amital imparted to those students who became officers. "He inculcated within us the notion that joining the army leadership was the order of the day. His main reason was the army's need for officers after the crisis of the Yom Kippur War, but he also spoke about the great privilege of serving in the military after the Holocaust." Less enthusiastic about the students joining the ranks of officers was Rav Lichtenstein, who was concerned that the students' prolonged service would harm their development in Torah study as well as the general academic atmosphere of the yeshiva. At first he did not explicitly articulate his opposition, but by the end of the 1970s, when the proportion of students who wished to enter the officers corps swelled to significant dimensions, he began to curb enthusiasm and limit the number of students in the officers' course. Rav Amital did not change his mind about the importance of the course, but he honored his colleague's opposition, and the number of yeshiva students becoming officers dropped. Rav Amital continued to maintain that becoming part of the military leadership ought not harm a student's spiritual progress. As proof, he pointed to Rabbis Cherlow and Hacohen, who served as officers and still became Rashei Yeshiva.

Rav Amital's positive attitude toward military service found expression in other ways as well. Col. Ben-Ner tells how Rav Amital made an astonishing proposal to him in the mid-1970s: he wished to establish emergency weapons storage units near the yeshiva, to be available to the students in case of emergency. The units were not built because the yeshiva did not have enough manpower to justify it, but the proposal demonstrates the importance that Rav Amital ascribed to his students' military service.

At the rabbinic liaison between the yeshivot and the military, the yeshiva boys' fitness was more important to Rav Amital than their terms of service. Ben-Ner recounts that Rav Amital would occasionally complain that the soldiers did not get sufficient mechanical or ammunition training. "When Rav Amital would express concern about the soldiers' battle-worthiness," Ben-Ner said, "the commanders would just melt and immediately make the necessary changes." R. Yuval Cherlow recalls how surprised he was as a soldier by Rav Amital's reaction to his students' complaints about the workload they carried in the army:

> We barely slept. It was a very cold winter, and they worked us to exhaustion because there was a fear of war. Rav Amital came and we thought, great, here's someone we can complain to. We started telling him about the difficulty, but he said, "Excellent!" We were quite confused. He then explained his views to us. He said, "I'm very happy to hear that the guys in the army are working hard, and for two reasons – so that they're really fit, and so that they're too busy to get involved in nonsense."

Recently, there have been frequent tensions between the army and the heads of the various *hesder yeshivot*. During Rav Amital's tenure as liaison between the sides, there were no recorded conflicts. He projected to the officers a sense that he was working with them as a partner, which prevented any conflict. Col. (Res.) Mordekhai Tzipori, who got to know Rav Amital while he was commander of the Armor School and of the

Armored Corps, attributes Rav Amital's good relations with the officers to the dual responsibility that he bore: "His responsibility was not only to Torah study, but also to making sure that his people took part in the country's defense. Even when he concerned himself with the needs of his students, he did so with an understanding of the army's needs." Major General (Res.) Moshe Nativ, who served as the head of the Manpower Directorate during the 1970s, believed that the emphasis placed by Rav Amital on his students' military service stemmed from his view that their period of service was an opportunity for positive interaction and bridging between religious and non-religious soldiers.

The importance that Rav Amital ascribed to military training occasionally impacted his halakhic rulings. Nissan Zisken, a student from the yeshiva's early years, recalls that about a year and a half after the Yom Kippur War, a state of high alert was declared, and he and his friends were required to train on Shabbat.

> They told us that the decision to train had already cleared all the necessary hurdles, so we trained. But as a tank driver, I tried to do some things in a backhanded manner to mitigate the degree of Shabbat violation involved. A week later I met Rav Amital and told him how I trained on Shabbat. He said to me, "There was no need for you to act that way. One cannot train for battle backhandedly."

One of Rav Amital's qualities that helped his soldier-students during their military service was his ability to decide halakhic questions quickly, without hesitation. R. Ya'akov Medan tells of one such incident:

> In August 1970, a month before the events of Black September, we were designated as the unit on alert for the Airborne Naḥal battalion in which we served. One Friday they informed us, about two hours before Shabbat, that they were taking us for training. They expected me to issue a ruling about training on Shabbat, and I had no idea what to do. I wandered around thunderstruck. I went to the war room, even though I was just a private, and resolutely told the woman in charge there that I must call Rav

> Amital urgently. She was alarmed and immediately let me call. Rabbanit Amital answered the phone and told me that the rabbi could not come to the phone just then. I gathered that he was taking a shower for Shabbat. I told her that I had to speak with him, and he was out of the shower in a second. He listened to me and said right away, "Don't worry. It's a mitzva." At that moment, a great burden was lifted off my heart.

Despite his concern and sympathy for security and military needs, Rav Amital knew how to be stubborn and not compromise on principles that he deemed important. When one of the heads of the Manpower Division asked him if female soldiers could instruct the yeshiva student-soldiers as part of their professional training, he completely rejected the idea. The senior officer tried to persuade Rav Amital, saying, telling him, "We'll get halakhic permission." Rav Amital responded that it was not a question of halakhic license, but of educational values. "I do not want female instructors for our soldiers." The officer gave in, and the issue was dropped.

In his visits to IDF bases in the context of his job as rabbinic liaison, Rav Amital did not view himself as a spiritual supervisor in charge of resolving halakhic issues, but as a rabbi coming to boost his students' morale. Menashe Goldblatt was a company commander in the Armored Corps Five-Hundredth Brigade, in which yeshiva students served, during the 1970s. Goldblatt, a religious man though not a yeshiva student, described a significant difference between Rav Amital's visits and the visits of rabbis from the military rabbinate:

> When Rav Amital would meet with his students, there was more warmth than when a father meets his sons. He would embrace the students, speak with them, pull one of them aside and speak with him privately, and then do the same for another. He would gather them together, teach them a *shiur*, and speak about the importance of military service. I witnessed a special bond between him and his students; it was quite exceptional. I also witnessed visits by the military rabbinate. The rabbis would come and make sure that the silverware was kosher, that there were enough prayer

> books, and that the synagogue had everything it needed. There was a huge difference between those rabbis of technicalities and Rav Amital, a real rabbi. Everybody noticed the difference. Rav Amital was a rabbi to his students. I think that with regard to *kashrut* he trusted that they would manage. He didn't come all the way to the base to solve halakhic problems. He came to speak with his students and to be with them.

R. Barukh Gigi, presently a Rosh Yeshiva at Yeshivat Har Etzion, was a student in the eighth class of the yeshiva. During his military service, he and his peers were privileged to be visited by Rav Amital and Rav Lichtenstein on many occasions. Rav Gigi describes a conspicuous difference between the natures of their respective visits:

> When Rav Lichtenstein came to visit, he would bring the yeshiva to the army. He came to give a *shiur.* Rav Amital brought a whiff of home, like a father. He offered a short idea about the weekly *parasha* and then spoke words of encouragement that lifted our spirits.

Rav Amital's frequent visits to his soldier-students were an emotional experience for him no less than for his students. Years later, in a letter that he sent to his students in the army, he described those visits as a spiritual experience:

> The encounter of a rabbi and Rosh Yeshiva with his students in uniform, somewhere out there in a camp or in the field, in the Israel Defense Forces, is always especially exciting for me. Something that rabbis throughout the ages never got the opportunity to do, I, despite my unworthiness, have been privileged by the grace of God to do. God, Who oversees history, gave us the task, among others, of belonging to a generation in which the beating of the wings of a unique history, guided by Divine Providence, can be heard even in the most routine of events.

Rav Amital's role as rabbinic liaison demanded his intervention in incidents that were personally difficult. Such an incident occurred in 1978 when a student from the *hesder yeshiva* in Yamit took his own life during a course in the Armor School. At first suspicion was raised that the suicide was caused by abuse that the soldier suffered at the hands of his commander. Rav Amital immediately traveled to the Armor School to investigate the incident. When details of the incident were leaked to the media, he even granted a wide-ranging interview on the subject to the newspaper *Yediot Aharonot*. In the interview with reporter Menaḥem Ro'i, he expressed shock at the soldier's suicide and reservations about hazing of soldiers, but refrained from blaming the army before the final conclusions of the investigation were submitted. In that same interview, he was asked why he does not insist that *hesder* units have only religious commanders. He answered: "We have no interest in creating a closed ghetto for religious soldiers only…our soldiers, the yeshiva students, must get used to living together with non-religious soldiers and serving under the command of non-religious officers." Rav Amital advocated dispersing yeshiva students throughout the units in which they served, since he wanted them to interact with other soldiers. But he had another reason to prefer their broader distribution: after the yeshiva's terrible loss of eight students in the Yom Kippur War, Rav Amital thought that it was worth it to break up the yeshiva students into different companies and not create separate companies. That way, during wartime, an entire company of yeshiva students could not be hit. Other Rashei Yeshiva preferred to concentrate their students in homogeneous companies. Their main reason was educational – to reinforce the shared religious steadfastness of all yeshiva students in the army. There was a technical reason as well – so that rabbis could meet with as many of their students as possible during their visits to the base. Ultimately, the students were not dispersed through the various companies, and Rav Amital's fears came true during the First Lebanon War when many yeshiva students who served together were injured at the battle of Sultan Yacoub. Only after the war did the gradual dispersal of yeshiva students begin.

Chapter Twelve

Steps from the Depths

The worship of God, in whatever form, cannot wipe out simple human feeling. The Rebbe of Kotzk would say about the verse: "And you shall be holy people to Me" (Ex. 22:30), that God, as it were, is saying here: "Angels I have in sufficient quantity; I am looking for human beings who will be holy people."

There has been a tendency in recent years to idealize great rabbis, to the point of total disregard of their human feelings and weaknesses. The Torah presents the opposite approach: every person has a human side, which must not be denied. Even the prophets had doubts and difficulties. The Torah recognizes that man lives in this world, and it has no expectation that one behave as if he were living in an ideal and unreal universe.[1]

1. Rabbi Yehuda Amital, *Commitment and Complexity* (Jersey City, NJ: KTAV Publishing House, 2008), p.68.

During the winter of 1973–74, right after the Yom Kippur War, the Gush Emunim movement consolidated. The movement, whose name means "Bloc of the Faithful," was established following the shock and despair that took hold of a large part of the population after the war. National desperation led to discussions about territorial withdrawal and disengagement. Young religious Zionists wished to alter this course and lift the nation's spirit by posing a new Zionist challenge – settlement in the areas of Judea and Samaria. Before the Yom Kippur War, very few Jewish settlements had been established in Judea and Samaria – a handful in Gush Etzion and the Jewish community of Ḥevron. Jewish re-settlement of the hills of Samaria had not yet begun. Among the creators of Gush Emunim were R. Moshe Levinger, R. Ḥayyim Druckman, R. Eliezer Waldman, Ḥanan Porat, and R. Yoel Bin-Nun. The latter two, the youngest of the group, worked hard to win over more rabbis to the new organization. As partners in the establishment of Yeshivat Har Etzion, they saw Rav Amital as a natural ally. His book *HaMa'alot MiMa'amakim* had just appeared to great acclaim in the religious-Zionist community. Even those who had not been familiar with Rav Amital until then became aware of his spiritual teachings and identified him with the same ideas that motivated the establishment of Gush Emunim. Ḥanan Porat states that when he was asked what book articulates the ideas of Gush Emunim, he pointed to *HaMa'alot MiMa'amakim*. Other Gush Emunim personalities like R. Yoel Bin-Nun and Uri Elitzur saw it as the foundational text of their movement. The late Professor Ehud Sprinzak, an expert on Israel's political right wing, stated to *Haaretz*'s Iris Milner that in his opinion, Rav Amital's book presented a theological solution to the confusion that plagued the founders of Gush Emunim after the war. According to Rav Amital's thesis, the war was another clear demonstration that the nation of Israel was in the midst of the era of redemption. This thesis was part of Gush Emunim's ideological platform.

Rav Amital did not swiftly reject the invitation to join the new movement, but neither did he show much enthusiasm for the organization. In his book *Gush Emunim*, Gershon Shafat quotes – in the name of the late Yitzḥak Armoni, a resident of Kiryat Arba, near Ḥevron, who served as the Gush Emunim's general secretary – the severe critique that Rav Amital leveled at the members of the movement when they visited his home with the goal of converting him to their cause: "You're crazy. You're delusional. You think you're angels, but you're powerless. Do you have the gall to rebel against the NRP leadership? This is all just idle chatter." Rav Amital referred to Gush Emunim's political plan to become an influential ideological element within the National Religious Party and to dictate a new agenda to the long-standing religious party. He was never such an enthusiastic devotee of the NRP leadership, but he nevertheless viewed the pretension of the young Gush Emunim activists to influence the party's direction as naïve.

Even though Rav Amital did not pin his hopes on the new movement, he nevertheless attended several of its meetings. Shafat's book names Rav Amital as a member of the movement's education and public relations staff, and a meeting that took place at his home on 20 Shevat, 5734 (February 25, 1974) is mentioned as well. But Rav Amital terminated his affiliation with Gush Emunim after only a few weeks, for several reasons. First of all, as previously mentioned, Rav Amital was disinclined to support protests and anti-establishment initiatives. He said of himself that he only participated in a single demonstration his entire life – a Gush Emunim protest against the American Secretary of State Henry Kissinger, who visited Israel in the winter of 1974 to advance the Israel-Egypt Disengagement Agreement. Rav Amital later regretted even his participation in that protest. Additionally, Rav Amital claimed that despite the certainty that he exhibited in *HaMa'alot MiMa'amakim* about the present era being the "beginning of redemption," and despite his unambiguous call to transition from political Zionism to redemptive Zionism, he never meant to encourage activities on the ground that purport to hasten the redemption. "It was not a call to action," Rav Amital said of *HaMa'alot MiMa'amakim*, "When I spoke of redemptive Zionism, I did not think that this concept would be used to advance messianic Zionism." Rav Amital maintained that the Zionism of Gush Emunim is messianic since it wishes to alter reality to hasten the arrival of the Messiah.

It can be demonstrated from the book that Rav Amital never

meant to call for human initiatives to hasten the redemption. In a discourse he delivered in yeshiva after the war, published in *HaMa'alot MiMa'amakim* under the heading "Redemptive Zionism," Rav Amital said: "The time has come for Zionism to make way for the Zionism of redemption in our consciousness" (p. 43). Apparently, even in his clearest call for a redemptive Zionism, he spoke only of consciousness, not practice. Professor Avraham Shapira, a member of Kibbutz Yizra'el and the author of many books, read *HaMa'alot MiMa'amakim* soon after its publication and identified it with the ideology of Gush Emunim. In the winter of 1976 he brought some American students then studying at the Schechter Institute of Jewish Studies to Rav Amital's home. He introduced Rav Amital as "a Gush Emunim man." Rav Amital immediately corrected him: "I am not a Gush Emunim man," and Prof. Shapira changed his description to "a man who espouses redemptive Zionism." After the visit, the professor reread *HaMa'alot MiMa'amakim* and admitted to Rav Amital that indeed his theories differed from those of Gush Emunim.

Beyond the ideological differences, a major reason for Rav Amital's break from Gush Emunim was his opposition to its subjugation to the rulings of R. Zvi Yehuda Kook. R. Yoel Bin-Nun recounts that when he asked Rav Amital to join Gush Emunim, Rav Amital replied that there was no point unless Rav Zvi Yehuda agreed to take part as an equal among peers. "I know Rav Zvi Yehuda, and I don't believe he would agree to that," he summed up. Rav Bin-Nun claims that Ḥanan Porat even asked Rav Zvi Yehuda if he would agree to join as an equal, and he refused. Porat denies this, claiming that he would never have suggested something like this to Rav Zvi Yehuda, as his leadership of the movement was natural and unimpeachable. Regardless, according to Rav Bin-Nun, Rav Amital and Gush Emunim parted ways over this issue:

> Rav Zvi Yehuda had his positions and was not willing to open them up for discussion. Rav Amital wanted there to be open discussion and opposed Rav Zvi Yehuda's total domination. He also understood, in his wisdom, that if Rav Zvi Yehuda were convinced of something, there would be no need to debate the

> issue with R. Moshe Levinger or the others, since they were all disciples of Rav Zvi Yehuda.

Rav Amital did not confirm the details of Rav Bin-Nun's story, nor did he deny the fact that Rav Zvi Yehuda's domination of the group did not sit well with him, and that this was definitely one of his reasons for leaving Gush Emunim: "At the end of one of our discussions, Ḥanan Porat said that now we must ask Rav Zvi Yehuda. I opposed. I said that political conduct should not be influenced by religious halakha. They are two different things." Rav Amital opposed the attitude that developed in Gush Emunim that gave all of Rav Zvi Yehuda's pronouncements the force of a binding halakhic decision. From Rav Amital's perspective, the movement's activities were political and beyond the purview of any rabbi's halakhic rulings. Rabbis could advise political leadership, but their opinions carried no halakhic force. He frequently repeated this position years later, when he embarked on his own active political career.

* * *

Rav Amital's attitude toward R. Zvi Yehuda Kook must be examined more broadly, not just against the backdrop of the establishment of Gush Emunim. He knew Rav Zvi Yehuda in his youth, as a member of a small group that studied the writings of the elder Rav Kook with his son. He developed a sincere and profound appreciation for Rav Zvi Yehuda, yet still had quite a bit of criticism of him. He did not like Rav Zvi Yehuda's purported ownership of his father's writings, the compartmentalization that characterized his publication of his father's writings, and the spiritual direction of Yeshivat Merkaz HaRav under his leadership. He was especially critical of the emphasis that Rav Zvi Yehuda placed on the indivisibility of Eretz Yisrael, an emphasis that found expression in the way he taught his father's ideas. Of all of the elder Rav Kook's books, Rav Zvi Yehuda prioritized *Orot*, which deals with issues relating to the people of Israel as a whole, and addresses at length the uniqueness of Eretz Yisrael, the people of Israel, and the process of redemption. Rav Amital believed that the elder Rav Kook's central work was *Orot HaKodesh*, which deals with morality. On various occasions, Rav Amital pointed out that the word for morality, "*mussar*," appears in Rav Kook's writings more often than the words "Eretz Yisrael." Moreover, Rav Zvi Yehuda often spoke about the mitzva of settling Eretz Yisrael, citing the Ramban's enumeration of this mitzva as one of the 613 mitzvot. On several occasions, Rav Amital embarrassed disciples of Rav Zvi Yehuda by mentioning that this position of Ramban is not even cited once in all of the elder Rav Kook's writings (eventually, a broadside that Rav Kook wrote to the *ḥaredi* community, in which he mentions this opinion of the Ramban, was found; yet it certainly did not occupy a major place in his writings). Rav Amital did not claim that Rav Kook was unaware of the Ramban's position on the mitzva of settling Eretz Yisrael – on the contrary. Yet, in contrast to his son's position, this mitzva was simply not so central to the elder Rav Kook's thought. Students from the yeshiva's first classes confirm that Rav Amital expressed reservations about the spiritual path of Rav Zvi Yehuda even before the establishment of Gush Emunim. He clearly stated that he wanted his yeshiva to remain free of the teaching and influence of adherents of Chabad or Merkaz HaRav, since those two groups thought they had a monopoly on truth and were not prepared to listen to other opinions.

Another area of disagreement between Rav Amital and Rav Zvi Yehuda was the Holocaust. Rav Zvi Yehuda explained the Holocaust as "a cruel Divine surgical procedure" whose objective was to extricate the Jewish people from exile (he expressed himself thus in a discourse he delivered on Holocaust Memorial Day, 1967). In his teaching, the Holocaust was necessary as a vital phase in the redemption of Israel, emphatically putting an end to the *galut*. Not only did Rav Amital oppose this description of the Holocaust as necessary for the redemption, he opposed defining it as a necessity in any form at all. He agreed that the establishment of the State of Israel helped to heal the wounds of the Holocaust survivors somewhat, and that the *kiddush HaShem* of the state's establishment helped heal the *ḥillul HaShem* of the Holocaust, but he opposed the idea of any sort of causal link between the two events. In a televised panel discussion on the Holocaust in 1977, Rav Amital said: "To see the State of Israel as compensation for the Holocaust, as though these tribulations were necessary for the state to emerge – I cannot begin to fathom this. I will continue to live with the questions that even the prophets did not always have answers for. That's faith." Years later, when he began to talk more about the Holocaust, he sharpened his opposition to Rav Zvi Yehuda's explanation for the Holocaust. In a talk he gave to his students in 1998 he said:

> In the past, very grave opinions were expounded regarding the Holocaust: there were those who claimed that the Holocaust was a sort of price that the Jewish People had to pay in order that the Jewish State could be established. There are those who claimed that the State of Israel is the divine compensation for the destruction of the Holocaust. There were even those who claimed that the Shoah was the only way – or, at least in practical terms, became the impetus – to compel the Jews of Europe to immigrate to the Land of Israel. These are very difficult claims, approaches that I find hard to countenance at all.

Although Rav Amital stopped participating in Gush Emunim meetings, he never openly opposed their activities. In the summer of 5734 (1974), attempts began to create a Jewish settlement in the abandoned Ottoman train station at Sebastia, and many Har Etzion students took active part. Rav Amital did not express support for these efforts and did not believe

Rav Amital speaks in New York at a panel discussion on the contribution of the hesder yeshivot (1976).

in their efficacy, but several students recall that he came to visit them at the gathering point prior to one of the attempts, and he even praised their participation. On *Ḥol HaMo'ed* Pesaḥ of 5735 (1975), Gush Emunim held a march through the heart of Samaria to Sebastia. It was approved by the IDF and did not include an attempt to settle the area. Rav Amital and his friend R. Mordekhai Breuer marched. On 1 Adar 5736 (February 2, 1976), in a panel discussion in New York on the contribution of the *hesder yeshivot*, Rav Amital said about that march: "In fact, there is currently a lot of sympathy in the army for Jews who demonstrate their faith in Eretz Yisrael. Tens of thousands of Jews went to Sebastia. Without discussing the political value of this, the fact that tens of thousands of people believe that we can resurrect Samaria made a big difference. How valuable is such faith!"

The only time that Rav Amital expressed vehement opposition to Gush Emunim activities in those years occurred in the summer of 5739 (1979). Several women from Kiryat Arba, led by Rabbanit Miriam Levinger, broke into Beit Hadassah in Ḥevron. Rav Amital did not publicly denounce Jewish settlement of Ḥevron, but he nevertheless criticized the move because he thought that an urban Jewish settlement in the midst of a large Arab population was likely to generate superfluous security tensions. He was not persuaded by the claim that the Jewish community in Ḥevron protected the Cave of Makhpela since he had no special sentiments for the site. He visited the traditional tomb of the patriarchs only once, immediately after its liberation in the Six Day War. "There were several mosques at the site," he reported, "I felt uncomfortable, and the site did not really speak to me." Nevertheless, Rav Amital understood and valued visiting the Cave of Makhpela far more positively than visiting the graves of any other Jewish saint or sage. When asked about the sanctity of such gravesites, he generally answered with a story: "Once, a large pilgrimage was organized to visit the grave of the first Sanzer Rebbe, R. Ḥayyim Halberstam, author of *Divrei Ḥayyim*. Hearing of this, his great-grandson R. Yekutiel Yehuda Halberstam, the Klausenberger Rebbe, quipped, 'My *alter zaide* has not been there for a long, long time.'" Rav Amital expressed his disapproval of rabbis who traveled to Europe to visit the graves of *tzaddikim*. His attitude toward these graves stemmed directly from his general outlook, influenced by the Rambam's opinion (Chapter four of the Laws of Mourning): "Monuments should not be built on the graves of the righteous, for they are remembered by their words. One should not visit these graves."

Chapter Thirteen

A Scale of Priorities

There is a scale of priorities in Judaism, and anyone who fails to differentiate between one level of holiness and another will end up unable to differentiate between the holy and the profane. The proper order is: the people of Israel, the Torah, Eretz Yisrael. Ḥazal address the importance of this hierarchy in Tana DeVei Eliyahu Rabba, *Chapter 14:*

> *He said to me, "My master, there are two things in my heart which I love greatly – Torah, and [the people of] Israel, but I do not know which of them takes priority." I said to him: "People usually say that Torah takes priority over everything else, as it is written: 'God acquired me at the beginning of His way' (Prov. 8:22), but I say that the holy [people of] Israel takes priority, as it is written, 'Israel is holy to God; the first of His produce' (Jer. 2:3)."*

In late 1977, six months after the "*Mahapakh*" ("Revolution") that swept Menaḥem Begin and his Likud Party into power, Egypt and Israel forged diplomatic ties. In Kislev 5738 (November 1977), Egyptian President Anwar El Sadat visited Israel, and by the end of December the Knesset had already approved the peace plan that Begin outlined after Sadat's visit. The plan mentioned, for the first time, the granting of political autonomy to the Arabs of Judea and Samaria. The joint staff of Gush Emunim and the Movement for the Greater Land of Israel decided to launch a series of PR operations against Begin's peace plan, which they claimed endangered the State of Israel. In contrast to them, Rav Yehuda Amital sang a completely different tune. In a discourse he delivered at the yeshiva on 11 Tevet 5738 (December 21, 1977), later published in the yeshiva's leaflet, he spoke about the importance of the emerging accords:

> Where will this lead? It's a mystery. Nobody knows whether there will be peace – a partial peace, a separate peace, or full peace. I don't know, but a lot has already been attained if war has been postponed... I thank God for every day that goes by without war, especially in the present era. Postponing war during the most critical period in the history of the Jewish people is a great thing.

This sheds light on some later developments in Rav Amital's leadership. Here, for the first time, Rav Amital expressed his anxiety about another war. While he never rejoiced at the prospect of war, he also never expressed apprehension about the Six Day War or the Yom Kippur War. He described the Six Day War as a "great event" and the Yom Kippur War in biblical-messianic terms. In 1978, he first spoke of a different path to redemption: "Remember that there are two paths to redemption: the path of war and the path of peace." Later in the same discourse, Rav Amital attributed spiritual significance to the peace agreement with Egypt:

> The inner meaning of the recognition of the State of Israel by

Celebrating the tenth anniversary of the return to Kfar Etzion, August 1977. Speaking: Prime Minister Menaḥem Begin. Seated (from right): Yoḥanan Ben-Ya'akov, Rav Amital.

> some Arab nations is the recognition of God's Kingship. If a large country like Egypt is prepared to recognize the State of Israel, it really means that they recognize God's *Malkhut*, for the dominion of Israel is the dominion of God... It has been a long process, fraught with pain. We hope and pray that from now on everything will proceed along the path of peace.

He continued and spoke, possibly for the very first time, about withdrawal from parts of Eretz Yisrael in order to obtain peace.

> There may be a situation in which we would need to relinquish [territories], and there may be a situation in which the interests of the people of Israel demand that we not surrender one iota. This is the central problem. Gentlemen, there is nothing that so completely aggravates me, that enrages me to the point of losing control, more than when I hear Jews talking about peace as a "gamble." Can peace be a gamble? Whoever says so is either a

> liar or hopelessly naïve. In a generation where one third of our people were consumed on the altar, they speak of peace in terms of a gamble? The danger in which the entire state may find itself – that's a gamble."

Further on in this discourse, Rav Amital hedged his pronouncements and criticized those who too easily relinquished parts of Eretz Yisrael, only to make life a bit easier for Jewish life in Israel and abroad. He stated that from his perspective, parts of Eretz Yisrael should be given up only if the alternative is danger. He likened it to amputating a limb to safe the rest of the body. He concluded with a prayer that redemption would thenceforth take the path of peace, not war:

> Peace is a challenge, a great spiritual challenge; we will not run away from this challenge. Were we to flee from challenges, we would not have built yeshiva high schools or *hesder yeshivot*. We would not have returned to Gush Etzion. We must face challenges, and with God's help we will succeed. As a natural process, real peace is indeed very far off. But I have faith. Perhaps, if we take the first steps, the Almighty will bring everything about through the path of peace.

To understand the significance of Rav Amital's support of the peace process with Egypt, it must be compared to statements by the leaders of Gush Emunim at the same time. In his *Dear Brothers – The West Bank Jewish Underground*, Ḥagai Segal quotes the official summary of a settlers' conference that took place the same week that Rav Amital spoke out in favor of the peace accords. Their statement made an emotional appeal directly to Prime Minister Begin: "Retract. Remain faithful to the deep Jewish roots that brought you this far. If you do not lead the people to their homeland at this time – 'relief and deliverance will come to the Jews from another quarter...who knows, perhaps you have attained royalty for just such a time.' (cf. Esther 4:14)" It can be argued that Israel's diplomacy vis-à-vis Egypt was the watershed moment at which the paths of Rav Amital and Gush Emunim clearly diverged. Although he had earlier expressed reservations about the *modus operandi* of Gush

Emunim members, the emerging accords with Egypt was the first political event that produced diametrically opposed responses on the parts of Rav Amital and Gush Emunim.

The Camp David Accords between Israel and Egypt, signed in Elul 5738 (September 1978), established that in the framework of the peace agreement Israel would withdraw its forces from the Sinai and evacuate all of the settlements that had been constructed there. The evacuation took place three and a half years later, in April 1982. Rav Amital, who had supported the peace accords, opposed Gush Emunim's struggle to prevent the withdrawal. In addition to the fact that he believed that the path of peace should be tried, even if it meant evacuation of settlements, he opposed the struggle also because the evacuation was the result of a government decision, and from his perspective such a decision was binding. Yamit, the largest Jewish settlement in the Sinai and the lightning rod for opposition to the pullout, was made a closed military zone in March. Despite the checkpoints, many young religious Zionists managed to infiltrate the area, where they began organizing resistance to the evacuation. Rav Amital gathered the members of the Kollel at Yeshivat Har Etzion and forbade them from going to Yamit: "Whoever wants to go can go – just don't come back." Ya'akov Shapira, then a young Kollel member, heard Rav Amital but nevertheless decided to go to Yamit. He felt that he was unable to continue sitting and learning while settlements were being evacuated. He was aware of the ramifications of his decision but nevertheless decided to close his Gemara and join the people of Gush Emunim in the Sinai. Before leaving, he wrote a letter to Rav Amital expressing his feelings. Rav Amital did not respond. After Pesaḥ, Shapira returned to the yeshiva and asked Rav Amital if he had to leave. Rav Amital answered in the affirmative, but let Shapira remain until the end of the year so that he could better organize his departure. At the end of the summer, Shapira left for Yeshivat Merkaz HaRav. He believes that had he tried to persuade Rav Amital, he would have been allowed to stay in the yeshiva, but by that point he had lost the desire to remain.

R. Ya'akov Medan, by then a *ram* in the yeshiva, explains that Rav Amital only forbade students from going to Yamit while the yeshiva was in session. He never intended to forbid them from going there during

Pesaḥ vacation, which began just a few days later. Rav Amital never told his students what to do during their free time. Rav Medan himself went to Yamit on the last day of *ḥoref zeman*. He was joined in the struggle on the rooftops of Yamit by thirty-five students from Yeshivat Har Etzion. When he returned to the yeshiva, two days after the beginning of the summer session, Rav Amital said nothing to him about it. Furthermore, Rav Amital did not prevent Rav Medan from giving a series of talks in the yeshiva in which he articulated his position against the evacuation of settlements.

On Purim of that year, as the situation in Yamit was intensifying, Rav Amital dubbed the students who were fighting against the withdrawal "Satmar Hasidim" due to their opposition to a government decision. Though said in a jesting, Purim atmosphere, the moniker expressed Rav Amital's feelings all too well. Shimon Siani, then a first year student at the yeshiva, remembers Rav Amital's sharp remarks, but notes that at that year's Purim party, Rav Amital joined in the singing of Naomi Shemer's "Al Kol Eleh," with its tagline "do not uproot what has been planted," which had become the anthem of the withdrawal's opponents. Siani viewed Rav Amital's conduct as an expression of the complexity of his personality and positions. "As he sang with his students, he was trying to express his overpowering love for Eretz Yisrael, despite his agreement with the concessions. Even when he shouted 'Satmars,' it was out of great love and intense pain."

Rav Amital similarly reacted sharply to another issue then current – the rumors that extreme rightist activists were planning to perpetrate terrorist acts against Egypt in order to prevent the evacuation. "If people decide to bomb Cairo, they must be stopped in any way possible. They have the status of a *rodef*," Rav Amital pronounced, making reference to a halakhic concept that permits a pre-emptive strike against a "pursuer" with intent to kill. Some saw his statement as a quasi-prophecy about the actions of the Jewish Underground, which was discovered several years later. In the aftermath of the Rabin assassination, Rav Amital's statement was quoted in the media to show that he – who attacked the way that right-wing rabbis used halakha in their struggle against the government – had previously invoked the law of the *rodef*. Rav Amital did not retract his strong statement, but clarified that at the time he spoke those words it was obvious to everyone that he was discussing a purely hypothetical scenario.

On the Shushan Purim before the withdrawal, Rav Amital hosted his friend Yehoshua Cohen, the former Stern Gang member. Cohen informed Rav Amital of his intention to begin a hunger strike at the Kotel plaza, protesting the evacuation of the settlements in the Yamit region. The Purim feast at Rav Amital's home was Cohen's final meal before beginning his fast. In the book *Desert Wind: The Story of Yehoshua Cohen*, author Yair Sheleg describes that meal as being festive and apolitical. Cohen, who got to know Rav Amital when the yeshiva was still in Kfar Etzion, said at the meal that if his doctor and Rav Amital instruct him to break his fast, he would. In conversations they had during that period, Cohen expressed his disappointment that most citizens of Israel did not view the Sinai as part of Eretz Yisrael. Rav Amital recalled that Cohen told him: "I asked the people who fought to conquer the Sinai whether they had the sense that they were fighting for Eretz Yisrael. They replied that they did not, that they only began to feel that way when discussion of evacuating Yamit began." For Rav Amital, this only reinforced his belief that the evacuation decision should not be opposed. If even the leaders of the fight against withdrawal acknowledge that the nation did not see the Yamit region as part of Eretz Yisrael, there was no reason to oppose its return to Egypt.

The week after the evacuation of Yamit coincided with Israel's thirty-forth Independence Day. In a discourse that he delivered at the yeshiva, later published in the newspaper *Hazofe*, Rav Amital stated that despite the pain of uprooting communities, there was still room to celebrate the resurrection of Jewish sovereignty. He also expressed amazement at the intensity of the crying and grieving that could be seen during the evacuation. "I was witness to many terrible events that befell the Jewish people ... and with them the nation's reaction and grief ... and I must say that this tremendous hue and cry that we have recently seen at Yamit is unprecedented." Rav Amital claimed that political considerations intensified the mourning over Yamit: "The *Yetzer HaRa*, Satan, and schism were partners in the eagerness to mourn." He then spoke about the dangers inherent in the struggle against withdrawal: "There was a great risk of divisiveness and hatred of fellow Jews, for there is no denying that tens of thousands of people in Israel did not feel any pain at the evacuation of this area and its exclusion from Eretz Yisrael." Rav Amital viewed the demolition by bulldozer of the houses in Yamit as a moment of solidarity in which the entire nation identified with the tragedy. He even described that difficult moment as a "great thing" since it created the pain that unified the Israeli public and prevented a rift.

In the same discourse, Rav Amital boldly cast aspersions on the sanctity of the Yamit region. "I view this as a symbol of the removal of the sanctity of this region. Halakhically speaking, the sanctity of Ḥevron and Shekhem persisted even when they were occupied by Jordan. But if you look at the halakha ... if the sanctity of Yamit derived from its conquest, that is, if conquest by the State of Israel is considered popular conquest, "*kibosh rabim*," then once it is occupied by others, its sanctity disappears."

Rav Amital then reiterated his stance that this is the period of the "beginning of redemption" and called for strengthening the land by strengthening its people. He emphasized the need for solidarity and criticized extremists on the right and left who did not accept the authority of the government. Regarding right-wing extremists who struggled against the evacuation, he said: "This was the first time that an organized, national-religious, Zionist group announced that they do not accept the authority of the Jewish state." Instead of speaking about the value of the land, Rav Amital proposed first strengthening the willingness to sacrifice for the sake of certain values and the belief that "we are living in the Messianic Era."

R. Moshe Zvi Neriya, head of the yeshiva high school at Kfar HaRo'eh, objected to Rav Amital's statements and published a response in the newspaper. Rav Amital later claimed that Rav Neriya's attitude toward him was never the same after that; he believed that Rav Neriya did not attend a banquet honoring Rav Lichtenstein and Rav Amital because of what the latter said about the sanctity of Yamit.

The evacuation of Yamit represents the first time that Rav Amital opposed the vast majority of religious-Zionist rabbis on a religious matter. Within the world of religious-Zionist yeshivot, rumors about the moderate views of the Rosh Yeshiva from Gush Etzion began to circulate. Yet the broader religious community, and certainly the secular community, remained unaware of Rav Amital's variant opinions. His speeches were intended for a yeshiva audience and thus did not reverberate beyond its walls.

The next landmark in the consolidation of Rav Amital's new public identity occurred a few weeks later, with the outbreak of the First Lebanon War. The *casus belli* was the attempted assassination of Israel's Ambassador to the UK Shlomo Argov on 12 Sivan 5742 (June 3, 1982). The government decided to bomb terrorist bases in Beirut, and the terrorists responded with massive shelling of Israeli communities along the border with Lebanon. In response to the shelling, the government decided to initiate Operation Peace for Galilee, as the war was initially called. The decision was reached at a government meeting on Saturday night, 15 Sivan (June 5). The objective of the plan presented to the ministers was to create a buffer zone that would protect the northern communities from terrorist shells. The ministers supported an operation with the understanding that the range of the terrorists' artillery was forty kilometers, and that the IDF would not advance beyond that range. On Sunday, 15 Sivan (June 6), three tank formations entered Lebanon, occupied the town of Nabatiyeh and the cities of Tyre and Sidon, and prepared to advance toward Beirut. Dozens of students from Yeshivat Har Etzion, mostly serving in the armored corps, were conscripted into the battle. Rav Amital bade an emotional farewell to his students as they got on the busses and then began following developments anxiously. As the liaison officer between the military and the yeshivot, he was in constant contact with senior officers and received news of what was happening at the front. At the same time, Rav Amital was in touch with NRP representatives in the government and received updates on the plans of the political echelons as well. On Thursday, the fifth day of the war, David Malek, a student in the yeshiva's twelfth class, was killed. Malek, who had switched to Yeshivat Har Etzion from the yeshiva in Kiryat Shemona, was killed in battle trying to break through a Syrian commando force in Khaldeh, Lebanon. That evening, an armored battalion in which many *hesder* students were serving was ambushed near the town of Sultan Yacoub east of Beirut. The battalion was forced to retreat, leaving behind damaged tanks, twenty killed, more than thirty injured, two POWs, and four MIAs. One of the missing soldiers, Zachary Baumel, was a student in the yeshiva's eleventh class. His fate remains unknown.

On Friday afternoon, a few hours after the Battle of Sultan Yacoub, the first ceasefire between Israel and Syria was declared. Fifteen minutes before the onset of Shabbat, the phone rang at the home of Deputy Foreign Minister Yehuda Ben-Meir of the NRP. Rav Amital was on the line. He knew that Ben-Meir received ongoing updates from the front, by virtue of his position, via the Foreign Ministry representative at the General Staff war room. Ben Meir had two phones in his home: a regular phone and a special "Shabbat phone," developed by the Zomet Institute – an organization that designs technological devices to meet the needs of halakha. Rav Amital called to urge Ben-Meir to use the regular telephone that Shabbat, as matters of life and death were at stake. He asked that the special phone be saved for when things returned to normal.

About a week later, Rav Amital went with Minister Ben-Meir and Minister Yitzḥak Moda'i of the Likud party to visit his soldier-students in the eastern sector of Lebanon. On that visit, Rav Amital was shocked to discover the gap between what the Israeli government and public knew and what was actually happening on the battlefield: Rav Amital expressed concern to his students serving in the Seventh Brigade, at the time – to the best of his knowledge – in the middle of the fighting, and was astonished by Minister Moda'i's response, in which he stated vociferously that there was no fighting since there had been a ceasefire. Later in the visit, it was Moda'i's turn to be surprised. Rav Amital and the ministers met with soldiers who informed them that despite the apparent ceasefire they regularly received orders to shoot, even when they were not being fired upon. The soldiers expressed confusion and lack of understanding of everything going on around them. During their discussion, the firing started again and the soldiers were called back to their tanks. Minister Moda'i was astounded that the declared ceasefire was not being observed at all in the field, and that IDF forces were continuing to advance toward Beirut. Rav Amital was troubled by what he heard from the soldiers, but he was even more troubled by the fact that a government minister had no idea what was going on. The greatest shock came when the officers in the eastern sector laughed upon hearing Minister Moda'i speaking about the ceasefire. At that moment, Rav Amital lost faith in the government ministers and in the updates he had

Major General Ariel (Arik) Sharon visits the fledgling yeshiva.

been receiving from them. He understood that Defense Minister Arik Sharon and Chief of General Staff Rafael Eitan were running the war by themselves. Rav Amital had long been suspicious of Sharon. Once, when he visited the yeshiva in its early years, he boasted in front of the students that had they wanted to, Israel could have reached Pakistan during the Six Day War. Rav Amital did not like Sharon's bravado, and from that moment on regarded him with suspicion.

The supposed ceasefire officially collapsed nine days after it was declared, and the battles resumed in earnest. The IDF completed its encirclement of Western Beirut, sparking a ferocious public debate in Israel about whether it was necessary to occupying the city. Rav Amital, who was in touch with senior officers, heard from them that the IDF's penetration of the Lebanese capital was liable to cost hundreds of lives. The officers expressed their concerns to him and asked him to work to prevent it. The officers' gloomy predictions, coupled with his mistrust of Sharon, put Rav Amital in a state of real anxiety, and he decided to carry out the officers' request. The natural address was the NRP and its government ministers: Yosef Burg, Zevulun Hammer, and Yehuda Ben-Meir. He focused his efforts on Burg, the Interior Minister and the leader of the NRP. Burg, who himself opposed the occupation of Beirut, assuaged Rav Amital, telling him that entry into Beirut was not in the offing. Rav Amital, who had been briefed by senior ministers about the impending entry, did not believe Burg. "If you think," he wrote to Burg, "that as a civilian I am not supposed to know about the invasion of Beirut, and you therefore deny such a possibility, that is fine. But if you actually believe what you wrote to me, then I am definitely concerned."

Rav Amital's opposition to the occupation of Beirut reached the media. In a conversation with *Haaretz* journalist Elazar Levin at the end of June, he called for an end to the fighting in Lebanon. Rav Amital's statements appeared in the same article as statements of support, by R. Tzefanya Drori, the head of the *hesder* yeshiva in Kiryat Shemona, and MK R. Ḥayyim Druckman, Rosh Yeshiva of Or Etzion, for continued fighting. The *Haaretz* article even found its way to the front, sparking debate among the *hesder* yeshiva students there.

Like during the evacuation of Yamit, Rav Amital again found himself in the minority of the religious-Zionist rabbis. Rabbis from Merkaz HaRav circles called for the military and the government to continue fighting and to conquer Beirut. R. Yisrael Ariel, the rabbi of the recently evacuated town of Yamit, called for Jewish settlement of occupied Lebanese territories in an interview with the *Nekuda* news-

Former President Yitzḥak Navon visits the yeshiva.

paper. R. Dov Lior, the head of the *hesder* yeshiva in Kiryat Arba, also told *Nekuda* that the mitzva of conquering Eretz Yisrael applied to all of the territories occupied by the IDF. Gush Emunim published a notice praising the IDF and the government for "restoring the territories of the tribes of Naftali and Asher to the borders of Israel." On the opposing side, Peace Now held a rally at the beginning of July in Rabin Square (then Kings of Israel Square), protesting the continuation of the war. The debate about occupying Beirut and continuing the war turned into a debate between the right and left wings of the political spectrum, and Rav Amital found himself as the lone Rosh Yeshiva in the camp calling for an end to the war.

At some point, the government authorized the Prime Minister and Defense Minister to decide whether and when to enter Beirut. The NRP ministers voted against this authorization, but it nevertheless passed by virtue of the votes of the Likud ministers. Ben-Meir and Hammer pressured Burg to go to Begin and demand that the invasion of Beirut be brought before the government for a decision and not happen solely on the authority of Begin and Sharon. Burg went to Begin's home on Shabbat to present him with the demand, and Begin was persuaded. Rav Amital was apprised of the development.

At the beginning of August, the IDF began bombing the besieged western part of Beirut. Two weeks later, the PLO capitulated and left the city. The invasion of West Beirut was avoided, Bashir Gemayel, leader of the Christian Phalange party, was elected President of Lebanon, and the mood in Israel calmed somewhat.

During those first months of war, Rav Amital and the yeshiva lost three students: Ram Mizraḥi, a member of the thirteenth class, David Malek of the twelfth class, and another student, Yeḥiel Weitzman of the ninth class, who had already completed his time in yeshiva. Weitzman, the son of Holocaust survivors, left a pregnant wife. Several months later, the young widow had a baby boy who was named for his father.

Like during the Yom Kippur War, the bad tidings were visible on Rav Amital's face. Anyone who met him during those days saw how events impacted his mood. In a discourse he delivered at the yeshiva during the war, he compared his worries about his students at the front to a mother worrying about her son: "There are times that your entire being is given over to worrying – what's happening with the boys? Every time the phone rings it alarms you, terrifies you. The fragmentary flow of current news, the great tension that accompanies every bit of dubious information, and when, God forbid, news like Job's does arrive – silence and grief 'as I sit in darkness.'" Nevertheless, even during those terrible, anxiety-filled days, Rav Amital continued to claim that this era is the "beginning of redemption," and that this latest war was yet another phase of its unfolding. "The sacrifices that Israel offered during this war are bound to the birth pangs of the redemption," he claimed in the presence of his students.

Chapter Fourteen

Warning Lights

I believe that to the extent that I have brought harm to the Greater Israel camp, I have at the same time done a favor to the Greater Israel cause. As a Rosh Yeshiva, I certainly would have preferred to distance myself from any public controversy, but I acted as I did out of a sense of "It is time to act for God." Far be it from me to tell my students, "Accept my view," but if the only thing that comes of my words is a clarification of ideas and an open debate, without fear of anyone – that shall be sufficient reward.

Discourse delivered at Yeshivat Har Etzion, 5743 (October 1982)

On 26 Elul 5742 (September 14, 1982), three weeks after his election as President of Lebanon, Bashir Gemayel, the leader of the Christian Phalange movement and an ally of Israel, was assassinated. That evening, the government convened a meeting and decided to insert IDF forces into West Beirut. As the IDF entered the western parts of the city, Phalangists entered the Sabra and Shatila refugee camps and slaughtered hundreds of Muslims in retaliation for the murder of their leader. Images of the massacre reached the media, sparking a storm of protest in Israel and throughout the world. The world pointed an accusing finger at Israel for turning a blind eye to the murderous actions of the Phalangists. The Israeli government claimed, in its defense, that the Phalangists entered the camps without its knowledge. The government refused to set up a commission of inquiry. Rav Amital thought that the government's shirking of responsibility for the slaughter was a moral transgression and a *ḥillul HaShem*. He was especially angry at the representatives of the NRP in the government, who indeed supported the establishment of a commission of inquiry, but not strongly enough. He felt that he could no longer remain silent, and for the first time in his life, Rav Amital decided to come out publicly against the government and its religious ministers. On Thursday, 6 Tishrei (September 23), he called the yeshiva office from his home and dictated a public statement in his own name to the yeshiva's secretary, Shosh Tal:

> The Beirut massacre, which took place under the occupation of the Israeli military, has caused – beyond the ethical aspects, which cry out to the very heart of the heavens – a great *ḥillul HaShem* in Israel and the other nations. We now stand four days before Yom Kippur, and my entire being quakes and trembles out of fear for the Day of Judgment, for as is known, Yom Kippur does not atone for the sin of *ḥillul HaShem*.
>
> "Where there is *ḥillul HaShem,* honor is not extended to a rabbi." It is unfortunate that the representatives of religious Judaism in the government and in the Knesset were not aware that by voting as they did yesterday, they gave priority to the honor of the Prime Minister over the honor of Heaven. I pray that our benevolent God atones for them and hope that they find the way to repair this sin.

The official addressees of this statement were the yeshiva students, and indeed it was posted on every door to the *beit midrash*. His real target, however, was the media. He consciously used the students as a conduit to get the word out, and it worked. Within a few hours, radio stations had gotten wind of his public statement and broadcast it in their news reports.

Even before the statement reached the media, Rav Amital called Minister Hammer to inform him of its contents. Hammer was hurt by the harsh accusations made about him and his colleagues. He explained to Rav Amital that the NRP ministers supported the establishment of a commission of inquiry, but since Begin was opposed, they did not insist to the point of threatening to leave the governing coalition. Rav Amital did not accept the rationale offered by Hammer and his colleagues. He viewed the failure to establish a commission as an evasion of responsibility and a *ḥillul HaShem* that justified bringing down the government. There was no consensus within the NRP vis-à-vis establishing a commission of inquiry: Ben-Meir and Hammer supported it, Rav Druckman opposed, and the leader, Yosef Burg, wavered between the two poles. Burg only came out in favor of establishing a commission after receiving an urgent message from R. Joseph B. Soloveitchik expressing his view that a *ḥillul HaShem* was indeed perpetrated.

Among Israeli rabbis, Rav Amital's stance put him in a tiny minority. Other than his colleague, Rav Lichtenstein, who openly supported establishing a commission of inquiry, all other rabbis came out against it. Chief Rabbi Shlomo Goren reasoned that the IDF's responsibility for Sabra and Shatila was negligible. R. Shaul Yisraeli, Rosh Yeshiva of Merkaz HaRav, told his students that the State of Israel need not take responsibility for Arab civil wars and crimes. Even the leader of the *ḥaredi* community, Rav Shakh, who had previously taken moderate positions and supported the peace agreement with Egypt, harshly criticized the left wing's demand for an investigation. He accused Alignment (Maarakh) party chairman and opposition leader Shimon Peres of being an informant and a *moseir* for inciting *goyim* against Israel. Rav Amital did not hesitate to attack the pronouncements of his old colleague from Yeshivat Kletzk, and he consequently was criticized within the *ḥaredi* community.

Rav Amital's statement sparked a public furor. *Yediot Aharonot* featured a long article under the headline "Rav Amital versus Gush Emunim." In *Haaretz,* Akiva Eldar published an article entitled "Something's Happened in the *Hesder Yeshivot.*" The media suddenly "discovered" the moderate rabbi from Gush Etzion and wrote about him as though they found a buried treasure. Passions flared in the religious-Zionist community. Most of the community disagreed with Rav Amital's statement and felt uncomfortable about his media involvement, but others expressed support for his actions. Two events that took place in Jerusalem the week after Rav Amital's public statement demonstrate the dichotomy of the reaction to it. At Yeshivat Merkaz HaRav, Defense Minister Sharon met with yeshiva students in a show of support against those calling for his resignation. Concurrently, a group of *hesder* alumni, students, and academics who were disappointed with the conduct of the NRP leadership met at an apartment in the Katamon neighborhood to discuss the establishment of a moderate religious faction within the NRP, as a counterweight to the Gush Emunim faction. *Haaretz* reported that Rav Amital was behind the meeting. It was reported on television that at a convention of *hesder* alumni in Bnei Brak organized by the NRP's young leadership, Rav Amital came out against the "Arik Sharon government" and called for forming a government with Alignment.

The media's interest in Rav Amital provided him with the opportunity to explain some of his general ideas that had nothing to do with the invasion of Beirut or the Sabra and Shatila massacres. He told the media about his long-standing opposition to Gush Emunim. "I was one of the first people in Gush Emunim, but I left right away," he said in an interview with *Yediot Aharonot*'s Michal Miron, "I argued that they were turning the people off their ideas by adopting such hawkish positions… I don't understand why they must combine the struggle for the Greater Land of Israel with complete faith in Arik Sharon." He blamed Gush Emunim for the nation's exhaustion from war and for causing Judaism to be hated. He called for the struggle over Judea and Samaria to be replaced by outreach and bridge-building, and opposed religious legislation based on coalition agreements. In an interview with *Hazofe*'s Naomi Golan, he publicly outlined, for the first time, what he believed to be the proper hierarchy of values, calling for the priority of the people of Israel over the whole Land of Israel. "If, God forbid, I would one day have to answer the question of which is preferable, more people or more land, I would answer without hesitation: more people."

Rav Amital's statements aroused numerous responses from Zionist rabbis. Chief Rabbi Shlomo Goren responded in *Yediot Aharonot* to Rav Amital's willingness to compromise territorially to save lives: "It is forbidden for him to issue halakhic rulings on matters of the utmost importance to us, entailing matters of national life and death. In any case, his statements – if he really said them – go against Rav A.Y. Kook's entire worldview." Rav Goren's words accurately reflected the feelings of Rav Kook's disciples about Rav Amital's statements. MK Rav Ḥayyim Druckman, among the closest disciples of R. Zvi Yehuda Kook and the rightmost representative of the NRP, conjectured that Rav Amital made his pronouncements precisely then, after the death of Rav Zvi Yehuda (six months earlier, on Purim 5742). *Hazofe* quoted a speech by Rav Druckman about his mentor at an NRP young leadership convention: "In the past, they were afraid of him. He was the pillar of fire walking before the camp." Ḥanan Porat made a similar claim. In an interview with *Nekuda,* he said: "I cannot shake the feeling that while Rav Zvi Yehuda was alive, nobody would have had the nerve to say anything so convoluted and place, as it were, the cardinal values of nation and land in opposition to each other."

Some responded to Rav Amital by mail. For example, Professor Yisrael Aumann, later a Nobel Prize winner, lost his son Shlomo in the First Lebanon War. He heard about Rav Amital's statement from his son Yehonatan, then a student at Yeshivat Har Etzion. On the day after Yom Kippur, he wrote a letter to Rav Amital, his son's Rosh Yeshiva, in which he quoted something that Rav Amital himself had said during the war's early stages, namely, that the nation must remain unified in times of danger. Aumann then asked: "Despite all the respect and awe I have for you, I must ask: does the need for unity and reconciliation apply only when we personally agree with every one of the government's actions? At a time of grave danger such as now, are we permitted to publicly criticize and denounce whenever some event or development appears to us to be negative?"

The public controversy surrounding Rav Amital continued through Sukkot and even beyond. The entire time, the students of Yeshivat Har Etzion were on holiday break. Many of them felt confused and uncomfortable with their Rosh Yeshiva's pronouncements. Some were even castigated by friends and family members who railed against Rav

Amital's positions. When they returned to yeshiva for *ḥoref zeman*, they wanted to hear Rav Amital's reasons for his positions and for going to the media with them. That first Saturday night, Rav Amital addressed a jam-packed *beit midrash*.

He began by apologizing to the students for the confusion he caused by going to the media. He told them that he was willing to pay a personal price:

> I am willing to go about with a feeling of "I am estranged from my brothers, an alien to my kin" – simply because, as King David said (Ps. 69:9–10), "Zeal for Your house has consumed me." I am convinced that those things had to be said for the sake of the honor of Heaven, for the sake of the honor of the Torah, and for the sake of the honor of Eretz Yisrael.

He explained that several warning lights had gone off in his mind with regard to the ideology sweeping through the religious public. He claimed that this ideology causes *ḥillul HaShem*, damages the cause of the Greater Land of Israel, and weakens Jews' connection to the Torah. Rav Amital then listed the warning lights that caused him to take action. The first was the religious-Zionist rabbinic voices that were heard during the second week of the war, calling for the occupation of Lebanon on the halakhic grounds of conquering Eretz Yisrael. The second was the statements by R. Shlomo Aviner, rabbi of Beit El, published in a booklet entitled *Artzi* at the height of the controversy about occupying Beirut, and saying that even if there would be peace, Israel would need to initiate a war to liberate and conquer those parts of Eretz Yisrael. Rav Amital argued:

> These words were spoken were spoken in the real, practical context of the debate about invading Beirut, which according to IDF estimates would have entailed the risk of hundreds of losses on our side and terrible damage to the civilian population… I had hoped to hear, at the very least, some hesitation like we heard from the Prime Minister, but the clearest, most resolute voice, the voice that was so certainly and decisively in favor of military action, came from the representatives of religious Zion-

> ism...What's the connection between the struggle for Judea and Samaria and the invasion of Beirut?...The fact that these ideas are peppered with verses, statements of Ḥazal, and expressions borrowed from the style of Rav Kook makes me shudder.

Rav Amital then mentioned the Sabra and Shatila massacre and came out against the pronouncements of Rav Druckman in support of the IDF and against setting up a commission of inquiry. The third warning light that Rav Amital pointed out was a series of statements by religious-Zionist rabbis that implied their satisfaction with expressions of anti-Semitism throughout the world resulting from the war. Rav Amital claimed that this satisfaction stemmed from a broader worldview that held that an increase in anti-Semitism would be good for the Jews. Such pronouncements, Rav Amital argued, belittle Diaspora Jewry, which is directly affected by any surge in anti-Semitism. He further suggested that neglecting world opinion and its effect on Diaspora Jewry stems from a corruption of priorities within religious Zionism. "What stands out here is the erroneous principle that places the interests of the State of Israel above the interests of the people of Israel." Rav Amital explained that the State of Israel has a responsibility to every Jew, wherever he or she may be, and therefore:

> If a chance came about for real and final peace with the Arabs, and in the wake of this there were chances of halting emigration and nurturing a great movement of *aliya*, and we were faced with the question of which is preferable – more Jews in Eretz Yisrael with less of the Holy Land under Jewish rule, or fewer Jews in Eretz Yisrael with more of the Holy Land under Jewish rule, I would choose the first option. I perceive the importance of this declaration not on the practical level, nor from the political perspective, but rather in the educational sphere; therefore, I regard it not as a political message, but rather as an educational one.

Rav Amital subsequently launched into a halakhic polemic against the rabbis who claimed that the conquest of Eretz Yisrael is a mitzva that supersedes all others. The mitzva of conquering Eretz Yisrael nowadays

(photo: Na'aman Kam)

(photo: Na'aman Kam)

Addressing students in the beit midrash of Yeshivat Har Etzion

hinges, he pointed out, on a dispute among the *Rishonim*. Therefore, absent the threat of attack such as prior to the Six Day War, there is no license to risk lives to conquer more tracts of land.

He then told his students that he was bothered by the fact that many secular Jews recoiled upon hearing the voices emanating from the religious-Zionist camp. "There is nothing that should cause us more worry than the possibility of another war... Every individual casualty wounds the souls of a wide radius of the Israeli population. Beyond this, though, every war weakens the Zionist commitment of masses of Jews in Eretz Yisrael." He concluded by calling on religious Zionism to change direction and declare itself ready for a real and final peace, in which context it would agree to concessions and territorial compromise.

The time had come for the students to ask questions. One of the first hands in the air belonged to Ḥanan Porat. Porat, still staunchly in the Gush Emunim camp, was by then a Knesset member of the Teḥiya party. In his book *Et Eḥai Anokhi Mevakesh*, he wrote that Rav Amital's speech caused him pain and insult. Due to these feelings, he could not stop them, he decided to respond. "It was very difficult for me to publicly defy and dispute Rav Amital, whom I love, but our Sages instructed us: 'Where there is *ḥillul HaShem*, honor is not extended to a rabbi.'" Porat recounts how Rav Amital noticed his extended hand and invited him with a flourish of the hand and a twinkle of the eye to ascend the pulpit and speak from precisely the same location from which he had just spoken. Many students were astounded by the openness and generosity of spirit that Rav Amital displayed by inviting Ḥanan Porat to reply. Not every day does a Rosh Yeshiva invite an outsider to speak to a packed *beit midrash* and object strongly to his statements. Porat called Rav Amital's willingness to compromise on Judea, Samaria, and Gaza "an educational disaster." He objected to Rav Amital's placement of the people of Israel ahead of the land of Israel, saying that only by educating toward a love of the land would it be possible to increase *aliya* to Israel. Finally, he argued that Rav Amital's words were exploited by the media to goad the land of Israel loyalists. Rav Amital, as was his wont, did not respond to Porat. As far as he was concerned, the students had already heard what he had to say and could judge for themselves. He saw no need to continue the argument. He later said, in retrospect, "I had faith that time would prove me right."

Several days after his address, which was quoted by the media, the newspaper *Ma'ariv* published a notice that took exception to Rav Amital's words. Though his name was not mentioned, the contents of the notice left no doubt about the identity of its target. Under the headline "On Truth and Peace in the Galilee" was written: "There is no real meaning to the separation of the land of Israel from the people of Israel." It stated that the First Lebanon War was an obligatory war ("*milḥemet* mitzva") whose attainments constituted a *kiddush HaShem*. Regarding the anti-Semitism the war provoked, the notice stated that this was merely "another link in the historical chain of Jew-hatred." It concluded: "We will not achieve peace with security by being weak-spirited vis-à-vis the nations of the world and submissive to their opinions and dictates." The notice was signed by more than thirty rabbis, including: R. Zvi Thau, Rav Amital's student at Yeshivat HaDarom; R. Elḥanan Bin-Nun, Rav Amital's student at Yeshivat Har Etzion; and R. Uzi Friedlich, the yeshiva's *mashgi'aḥ*.

Rav Amital's address was printed in its entirety, with the exception of the halakhic discussion, in *Nekuda*, where it again sparked many reactions. His student, R. Yoel Bin-Nun, admitted that the militancy that characterized elements of the religious-Zionist public troubled him as well, but he opposed the manner in which Rav Amital pitted the people of Israel against the land of Israel. He argued that Rav Amital's statements about the priority of the people over the land contravened the teachings of his mentor, Rav Ḥarlap, and provided an excuse for Jews who wished to remain in the Diaspora. He accused Rav Amital of attempting to present a political stance as an educational stance. R. Yisrael Ariel wrote, "The People of Israel and the Land of Israel are one thing that cannot be divided" and compared Rav Amital's view to that of the biblical spies who despised the land. R. Moshe Levinger, one of the heads of Gush Emunim, argued that Rav Amital's positions stemmed from his lack of understanding of the Torah of Eretz Yisrael, in which there is no division or separation between the people and the land, and described Rav Amital's approach as exilic ("*galuti*").

Unforgiving reactions to Rav Amital's address arrived from alumni as well. Several of them penned an open letter, in which they explained at length why they disagreed with him. The letter was unsigned – its authors did not want to get into a disagreement with their Rosh Yeshiva. Although the letter was addressed to Rav Amital, its authors knew that Rav Lichtenstein shared Rav Amital's opinions – he spoke at a rally of the religious left just after Rosh HaShana, as the details of the Sabra and Shatila massacres were emerging, and he added his signature to the public statement that Rav Amital posted in the yeshiva. Nevertheless, since he did not give many media interviews, and took a more restrained approach than his colleague, the students were more forgiving of him.

Chapter Fifteen

From a Zionism of Redemption to a Zionism of Sovereignty

I believe that we merited a Jewish state only because of God's desire to sanctify His Name in the aftermath of the terrible ḥillul HaShem *of the Holocaust. The establishment of the state and its military victories over the Arab armies that rose up against it constitute a response involving* kiddush HaShem. *Precisely for this reason, the obligation to sanctify God's name has special significance in our time for those of us who live in the State of Israel, the entire establishment of which stemmed from the principle of* kiddush HaShem. *This is why on various occasions over the years I felt obligated to protest against instances of* ḥillul HaShem. *This was the only cause for which I felt a need to speak out publicly.*

Jewish Values in a Changing World, 2005, p. 155

The religious-Zionist public perceived Rav Amital as having changed his views; this raised the obvious question of why he changed his views. But in order to answer this, one must first agree that Rav Amital indeed changed his views and then specify exactly how these changes were manifested. It is not at all clear that Rav Amital changed his political stance. Those who claim he changed bring as evidence his book *HaMa'alot MiMa'amakim*, considered by several Gush Emunim leaders as the movement's fundamental text. They believe that the proponent of redemptive Zionism who said "we should mention and emphasize *Mashiaḥ* incessantly" was not the same man who supported the peace accords with Egypt, opposed the movement to prevent the withdrawal from Sinai, actively opposed the occupation of Beirut during the First Lebanon War, criticized the government after the Sabra and Shatila massacre, and ultimately founded Meimad. Yet Rav Amital denied that he changed his views in this area. He insisted that *HaMa'alot MiMa'amakim* does not articulate the same views as Gush Emunim. He claimed that when he spoke about redemptive Zionism in the 1970s, he never meant that the redemption must be implemented by settling Judea, Samaria, and Gaza, by opposing peace agreement, or by occupying Lebanon. "There is nothing that we must do just because we are in the era of the beginning of redemption," he said, "We must proceed along a realistic path." In this context, he also mentioned his early departure from Gush Emunim and his absence from the Sebastia demonstrations. He claimed never to have espoused the same ideas as the settler leaders, and that those who argue that he changed his political opinions never understood them in the first place. "It took them a while to comprehend that I speak differently," he said.

As previously noted, Rav Amital's personality was not suited to the type of activity undertaken by Gush Emunim in its early years. Then, as always, he took a statist approach that did not support or believe in antiestablishment activity. He did not believe in protest rallies or in establishing "facts on the ground," an approach reflected during the yeshiva's early years, when approval to build in Alon Shvut was delayed. Even those who argue that his positions changed are forced to admit that his attitude toward the settlement project never changed dramatically: he always viewed settlement of Judea, Samaria, and Gaza positively, as long as it was with government approval and did not constitute a real obstacle to peace. He had no doubts that Jews had full rights to these territories, but he was prepared to make territorial compromises to prevent bloodshed.

Even if Rav Amital held the same political views all those years, the fact that he only went public with those views in the early 1980s requires explanation. What led him to shift the contents of his discourses and emphasize his scale of priorities, which placed the people of Israel before the land?

As noted, the first time Rav Amital presented his moderate political doctrine was during the Israeli-Egyptian peace negotiations in late 1977. On that occasion, his speech to the limited audience of his yeshiva did not reverberate significantly. His opposition to the struggle against the evacuation of Yamit won a bit more publicity, but it was not as yet addressed to the broader community. He first began actively involving himself in the public sphere during the First Lebanon War, when he lobbied government ministers to try to prevent the occupation of Beirut. The next, decisive phase in the public exposure of his position was during the aftermath of the Sabra and Shatila massacre.

With the exception of this latter incident, the common denominator of the other events was the chance for peace and the risk of war. Many of Rav Amital's students and confidants thus concluded that his primary motivation for disclosing his moderate views was fear of war and its effects. Fear of war, they claimed, explained his willingness to make concessions and territorial compromises. Many of those closest to him theorize that his anxieties originated with the Yom Kippur War. The loss of students in the war was a heavy blow for him and led him to adopt the positions that he began publicly espousing during the First Lebanon War. Professor Moshe Bar Asher, a student of Rav Amital's in Yeshivat HaDarom, claims to have noticed a transition when Rav Amital eulogized his fallen students.

> At one of the funerals, I was standing with two friends from Yeshivat HaDarom as Rav Amital eulogized. Listening to what he was saying, I told my friends that this speech marks Rav

> Amital's passage from right to left. He spoke of wars whose cost is too heavy to bear. When the funerary booklet *Eight Princes of Men* came out, I told Rav Amital that I noticed a transformation. He told me that a Rosh Yeshiva who loses eight students is like a father who loses eight sons.

Other students from the yeshiva's first classes, who studied under Rav Amital before and after the Yom Kippur War, believe that the deaths of his students influenced his worldview.

Yet Rav Amital dismissed this theory out of hand. "Nonsense that the Yom Kippur War affected me," he said, "it had nothing to do with politics." He contended that his political stances did not change. He listed his reasons for starting to publicly articulate his positions in the early 1980s in a discourse he delivered at the yeshiva after the Sabra and Shatila massacre. These were the "warning lights" – calls for conquering Beirut that various rabbis made on halakhic grounds, the worrying gap between government decisions and the reality on the ground, and his concern for unnecessary loss of life. He explained that he went to the media after Sabra and Shatila because he felt that the massacre had created a *ḥillul HaShem*.

R. Shlomo Brin, a son-in-law and close confidant of Rav Amital, speaks of a personality change that brought about a later ideological change: "After the Yom Kippur War, people noticed a change in his personality. He was more hesitant. He reacted to events like a wounded man. He lost some of the optimism and certainty that he had before the war. But the ideological changes came later."

Some connect the impact of the Yom Kippur War on Rav Amital with a delayed impact of the Holocaust and view the combination of these two traumas as the reason for his public stance during the First Lebanon War. For example, Dr. Danny Tropper, a close friend of Rav Amital and co-founder of Meimad, connected the two events: "The war showed that annihilation is possible here, too." Moshko also thought that the trauma of the Yom Kippur War revisited the trauma of the Holocaust on Rav Amital. Rav Amital preferred not to address psychoanalytic explanations of his motives. "I don't know enough psychology to say things like that," he said, "and I can't psychoanalyze myself."

Although Rav Amital insisted that his political stances never varied, he agreed that his national-religious worldview indeed changed. He admitted that his religious conception of the State of Israel and his attitude toward the process of redemption underwent changes; he even conceded that the changes were the result of the delayed impact of the Holocaust. Moshe Maya is partially to "blame" for Rav Amital's admission. Maya, a historian from Mitzpeh Hoshaya in the Galilee, was never a student of Rav Amital. He studied at the *hesder* yeshiva in Sha'alvim and became familiar with Rav Amital via army comrades from Yeshivat Har Etzion. Maya read Rav Amital's essays that were published in the yeshiva's journals and sent to students at the front. He was so deeply impressed that he purchased the newly published *HaMa'alot MiMa'amakim* on one of his first furloughs. Fifteen years later, prompted by the questioning of his students at Ulpanit Tiberias religious girls' high school about faith after the Holocaust, Maya decided to explore Rav Amital's understanding of the Holocaust. In order to analyze Rav Amital's views objectively, Maya refrained from meeting with Rav Amital and relied solely on works published in various forums, finally meeting with him only after completing a first draft. Rav Amital told him that he generally did not like it when his personality and worldview were studied, but that he would

With author Elie Wiesel at an event honoring the publication of A World Built, Destroyed, and Rebuilt.

agree to allow Maya to publish his work specifically because he wrote as an outside observer, not as a close disciple.

Maya's book appeared in 2002, and in 2004 an English translation, *A World Built, Destroyed, and Rebuilt: Rabbi Yehuda Amital's Confrontation with the Memory of the Holocaust,* was published. In the book, Maya points out, *inter alia,* the gradual shift in Rav Amital's religious view of the state and his certainty about the process of redemption. In the 1970s and early 1980s, Rav Amital spoke about the State of Israel in terms of redemption, but starting in the mid-1980s he spoke about the state in terms of a national home and the attainment of sovereignty, likening it to the Second Temple era. The messianic terminology of Rav Kook's circle was replaced with existential terms such as rescue, sovereignty, and safe haven. Maya points to the Sabra and Shatila massacre as the watershed event, a blow that revivified the images of the Holocaust for Rav Amital and transformed his worldview. If at the beginning of the war Rav Amital still spoke of casualties as part of the birth pangs of redemption, he almost completely ceased after the massacre. Maya argues that that the delayed influence of the Holocaust did not merely alter Rav Amital's religious view of the state, it also caused reservations about the certainty that he had previously projected regarding the progress of the redemption. Whereas in the 1960s Rav Amital decisively upheld the validity of Rav Kook's statements identifying the present era with the process of redemption, he had expressed doubts – mainly prompted by the Holocaust – by the 1980s, and more vigorously in the 1990s.

In a discourse delivered on Yom HaAtzma'ut 5747 (1987), Rav Amital spoke about his expectations at the time of the establishment of the state: "We anticipated great things, that the physical redemption would be accompanied by a spiritual redemption... but the disappointment is great, the steps so slow that they sometimes cannot be discerned." Six years later, in his discourse on Yom HaAtzma'ut 5753 (1993), he first explained his skepticism about the progress of the redemption with respect to the Holocaust:

> The students of the Vilna Gaon spoke of the "beginning of the redemption," R. Eliyahu Guttmacher of Graidetz spoke of the "beginning of the redemption," and Rav Kook also spoke of the

> "beginning of the redemption." Yet after all of these came the Holocaust.

Several months later, in an interview with Shaul Schiff of *Hazofe*, Rav Amital said: "This idea of 'the beginning of redemption' did not start with the establishment of the state. The Vilna Gaon, the students of the Ba'al Shem Tov, and Rav Kook all related to it … and despite all of these predictions, we witnessed the Holocaust."

After the signing of the Oslo Accords, which included an Israeli commitment to withdraw from broad areas of Judea and Samaria, the religious-Zionist community's concern with the progress of the redemption increased. In 1995, Rav Amital, Rav Lichtenstein, and Rav Druckman participated in a panel discussion in New York. A member of the audience asked whether it was still possible to describe the State of Israel as "the first flowering of our redemption" once cities were ceded to the Palestinians as part of the Oslo framework. Rav Druckman answered that if seventy years earlier Rav Kook could call the fledgling Zionist project the first flowering of our redemption, the same could certainly be said of the State of Israel. Rav Amital quickly responded, "How can you speak with such certainty? There was a Holocaust in between!" Similarly, in a discourse delivered in yeshiva on Chanukah 5757 (1996), Rav Amital said:

> Rav Kook did not witness the Second World War, which made the First World War seem like child's play. He did not see Hiroshima and he did not see the terrible Holocaust …
>
> We know more than Rav Kook. We saw the Second World War and the Holocaust. He never had a dilemma – the only possibility that he saw was the beginning of the great redemption.

In Maya's understanding, the Holocaust was the major cause of the erosion of Rav Amital's faith in the progress of the redemption. An intriguing question remains: what caused Rav Amital, who experienced the Holocaust bodily, to suddenly "remember" it in the 1980s? As noted, Maya claims that the Sabra and Shatila massacres revivified the Holocaust for him. Rav Amital himself said, "It was not one event. The further I got from the Holocaust, the closer to it I became."

Not everyone agrees with Maya's assessment that the Holocaust was the major catalyst for the shift in Rav Amital's worldview. Some argue that delays in the redemptive process and disappointment with the moral condition of the State of Israel led to Rav Amital's reservations about the process he once spoke of with such certainty. This is how Dr. Yoḥanan Breuer, the son of R. Mordekhai Breuer and a student of Rav Amital, sees things. "Rav Amital continued to see God's hand in history and speak of redemptive Zionism long after the Holocaust," Breuer explains, concluding that a realistic outlook, and not a delayed reaction to the Holocaust, led Rav Amital to change. "Until the Six Day War," he explains, "they thought that redemption was nigh and everyone would repent. Rav Kook's redemptive Zionism was possible." But as time went by and nothing happened, a relevant alternative had to be proposed. "Of course, it is possible to remain oblivious to what's going on around you, but Rav Amital, despite the strong influence of Rav Kook on him, was a realist. He saw what was going on around him and shifted his focus from redemptive Zionism to 'safe haven' Zionism."

R. Hillel Raḥmani, a student of Rav Amital and a *ram* at Yeshivat Har Etzion, tends to view other developments in the State of Israel as the reasons why Rav Amital's anticipation of the redemption was dulled. "Rav Amital never placed much value on pie-in-the-sky redemption. His approach was always realistic. Until his later years he felt that he could chart a path that combined redemption with realism. In his later years, due to his realism, something about his attitude to the redemption dimmed and shattered. I do not thing it was related to the Holocaust, but to developments in the state." R. Shlomo Brin charts a middle course in this dispute as well. He believes that two things caused Rav Amital to question the vision of redemption: "The first thing was the constant wars and the moral condition; the Yom Kippur War, the First Lebanon War, the unraveling of the Oslo Accords and its bloody cost; and also the inferior moral condition of the state. The second thing was the Holocaust, whose influence on him was delayed."

I interviewed Rav Amital for *Nekuda* in 2004, and what he told me then strengthens the claim that the Holocaust alone did not cause the change in Rav Amital's attitude toward the state:

> I constantly said that the establishment of the state and the Six Day War opened a door, an opportunity to create a much better situation. Unfortunately, I cannot say that our situation is better now. There are difficult, troublesome problems. So how can I say with certainty that this is the "beginning of redemption"?

R. Yoel Amital believes that his father's seemingly sharp switch from redemptive Zionism to sovereignty-based Zionism is in the eye of the beholder:

> One of the reasons that they see such a sharp contradiction in my father's views is that they are used to thinking in slogans and viewing everything as black or white. In the religious-Zionist community, there are only two approaches: The approach of R. Zvi Yehuda Kook on the one hand, and the non-messianic approach of Rav Soloveitchik or Rav Reines on the other. My father's approach was that everything that happened in Eretz Yisrael must be viewed with prophetic eyes, that is, as the actualization of prophecies. On festive occasions, my father frequently spoke about the prophecies of Zekharya that the streets of Jerusalem would once again be filled with boys and girls at play. He continued making those speeches even after casting doubt about the "beginning of redemption." According to him, even if our generation corresponds "only" to the salvation achieved during the Second Temple era, everything must still be viewed prophetically – but not messianically, at least not in the deterministic sense. My father's recoiling from the words "beginning of redemption" began after the First Lebanon War, during which it became patently clear that this concept had become a practical political prescription. Today, the "beginning of redemption" carries connotations of belligerence and militarism, of elevating a non-realistic view of things into some sort of ideal. Obviously, my father could not identify with such an interpretation.

Still others attribute the change in Rav Amital's thinking to the influence of his co-Rosh Yeshiva, Rav Lichtenstein, who had long expressed skepticism about viewing the state as the beginning of redemption. In the yeshiva's early years, when the messianic euphoria that followed the Six Day Way still prevailed, Rav Lichtenstein often took steps to cool things off. He never flinched from telling students that he did not discern any messianic indications in Israel's victory, and frequently engaged them in passionate debates on this issue. Most of the students then believed, as Rav Amital did, that the establishment of the state and the miraculous Six Day War justified messianic fervor and the belief that they were living through the process of redemption. Rav Amital and Rav Lichtenstein never openly debated the issue, but the students were well aware of the wide rifts between the respective positions of the Rashei Yeshiva.

Thus, when Rav Amital began questioning his certainties about the redemption, several students chalked it up to Rav Lichtenstein's influence. Rav Amital did not believe that Rav Lichtenstein caused him to change his positions, but Rav Lichtenstein neither confirms nor denies the possibility that he influenced his colleague, even if indirectly. "We never spoke about these subjects," he reports, "but I managed to create a slightly different atmosphere in the yeshiva." Regarding the changes in Rav Amital's positions, Rav Lichtenstein observed:

> That was part of his greatness. He was able to change his mind about matters close to his heart as realities shifted. From his per-

With his son, Rav Yoel Amital.

> spective, this was not a concession of principles or a changing of his spots, but a way of maintaining principles. When reality changes, your practical attitudes must change along with it. Otherwise, you essentially turn your back on those principles, since principles must be implemented in the prevailing reality.

Perhaps the explanation for Rav Amital's changing positions lies, as Rav Lichtenstein put it, in his complex personality. In addition to being a visionary who displayed the ability to see things from a great distance, to the point that some viewed him as something of a prophet, Rav Amital was also a sober realist, sometimes in the extreme. The wide gap between his own foresight and sobriety can perhaps explain the change in his positions.

R. Yuval Cherlow, an alumnus of the yeshiva, offers another explanation for the changes in Rav Amital's positions. This explanation relates to Rav Amital's realism but focuses on another aspect of his personality, which Rav Cherlow believes can explain his conduct:

> In my opinion, the fact that Rav Amital was one of the only Rashei Yeshiva in Israel who would go to museums explains quite a bit. It signifies the pride of place he gave to natural morality and human sensibility. I believe that his connection to reality also explains his support for religious-secular social covenants. I believe it came from the same place. The fact that he valued authenticity, creativity, and the individual human voice explains his positions.

Indeed, Rav Amital saw no contradiction between a content- and meaning-filled spiritual life and worthwhile cultural pursuits. In 5756 (1995), on the occasion of his appointment as a government minister, he made a guest appearance on a television show hosted by Kobi Meidan and was asked about his habits of consumption of secular culture. He responded that he did not go to the movies because he found them boring ("when I was in the army I watched movies and fell asleep"), but he confirmed that he occasionally read, when he had time, secular literature. The Israeli authors whose works he read include Ḥayyim Gouri, Amos Oz, A.B. Yehoshua, and David Grossman. Rav Amital explained to the interviewer that through these books he was able to keep a finger on the country's cultural pulse. Rav Amital also felt that reading the works of secular authors was an integral part of his relationship with them, and they often reciprocated by seeking out his friendship. He saw this as evidence of their deep desire to be close to Judaism. Rav Amital also greatly admired the works of R. Haim Sabato. When *Haaretz* ran a negative review of one of Rav Sabato's books, Rav Amital phoned him to compliment his writing and express his disagreement with the substance of the critique.

When Meidan asked about Rav Amital's affinity for Dutch cigars, he responded with his characteristic smile and humor, "You're reminding me of my sins, of when I smoked. My father-in-law was against my habit, but I told him: 'When I arrive at the heavenly courts, I don't want them to be able to claim that I listened to the doctors but not to God. I want to be able to say that I didn't listen to the doctors either…' But since then I've grown up, gotten a little wiser, and quit smoking."

Rav Amital's openness was one of the qualities that charmed many students over the years. They enjoyed discovering his love of the arts and describing him as "someone who knows what life has to offer beyond the pages of the Talmud." However, visitors to Rav Amital's home would always find him diligently studying some holy book; with all due respect to the arts, his Torah was his art.

Nevertheless, Rav Cherlow viewed Rav Amital's attentiveness to the wide world as one of the reasons for the changes he underwent. "The same applied to political matters. He saw that the Palestinians were here to stay, and he experienced dissonance. He felt that dissonance very deeply and therefore supported a solution. Rav Breuer once said that Rav Amital's problem was that he viewed the world through the lens of *Haaretz*. I think that's significant, too. He was the only Rosh Yeshiva to keep reading *Haaretz* over the years."

Indeed, Rav Amital felt it important to always keep open channels of communication with secular public intellectuals. As mentioned, he forged relationships with secular writers such as Ḥayyim Gouri, A.B. Yehoshua, and Amos Oz, public intellectuals like Professors Eliezer Schweid and Shlomo Avineri, and he generally ascribed significance to finding a common Jewish denominator with every current of Israeli society. No doubt, Rav Amital's connection with the secular elite – a connection that was very important to him – influenced his decision to voice his opinions publicly. A story that Rav Amital often repeated when explaining why he went into politics relates to his relationship with the poet Abba Kovner. In 1977, Kovner and Rav Amital participated in a televised panel discussion on the meaning of the Holocaust. Kovner, a member of Kibbutz Ein HaḤoresh, was a leader of the Jewish resistance fighters in the Vilna Ghetto. After the program, they began discussing faith after the Holocaust. Kovner asked Rav Amital how he could continue to believe in God after the Holocaust. Rav Amital asked Kovner how he could continue to have faith in man. "I *believe* in God," Rav Amital told Kovner, "I don't *understand* Him. But we're supposed to understand man." Kovner summed up by saying, "Let's just say that we both have questions for which there are no answers."

The two of them remained in touch after the symposium. In the early 1980s, Kovner had an idea for a collaborative effort. He wanted to strengthen the connection of young, secular kibbutzniks with Jewish sources. He proposed to Rav Amital that they publish weekly *parasha* sheets to distribute in the *kibbutzim*. "I'll contribute selections from modern Hebrew literature, and you'll contribute *midrashim* and rabbinic literature," Kovner proposed. Rav Amital agreed, but the plan was delayed. They met again during the First Lebanon War, and Kovner said to Rav Amital: "Everything has gone down the tubes. We've lost a generation; as far as Judaism is concerned, they won't listen even to me anymore." He told Rav Amital that the rabbis' call to occupy Beirut caused the secular kibbutzniks to despise religion and Judaism. Rav Amital tried to reassure him, but he would not be reassured. Kovner died in 1987 at the age of sixty-nine, and Rav Amital believed there to be a connection between his early demise and the despair of his last years. Rav Amital viewed Kovner's statement as definitive proof that expressions of militancy in the name of halakha distances people from Judaism and the Torah. Once again, he identified *ḥillul HaShem* as the root of the matter; this is what caused him to act. All of his public statements, the establishment of Meimad, his willingness to be its head, and his eventual appointment as a minister in the Peres government – he explained them all by the desire to demonstrate that there is another Judaism, and thereby to sanctify God's Name.

To a large degree, it can be argued that Rav Amital's entire life hinged on the axis of *ḥillul HaShem* and *kiddush HaShem*. He described the Holocaust as the greatest *ḥillul HaShem* and the State of Israel as a *kiddush HaShem*. Extremist behavior and militant pronouncements in the name of religion constituted *ḥillul HaShem* for Rav Amital, and any action or statement done or said as a reaction to a *ḥillul HaShem* is a *kiddush HaShem*, and that is its primary importance. Rav Amital recounted that a rabbi once came to him with a grievance, namely, that he chose to protest only certain phenomena while remaining silent in the presence of others. "I told him: Note that I only yell about what the religious do. That's due to the issue of *kiddush HaShem* and *ḥillul HaShem*."

Chapter Sixteen

For It Is in Our Soul

The Sages of Israel were well aware of the spiritual price exacted by involvement in community affairs, but they did not see that price as sufficient reason to abstain from community service. The Mishna in Avot (2:2) cites the words of Rabban Gamliel, the son of Rabbi Yehuda HaNasi:

> *Let all those who occupy themselves with [the affairs of] the community do so only for the sake of Heaven, for the merit of their ancestors sustains them, and their righteousness endures forever. And as for you, I credit you with great reward, as though you accomplished it.*

The Rambam explains (Commentary to the Mishna, *ad loc.):*

> *'I credit you with great reward, as though you accomplished it' – these are the words of God to those who toil on behalf of the community, for they are sometimes prevented from performing*

> *a mitzva when they occupy themselves with [the affairs of] the community. God, blessed be He, says that He will credit them with reward as if they had performed the mitzva, even though they did not do it, since they occupied themselves with the heavenly affairs of the community.*

In other words, even though public service extracts a spiritual price, a person should occupy himself with community affairs, and God will reward him as if he had performed the mitzvot that he had missed as a result.

Jewish Values in a Changing World, 2005, pp. 159–160

Rav Amital kept his distance from the political arena until the late 1970s. His attitude toward the NRP, the party for which he cast his ballot for forty years, was ambivalent. On the one hand, he felt it important that a party represent the interests of the national-religious public. On the other hand, he often showed contempt for party hacks who he felt wanted too much glory. Over the years, he developed close relationships with NRP Knesset members, especially Zevulun Hammer and Yehuda Ben-Meir, the two party members who dismantled the historic alliance between the NRP and Labor/Alignment in 1976. In the 1977 elections, when Likud rose to power, the NRP won twelve seats and became an instrumental part of Begin's government. During the coalitional wrangling, the NRP won the education portfolio for the first time; prior to that it had always gone to someone from Alignment.

As soon as it was announced that the NRP would hold the education portfolio, R. Zvi Yehuda Kook began declaring his disciple, Rav Druckman, "our Minister of Education" – even though Zevulun Hammer saw himself as a natural candidate for the position. Rav Zvi Yehuda's declaration caused Rav Amital's first political intervention. Just as he criticized Rav Zvi Yehuda's coercive interference with Gush Emunim decisions, he now objected to the latter's interference in internal NRP matters. In response to Rav Zvi Yehuda's support for Rav Druckman, Rav Amital expressed public support for Hammer's appointment. Many were astonished by his brash dispute with Rav Zvi Yehuda, but he, as always, was not fazed by his detractors. "Rav Zvi Yehuda is not an oracle," he said – which proves that Rav Amital did not fear expressing his own position even while Rav Zvi Yehuda was still alive, as some later claimed. In the end, Hammer held on to the education portfolio in the next government.

The signing of the peace accords with Egypt created rifts within the NRP. The Gush Emunim faction revolted against the party mainstream, which had decided to support the agreement, and several of them left the government. In 1979, the Teḥiya (Revival) party was founded by Geula Cohen and Moshe Shamir, who broke away from Likud in response to the treaty with Egypt. The party attracted disaffected NRP members such as Ḥanan Porat. The Gush Emunim people who stayed in the NRP, such as R. Ḥayyim Druckman, founded a separate faction within the party – the Eitanim faction. Prior to the 1981 elections, Eitanim demanded from the other two factions – Burg's LaMifneh faction and Hammer's HaTze'irim faction – that two of their members be included on the party's Knesset list. Hammer and his allies suggested Rav Amital as a candidate, but ultimately only one spot on the list was reserved for Eitanim, and it went to Rav Druckman. In the elections, which took place that June, the NRP lost half of its mandates; its right wing bolted to Teḥiya and many of its Mizraḥi voters voted for Tami, a new NRP breakaway party, headed by Aharon Abuḥatzira.

In the wake of the NRP's electoral collapse in the 1981 elections, the internal rift between Burg's LaMifneh faction and Hammer's HaTze'irim faction became more pronounced. In response, several religious-Zionist rabbis, including Rav Amital, established a new religious body called Ḥatam – *Ḥativa Toranit Mamlakhtit,* the Organization for State and Torah. This body called for the rehabilitation of the NRP and threatened to establish a political alternative. The rabbis and activists who participated in Ḥatam's establishment were not identified with any particular political stance or ideological circle. In addition to Rav Amital, Ḥatam included: R. Ya'akov Filber, a student of Rav Zvi Yehuda;

R. Yehoshua Ben-Meir, the brother of MK Yehuda Ben-Meir; and Shilo Gal, the head of the Gush Etzion Regional Council. A public declaration by Ḥatam's leaders stated that "factional disagreement and non-ideological disputes completely annihilate and eliminate any good that comes from the organizational power of the religious camp. The political leadership has not learned a lesson from its electoral collapse and has not moved towards rehabilitation. Therefore, we have decided to establish Ḥatam to constitute a central and leading force within religious Judaism, and which will keep all political options open." In an interview with *Ma'ariv* reporter Avi Bettelheim, Rav Amital explained, "we do not wish to bury or replace the NRP. Our objective is to jolt the party leadership, and force them out of the current, unprogressive framework. If they fail to do so, we may have no recourse other than to establish a new religious center."

Ḥatam ended up being short-lived. In another interview with Bettelheim, Rav Amital related that he withdrew from the organization as soon as he realized that it would occupy the majority of his time. He also claimed that meddlesome political activists made it clear that politics were not for him. Around that time, Zevulun Hammer officially offered Rav Amital a position among the party elite. Rav Amital refused. He did not believe that the offer was sincere. He felt that they wanted him as a decoration on the party list, not to be a real partner in making decisions about the party's direction.

The Yamit evacuation and the First Lebanon War widened the rifts within the National-Religious Party. Supporters of Gush Emunim protested the passivity of the party members during the Yamit evacuation and the moderate stances taken by Hammer and Burg during the evacuation and the war. On the other side, the party's more moderate elements joined Rav Amital in protesting the lackluster behavior of the NRP ministers during the Sabra and Shatila affair. In the numerous interviews that he granted to the media during that time, Rav Amital disparaged the hawkish line that Gush Emunim imposed on the NRP and called on the party's leaders to renounce it. In the context of his opposition to Defense Minister Sharon's actions, Rav Amital expressed hope that the alliance between the NRP and Alignment would be renewed. MK Rav Druckman criticized Rav Amital's moderate positions and willingness to replace NRP cooperation with Likud with a new government headed by Alignment.

In December 1982, the leftist religious movement Netivot Shalom was founded. The movement's founders declared that they had no intention of creating a new religious political party; they merely wished to form a counterweight to Gush Emunim within the religious camp. The founding convention was attended by Professors Yeshayahu Leibowitz and Uriel Simon as well as Rabbis Amital and Lichtenstein, who came to praise the movement's founding. In his speech to the convention, Rav Amital labeled the willingness to fight at all costs for the principle of Greater Israel, and the idea that the solution to all of the problems of the Jewish people lies in war and military might, "false messianism." On the other hand, he also disparaged the outlook of Peace Now, cautioning the members of Netivot Shalom against getting carried away and espousing positions that he characterized as a danger to the Jewish people. Rav Amital rejected an offer to head Netivot Shalom. In an interview with *Ma'ariv*, he said: "It's a movement of inexperienced youngsters. There is no leader who can lead the others." Although he declared his reluctance to become politically active, he nevertheless conceded that "there may come a time when my colleagues and I will have to become engaged politically. I hope we never get to that point, but who knows..."

In December 1983, several Alignment MKs, including Yitzḥak Rabin, visited Yeshivat Har Etzion to meet with Rav Amital, Rav Lichtenstein, and several NRP dignitaries and to discuss the renewal of the historic alliance of the two parties. For the Alignment members, the meeting had a political objective, but the NRP contingent preferred just to engage in dialogue. At the meeting, Rav Amital spoke about the importance of dialogue; he told the Alignment members that the fundamental problems of state and society would not be resolved by political means alone. He predicted that the Likud government would be replaced in the next election or the one after that. Regarding the political leadership of the religious public, he remarked: "Our political apparatus is disintegrating. No political figure speaks to our youth here. If a few Jews would get up from this table and say that they are forming a list and running for the Knesset, fear would grip the entire political apparatus." At a conference of the Religious Kibbutz Movement held around that time, Rav Amital called for the removal and replacement of all six NRP Knesset members.

In 1984, the existence of the Jewish Underground was exposed. Rav Amital, who had cautioned against extremist activities by right-wing activists since the Yamit evacuation, was dubbed "The Rabbi who Foresaw the Underground" in a wide-ranging interview with *Yediot Aharonot*. In the interview, he said to journalist Amos Nevo, "All of the indications and phenomena that were recently discovered in the Underground were already visible during the Yamit evacuation." He related that after the evacuation there had been a meeting of *hesder* Rashei Yeshiva at which he cautioned vigilance against Jewish terrorist operations aimed at thwarting the Camp David Accords. "I told my colleagues: 'What will you say if they find a weapons cache near one of you tomorrow?' They looked at me like I was crazy." Among the Underground arrests was Yehuda Etzion, an alumnus of the yeshiva's second class. Another yeshiva alumnus, Yossi Eindor, was suspected of being a member of the organization, but was not arrested. Rav Amital told the reporter that he was not surprised: "I knew they were that type." In the same interview, Rav Amital cautioned that if the NRP did not revert to its original, moderate path, it would disappear from the political map.

Prior to the 1984 elections, Rav Amital said that he was not opposed to a renewal of the historic alliance with Alignment, but preferred a national unity government. The NRP approached those elections with a more moderate stance than the previous ones. Rav Druckman and other members of the NRP's hawkish wing broke away and created the created the Matzad faction. They ran for the Knesset in the 1984 elections as part of the Morasha party, on a joint list with Avraham Verdiger's Poalei Agudat Yisrael faction. In those elections, the NRP won an all-time low of four mandates. The more right wing of its voters defected to Morasha, which won two mandates, and others – mainly Mizraḥi voters – preferred Shas, the new Sephardic religious party that won four mandates in its first Knesset campaign. Although the NRP joined the national unity coalition that was established after the elections, due to its decline in strength it lost the education portfolio that it had held for seven years.

Soon after the 1984 elections, Danny Tropper began pressuring

Rav Amital to work toward a fundamental shift in religious-secular relations in the State of Israel.

* * *

Rabbi Dr. Danny Tropper had been in touch with Rav Amital – for both ideological and social reasons – since around the time of the yeshiva's founding. Tropper, then a new immigrant from the U.S., had founded Gesher and begun organizing seminars that brought together religious and secular youths, in the attempt to forge a common ground and language. The connection between Gesher and the yeshiva was made by Ḥanan Porat, who assisted Tropper in Gesher's founding. The organization's first seminar, on Sukkot of 5730 (1969), was held in the dormitory of the yeshiva, then on vacation. Many in the yeshiva community did not look favorably on the young movement, as they were concerned about the meetings between religious and secular youth. But Rav Amital gave these activities his unconditional support. "He always gave us support and encouragement," Tropper relates. Regarding the concern that religious youths would "go off the path" due to their encounters with secular youths, Rav Amital remarked, "Whoever would go off the path in Gesher would go off the path alone, too." To those who cast aspersions on the point of these meetings, he said that there are two models of educating toward spiritual growth: one model is to help one person take ten steps forward, and the other is to help ten people take one step forward. "Who can calculate which is preferable?" Rav Amital asked Tropper rhetorically, "It's for God to calculate. Do what you believe in, and don't worry."

Rav Amital gave a particularly interesting response to one young woman who wished to become religiously observant as a result of one of these seminars. The girl asked what observances she should take on first. Rav Amital responded that the Israelites asked the very same question before receiving the Torah at Mt. Sinai. Soon after they left Egypt but before reaching Mt. Sinai, they stopped in Mara, where bitter waters miraculously turned sweet and potable. That verse (Ex. 15:25) continues to say that "there He set a rule and a law for them, and there He tested them." Ḥazal understood this verse to mean that God gave the Israelites three mitzvot prior to Mt. Sinai: Shabbat, honoring one's parents, and the red heifer. In the same vein, Rav Amital suggested that this girl begin with the observance of three mitzvot: Shabbat, through which she would be able to observe mitzvot at least once a week; honoring her parents, an interpersonal mitzva, so that she would internalize the notion that the Torah addresses the social realm and not only man's relationship with his Creator; and a third mitzva, one that, like the red heifer, is hard to rationalize, so that she would understand that some mitzvot are hard to explain – but nevertheless must be upheld.

Over time, the relationship between the yeshiva and Gesher became closer, and many yeshiva students joined the movement in order to staff the seminars.

In 1984, Tropper began urging Rav Amital to take action. He relates, "We both understood that the established patterns of behavior in the religious community had to change, as they were causing terrible alienation and endangering the Jewishness of the state. As a first step, we spoke about the need to stop religious legislation." The meetings between Tropper and Rav Amital resulted in the formation, in early 1986, of Hagut – an intellectual circle of rabbis and academics, designed to formulate ideas and strategies for tackling questions of religion and state. Political issues were bracketed, mainly so that they would not impede the growth of the new initiative, but also because they did not dominate the public agenda at the time. The circle's first publication, issued at a July 1986 press conference, called for the end of religious legislation and for a renewal of religious-secular consensus. The document was signed by rabbis and public figures from the right and from the left. Among the signatories were R. Ya'akov Ariel and R. Yehoshua Zuckerman of Merkaz HaRav; R. Yoel Bin-Nun; Ḥanan Porat; R. Shlomo Riskin, rabbi of the community of Efrat; R. Menaḥem Froman, rabbi of the community of Tekoa; Professor Shalom Rosenberg, then the Head of the Department of Jewish Thought at Hebrew University; Professor Michael Albeck, president of Bar-Ilan University; and of course Rav Amital and Dr. Tropper. Tropper, who worked hard on the wording of the position paper, describes his arduous campaign of shuttle diplomacy to find an agreeable formulation, which succeeded largely due to Rav Amital's involvement:

> I worked on that document like the American Secretary of State Henry Kissinger. I went from one to the next, and every time we got close to a final draft, someone began waffling about one clause or another and nitpicking the words. During the debates, Rav Amital sat quietly to the side, until finally he interjected, "What do you think, that we're talking about novellae of the *Rishonim*? Why are you nitpicking about every word? Who's going to pay attention to it? We need to get the message across. That's the main thing." His ability to transcend the wrangling over wording was characteristic of his personality.

Hagut's second document dealt with the cultural consensus about the Jewishness of the state. It called for a distinction between the private domain, in which everyone has the right to act as he wishes, and the public domain, which must have a Jewish character, as befits a Jewish state.

Having issued two position papers, Tropper and Rav Amital felt that if they wished to create something meaningful that would connect the religious and secular populations; they could no longer ignore sensitive political issues that divided elements of Israeli society. "And then," Tropper relates, "in one of our discussions at his house, he brought up the idea of founding a political party."

The reasons that motivated Rav Amital to voice his opinions during the First Lebanon War were the same reasons that later led him to establish Meimad. The founding principle of Meimad was the desire to articulate a different, more moderate voice of the Torah world. By means of that voice, Rav Amital wished to forge a connection with secular populations who were intimidated by what they saw as the religious and nationalist radicalization of the national-religious public. Additionally, the new party proposed Judaism without religious coercion, putting the people of Israel before the land of Israel, and willingness to make concessions for the sake of peace. These were all messages that Rav Amital considered important to impart, and the party served as his vehicle for their dissemination. Rabbanit Miriam Amital relates that establishing the party positively affected her husband's mental state. "He had a lot of internal pain because all these things he wanted to say had accumulated in his gut. For him, the party was a way to express his opinions. After its establishment, he calmed down."

Until that point, Tropper, too, had tried to keep away from politics, and was therefore a bit wary of the idea of a new party. Ultimately, both he and Professor Shalom Rosenberg bought into the idea, and the three began meeting to discuss formulating the principles of the new party. Over time, a nucleus of ten to twelve activists consolidated around the three founders, and they began holding meetings to prepare for the party's launch. In those first, secretive stages, meetings were attended by several prominent NRP activists, including: Adv. Yeshayahu Prywes, the head of the Committee to Rehabilitate the NRP, who became a major factor in Meimad's establishment; Professor Moshe Bar Asher, Rav Amital's student from Yeshivat HaDarom and a member of the Committee to Rehabilitate the NRP; Adv. Naḥum Langenthal, Chairman of the NRP's Young Generation; and Moshko Moskovic, the Director of Yeshivat Har Etzion, who was also a member of the NRP Central Committee. Another major NRP figure who later joined the group was MK Yehuda Ben-Meir.

The addition of Ben-Meir was connected to developments that took place within the NRP in 1987–88, contributing decisively to the establishment of a new, more moderate religious party. In the wake of its stinging defeat in the 1984 elections, the NRP established a reorganization and rehabilitation committee, which recommended a series of reforms to repair the party, primarily by democratizing its election campaigns. As part of the rehabilitation process, the Matzad faction returned to the party in July 1986. The struggle between the various factions was renewed, but this time through democratic means. Several months later, Dr. Yosef Burg resigned as party head, and Zevulun Hammer replaced him. Hammer had to work hard to consolidate his power in those first months. In 1987, the NRP held a convention to discuss its ideology, a large part of which was dedicated to foreign policy. Hammer and Ben-Meir attempted to gain the party central committee's support for the Camp David Accords, but the Matzad faction obtained a majority on the vote, and the central committee rejected the accords. This decision, considered surprising, indicated the NRP's rightward shift, to the chagrin of the more moderate elements. It led Ben-Meir and other prominent party activists to take interest in the new political organization of Rav Amital and his colleagues.

The existence of the new organization was first made public in January 1988, ten months before the elections for the twelfth Knesset. *Yediot Aharonot* reported briefly that Rav Yehuda Amital was considering founding a new party; *Ma'ariv* reported that the new party would represent a centrist and moderate political platform that accepts the "land for peace" formula. In response to these reports, Rav Amital confirmed that indeed feelers had been put out regarding the establishment of a new party if the NRP did not return to its original stances. Nevertheless, he made it clear that he had no intention of trading the benches of the *beit midrash* for the benches of the Knesset: "I am a Rosh Yeshiva. That is my mission," he told *Hazofe*'s Shaul Schiff.

The new organization gained momentum several months later, when the NRP list was set for the upcoming elections. A week and a half before the NRP primaries, there was still discussion of Meimad remaining an interest group and not running in the elections, but the NRP primary results pushed Meimad closer to a decision to run. Hammer lost the party leadership to Professor Avner-Ḥai Shaki. Ben-Meir was pushed down to the unrealistic seventh spot on the party list, behind Ḥanan Porat, R. Yitzḥak Levi, and Yigal Bibi. The NRP took on a more hawkish complexion, persuading Rav Amital that there was indeed room for a new political organization. Immediately after the publication of the NRP primary results, he called for the establishment of a new religious-Zionist party, since the moderates had been pushed out of the NRP. The results also led to Ben-Meir's final departure from the NRP. He officially joined Rav Amital's group and, due to his political experience, became a dominant figure in the new party.

From the moment it became clear that Meimad intended to contend in the upcoming elections, the NRP began trying to prevent it from running. Members of the Matzad faction, which had become dominant within the NRP, set up meetings with Meimad people to try to persuade them to join their list. At the same time, Naḥum Langenthal was pressured to sever his ties with Meimad, and he acquiesced. Dr. Yosef Burg, for the first time not running for the Knesset, went to Rav Amital's home to try to persuade him to give up his idea: "You will not succeed; you have no chance," he warned, but Rav Amital was determined. On 16 Sivan, 5748 (June 1, 1988), exactly five months before the elections, he convened some fifty activists at his home, and it was resolved: they were running. As at other junctures in his life, he again spoke about the need to sanctify God's Name. He saw the party as no less than an opportunity to impart the message of *kiddush HaShem*.

To encourage the activists, Rav Amital spoke to them about the experience of freshness that they would be privy to as founders of a new party. He mentioned Rashi's comments at the beginning of *parashat BeHa'alotekha* (Num. 8:2) that the high priest Aharon was sad that he was unable to participate in the Tabernacle's inauguration like the tribal princes. "Why was Aharon saddened," Rav Amital asked, "when he was in charge of the entire Tabernacle?" He answered, "Perhaps Aharon missed that sense of primal freshness that was felt by the tribal princes when they offered the first sacrifices on the altar. It is hard to replace that sense of being first, or creating a new entity."

The new party was described as a centrist party, and hence its name: Meimad stands for "*Maḥane Yisraeli Merkazi Dati* – the Centrist Israeli Religious Camp. The name was coined by Yitzḥak Meir, an employee of the Foreign Ministry who helped organize the new party. The campaign slogan chosen for the election was "Meimad – Because it is in our Soul." (In Hebrew, this phrase also connotes something that is of the utmost importance to us.) Meimad wished to champion two main causes: one in the realm of religion, and one in the realm of pure politics. In the religious realm, it called for "more Judaism, less coercion." It opposed coercive religious legislation, called for the Chief Rabbinate to be disconnected from politics, advocated reforming the rabbinical court system, and encouraged the inclusion of women into all areas of life. On the political side, Meimad did not formulate a detailed platform, but it declared its preparedness for painful territorial concessions for the sake of real peace.

As opposed to the 1990s incarnation of Meimad, which had a more left-wing bent, the original Meimad was truly a centrist party. Its leaders included rightists like Professors Bar Asher and Rosenberg as well as avowed leftists like Professor Avi Ravitzky and MK R. Menaḥem Hacohen, who left Alignment. Rav Amital even explained to the leaders of the dovish religious movement Netivot Shalom that he could not include them on his list out of concern that they would give it too much of a left-wing look. Leftist Professor Yeshayahu Leibowitz called Rav Amital just prior to the election to hear more about Meimad's political stances. What he heard did not satisfy him. He told Rav Amital that he could not see himself voting for the new party, as it was not left-wing enough for his tastes.

Even Professor Ravitzky, who did join Meimad, later related that he was reluctant to join because its dovish stances were not decisive enough. He ultimately decided to join the new party after hearing an interview of Rav Amital on the radio. Rav Amital was asked if he would be interested in becoming Minister of Religious Affairs in the event that he was elected to the Knesset. At the time, there was a health services strike, and the media reported about elderly men and women who were sent away from hospitals and nursing homes due to budgetary constraints. Rav Amital thus told his interviewer: "From a religious perspective, the question of how to run the Ministry of Health is more important than how to run the Ministry of Religious Affairs." This answer impressed Ravitzky, who decided to join the ranks of Meimad.

Rav Amital, who was the chairman of the party's presidium, did not plan to head its Knesset list. He characterized his activity as "a push for the organization to get off the ground." In the first phases, party members did not yet address the question of appointments, but from the moment it was decided to run for the Knesset, it was clear that this issue would have to be raised. Professors Rosenberg and Bar Asher refused to head the party, as did Danny Tropper. The pressure on Rav Amital to place himself at the top of the list gradually increased. After six weeks of failing to find a party chairman, Rav Amital understood that he would have no choice but to undertake the task himself. Before notifying his party colleagues, he gathered his family together and told them of his intention to head the list. He later called his partners and announced his decision. Meimad rejoiced over the decision, but others raised eyebrows upon hearing that the rabbi who often spoke out against rabbinic involvement in politics was running for the Knesset. In an interview with *Ma'ariv*'s Menaḥem Rahat several days after his decision, he explained:

> Now, as before, I believe that the place of the rabbi is in the *beit midrash*. I considered several candidates, all good and worthy of serving in the Knesset, but when I saw that each of them thought of his family and job first, I realized that we have a real problem. The question was to be or not to be. I saw that this is the need of the hour and was forced to make a difficult decision. I can't remember if I ever faced a more difficult decision. I always saw myself as one who dwells in the *beit midrash*. But I also believe that men of Torah and spirit should voice their opinions on the nation's existential questions. When we could not find someone to take the lead, I took it upon myself with a heavy heart. Ḥazal say, "Where there are no men, strive to be a man."

Years later, Rav Amital explained that the message that rabbis should not get involved in politics could only be delivered, from a Torah perspective, by a rabbi who engages in Torah. Only a rabbi can oppose the use of halakha in political debate.

In Yeshivat Har Etzion, Rav Amital's decision to run for the Knesset was received with mixed feelings. Many students and faculty members lamented the decision that turned their Rosh Yeshiva into an official political figure. R. Ya'akov Fisher, a student of Rav Amital and at that time the *mashgi'aḥ ruḥani* of the yeshiva, describes feelings of confusion mixed with understanding and admiration:

> On the one hand, all of a sudden my rabbi breaks out into the public sphere, so there's confusion and lack of comprehension. On the other hand, I put virtually unreserved trust in him, regarding this step as well. I thought that perhaps I do not understand this step, but he, with his sense of history, is certainly acting properly.

Yeshayahu Yeḥieli, a member of the yeshiva's first class, described primarily harsh feelings:

> I will never forget how one Friday I saw Rav Amital's picture on a full-page election notice in the newspaper. I thought I was hallucinating, not just because of the political angle, but because

> of the step he took and his willingness to leave the yeshiva. It wasn't only that I couldn't understand – it was a true crisis. An image was shattered.

R. Yuval Cherlow, then a *ram* at the *hesder* yeshiva in Hispin, wrote to Rav Amital prior to Rosh HaShana of that year:

> Your turning away from eternal life to engage in temporal life, without relating in any way to the substance and objectives of the movement, is difficult for me – are you laying out on a path in which influence over the people of Israel is centered in the Knesset and not the yeshiva? This is hard for me.

Nevertheless, at the end of his letter, Rav Cherlow hedged his musings by citing a passage from the Talmudic tractate *Sanhedrin*: "One who second-guesses his mentor is like one who second-guesses the Divine Presence."

Rav Amital had the full backing of his co-Rosh Yeshiva. Rav Lichtenstein publicly supported Meimad even though he was a member of the NRP's rehabilitation committee. His wife, Dr. Tovah Lichtenstein, the daughter of R. Joseph B. Soloveitchik, was even more involved; at one point she was even in the third slot of Meimad's Knesset list. Within the yeshiva's administration, Rav Amital won the support of his friend Moshko. "My joining Meimad," Moshko relates, "stemmed from my support for Rav Amital's positions. I was more attracted to the social platform regarding religion and state than to the political platform. Although I was a member of the NRP Central Committee, for me Meimad was an intellectual circle that I had no problem joining."

Rav Amital's placement at the top of Meimad's Knesset list greatly helped the fledgling party gain media exposure. Numerous journalists congregated by the door of the Rosh Yeshiva who dared to challenge the NRP. From the perspective of Rav Amital, who viewed Meimad as a vehicle for spreading certain messages, some of the party's objectives were attained even before it was tested at the ballot box. During the run-up to the election, his positions won respectable exposure in major newspapers; he viewed this as a *kiddush HaShem*. "Over the years," he told Tropper, "I've taught Torah, I've spoken about ideas, and nobody has noticed. Only now that I'm part of a political entity does the message get out." In contrast to the dissemination of his messages, the personal exposure was not easy for Rav Amital. In an interview with Amos Nevo of *Yediot Aharonot*, he confessed: "The large notices and pictures are bad for my soul. In yeshiva I speak about modesty and humility, and it's not simple. I insisted that my picture not appear more than once in the election notices."

At the beginning of September, the composition of Meimad's Knesset list was completed. Slotted after Rav Amital were Ḥayyim Rippel, an educator from Safed who served as the movement's secretary; Tovah Ilan, a prominent figure in the Religious Kibbutz Movement; Professor Shalom Rosenberg; Sara Meltzer of Emunah Women; and Professor Moshe Bar Asher.

At the beginning of October, a month before the elections, the party's first convention was held at Beit HaRofeh in Tel Aviv. At the convention, Rav Amital said that it is absurd to quote and follow Torah sages whose entire expertise and greatness is in the areas related to Greater Israel, but remain ignorant of every other facet of the Torah. Meimad's message, he said, is not limited to *kashrut* or the integrity of Eretz Yisrael, but addresses every facet of Israeli society. He added that it was clearer to him than ever that one day soon his detractors in the religious-Zionist camp would admit that he was correct to establish Meimad, and that it is a *kiddush HaShem*.

Most published surveys at the time were favorable to Meimad and predicted that it would pass the electoral threshold. Nevertheless, two weeks before the elections, the NRP decided not to sign a surplus votes agreement with Meimad, despite Rav Amital's warning that this decision was liable to cost the religious-Zionist public a Knesset seat. Uri Elitzur, head of NRP's public relations campaign during those elections, wrote in *Nekuda* around that time: "The Rav Amital phenomenon is politically marginal but very significant spiritually and educationally." Elitzur warned that if Rav Amital was not defeated by a wide margin, it would have a major impact on the mood of Bnei Akiva. "Whoever is attentive to the whispers and currents in today's Bnei Akiva," Elitzur wrote, "knows that the process has already begun." Over the long term, he wrote, the contest within the national-religious public is no less significant than the race for the premiership.

As the elections neared, Rav Amital came under pressure to declare who he would support to build the coalition after the elections: Shimon Peres of Alignment or Yitzḥak Shamir of Likud. Rav Amital refused to make a pronouncement. At one point, Meimad was offered a large donation by Jewish philanthropist Charles Bronfman, but with the stipulation that the party would only enter into an Alignment-led government. Rav Amital did not agree to make such a commitment. In an interview with *Ma'ariv*, he said: "I do not disqualify any party except for the Communists and the Progressive List for Peace on the left, and Kahane on the right."

On 21 Ḥeshvan, 5749 (November 1, 1988), elections for the twelfth Knesset were held. Before Channel One published the results of their exit polls, Rav Amital and party activists gathered at Meimad's Jerusalem headquarters. The atmosphere was optimistic. Several minutes before 10:00, Ḥayyim Rippel, number two on the party list, estimated that they had won two seats. When the results were publicized, there was silence at the headquarters. According to the exit polls, Meimad had not passed the electoral threshold. After two minutes of silence, Rav Amital recovered, got up, and said: "Friends, we sanctified the Name of Heaven." When reporters asked whether he regretted founding Meimad, he answered, "We wrought a revolution in religious Zionism. Our ideas are penetrating the broader public, religious and secular. One message we did not succeed in imparting: that even people like us can be Knesset members. Today's results are definitely a great failure for religious Zionism."

Meimad received 16,700 votes, about 6,000 votes shy of the threshold, which was close to 23,000 votes in that election. The number of votes it received was close to one mandate. In the 1988 elections, every mandate was 18,563 votes.

The religious right did not mask their satisfaction with Meimad's failure. In a *Nekuda* editorial after the elections, Editor Yisrael Harel wrote, under the headline "Defeat for Submissiveness":

> To be brutally honest, Meimad's downfall was received with great satisfaction in the communities of Judea, Samaria, and Gaza. Had they succeeded in winning even one seat, their success would have meant more than just another Knesset seat in the service

> of Alignment and Ratz. It would have attested to a weakening of faith and endurance among a significant part of the public.

In the post-election analysis, several reasons were offered for Meimad's failure: a major reason, which Rav Amital alluded to immediately after the results were announced, was the party members' lack of political experience. In many ways, the party was too elitist; its members were not thrilled about engaging in politics, and therefore they failed to generate an electoral critical mass that would allow them to succeed. Aviva Shabi, reporting on Meimad's convention a month before the elections, wrote in *Yediot Aharonot*: "The event was similar to an academic conference. It was very neat, very civilized, and all the pathos of an election campaign was absent." Moshko, a man of action to whom the political realm is not foreign, also pointed out the lack of professionalism among Meimad's membership as a major reason for their failure: "There were generals without soldiers. Rav Amital, for example, is not built to establish an organizational machine, to fundraise, or to organize propaganda and advertising. At some point I realized that these guys just are not cut out for it." Another reason for their defeat at the ballot box, mentioned by the party heads, was the conservatism of many NRP voters, who identified with Meimad's messages but could not bring themselves to turn against their familiar political home. In an interview with *Haaretz*'s Ronit Matalon, Rav Amital said: "Though it was not reflected in the votes, a large population bought into our ideas. This public is conservative, and the word 'separatism,' used by the NRP to describe us, scared them away. The NRP has some sort of religion that forbids separatism…" In the same article, Rav Amital said about NRP voters, "There was a sense that their house was burning down, so they ran to the rescue." In an interview with *Davar*'s Yoram Levi, Rav Amital claimed that the extra Knesset seat won by the NRP (they went up from four to five) should be credited to Meimad: "When NRP supporters saw that it was endangered by Meimad, it galvanized them to support the NRP again."

Another reason for the failure, mentioned by Rav Amital in the *Haaretz* interview, was its amorphous stance on foreign affairs. "The public wanted to hear a clear pronouncement one way or the other. It could be that we lost votes because of our centrist platform." In that same article, Prof. Ravitzky made the same argument: "Meimad's ideals were clear and lucid. Its message was very unclear. They wished to attract the moderate right, and they had some success. On the other hand, people who were afraid of a Likud government, the religious doves, did not vote Meimad... if you add Shalom Rosenberg to Avi Ravitzky and then divide by two, you get the feeble line that sometimes characterized Meimad's political explanations." Rav Amital later characterized Meimad's initial political ambiguity as a complex message that many in the religious public simply did not understand. "People want something far more unequivocal," he said.

Despite the defeat, the feeling in the NRP after the 1988 election was that Meimad won a moral victory simply by running. The national-religious leadership learned to recognize and consider the existence of a moderate stream within religious Zionism. With regard to its ideas, even if Meimad did not impact the political mood of the national-religious public, in the social realm of the relationship between religion and state, its messages began to percolate and occasionally even became the majority position.

Chapter Seventeen

With a Broken Heart

When the eternal character of Ecclesia Israel *was at stake, it was clear to Yosef that even with all the distress he caused his father, he was operating as his agent. He therefore arranged that the brothers would once again face the same situation that they faced with him. They again had to face the possibility of hurting their father – "For how can I go back to my father unless the boy is with me? Let me not be witness to the woe that would overtake my father!" The internalization of this message, that fraternal hatred damages* Ecclesia Israel *as a whole, constitutes a necessary condition for shaping the character of the nation. Clearly, this eternal lesson could not prevent occasional bouts of fraternal strife throughout our history, but at every such moment, this warning accompanies us like a torch, a torch with the capability to illuminate our history, to guide and enlighten, but also, Heaven forbid, to burn and destroy.*

From a discourse at Yeshivat Har Etzion, 1998

Right after the 1988 elections, Rav Amital returned to his routine in the yeshiva. Many of those who feared his entry into the world of politics breathed a sigh of relief when they saw him back in his natural habitat, the world of Torah. Meimad, left out of the Knesset, became completely dormant; nobody undertook to ensure its continued existence.

Although the party ceased to be, it left a mound of debt behind. Rav Amital was forced to pay thousands of shekels out of his pocket, even though it was not his personal debt. "Had I defaulted," he explained, "it would have been a *ḥillul HaShem*." Although an anonymous donor sent Rav Amital enough to pay off a fair portion of the debt, the whole situation had a lingering effect on Rav Amital. This was one of the reasons that Meimad never again ran in an election.

The 1988 elections strengthened the right. Another national unity government, headed by Yitzḥak Shamir, was formed after the elections, but it did not last long. A year and a half later, in early 1990, Alignment and Shas tried to topple the government by a vote of no confidence, but they did not manage to cobble together an alternative coalition. A narrow right-wing government was later established. It, too, survived for a

Speaking at an event organized by the Menora organization, on the occasion of bringing Torah scrolls from Hungary to Israel. Among those seated at the table is Prime Minister Yitzḥak Shamir.

(photo: K. Weiss)

Prime Minister Yitzḥak Rabin visiting Yeshivat Har Etzion during his first term.

year and a half, falling in January 1992. Another election was called, and the NRP positioned itself firmly on the right, declaring that it would not enter a government headed by Labor. Its campaign slogan was "The NRP is at your right side." The religious left again felt homeless and waited to see if Meimad would be re-established.

In February 1992, Yitzḥak Rabin defeated Shimon Peres to become the head of Labor. Rabin's return to the forefront of the political arena and the possibility that he would be elected Prime Minister again significantly influenced the return of Rav Amital and Meimad to the public sphere.

Rav Amital first met Yitzḥak Rabin in the mid-1970s, during Rabin's first term as Prime Minister, when he visited Yeshivat Har Etzion together with Minister Yisrael Galili, and met with students and the Rashei Yeshiva. The common language forged in the meeting with the Rashei Yeshiva left Rabin and Galili wanting more. "I have an idea," Galili said to Rav Amital at the end of the meeting, "We're so immersed in the public's needs that we have no time to discuss the truly important things. Let's institutionalize these meetings. We'll meet once a month to talk about the people of Israel." A date was set, and Rabin even requested that the meeting be without spouses, "so that it would be topical, not social." The meeting never took place as Rabin's government fell a few days later.

Rav Amital's next meeting with Rabin took place six years later, in December 1983, during the discussions about renewing the alliance between Labor/Alignment and the NRP. That meeting triggered another, less political meeting which author Amos Oz attended as well. Rabin's relationship with Rav Amital became closer with every meeting. In Rav Amital, Rabin felt that he had found a moderate and open rabbinic figure after his own heart. Rav Amital admired Rabin's sincerity, and it is quite possible that he was also impressed by Rabin's military accomplishments. Rabin served as Defense Minister in the national unity government from 1984–90. During his tenure, he offered Rav Amital the position of Chief Rabbi of the IDF instead of R. Gad Navon. Rav Amital rejected the offer: "I asked Rabin if he wants me to be silent. After all, if I would be appointed Chief Rabbi of the IDF, I wouldn't be able to express myself about controversial matters. He replied that he hadn't really thought of that..."

Rabin's victory in the Labor primary, coupled with the NRP's declaration that they would not join a Labor-led government, led Yehuda Ben-Meir to the conclusion that he must publicly support Rabin and thus present a moderate religious alternative to the NRP. Ben-Meir sought backing and support for his idea and therefore turned to Rav Amital, who agreed to stand by him. Rav Amital was bothered by the rightward turn of the religious public along with the NRP and feared that once again the Torah would be identified with a right-wing approach. Like when he founded Meimad, Rav Amital wanted another position to be voiced – one that would make it clear that left-wing positions could find an audience in the religious population. The two of them consulted on how to present voting for Rabin's Labor as a suitable alternative for the religious public. Ben-Meir notes:

> It's important to remember that the 1992 elections still had a single ballot. Voting for Rabin meant casting a ballot for the Labor party – not so simple for religious voters. Here's where Rav Amital's courage and originality came into play. He proposed that

> he get a letter of support for religious education from Rabin, and only then would I publicly endorse him. Rav Amital himself did not want to publicly call for Rabin's election, and I understood him. For a rabbi, endorsing the Labor party is like eating *treyf*.

Ben-Meir met with Rabin, informed him that he supports him, and told him about Rav Amital's idea. "I told Rabin that we wanted a letter of support from him for religious education. He told me to draft the letter and bring it to him." Ben-Meir sat with Rav Amital, and together they prepared a letter. It was important to Rav Amital that Rabin's support for religious education should not depend on the composition of his coalition if he won the premiership. Ben-Meir recounts: "Rabin accepted the letter and made just one change. Wherever we mentioned 'religious education,' he amended it to 'religious public education,' explaining, 'I know who serves in the army and who doesn't.'"

The letter, addressed to Rav Amital personally, was "sent" on June 4, 1992, three weeks before the elections. It stated:

> I am aware that many former Meimad supporters, as well as many others in the religious-Zionist public, are deliberating who to vote for in the upcoming elections. On the one hand, they desire regime change and the advancement of the prospects of peace, and on the other hand they are concerned about the future of religious education in Israel. I give you my word that any government that I lead will ensure the welfare and development of religious public education – that is, religious-Zionist education with all it entails – and the preservation of its autonomous character…
>
> It is plain that these positions are not dependent or conditioned on any coalitional composition whatsoever. I would be happy to make myself available to you in the future to the degree that I can, and would be grateful if you make these statements known publicly.
>
> Respectfully, Yitzḥak Rabin

Ben-Meir made sure that the letter was published in media outlets and enlisted other former Meimad members to sign a letter of support for

Rabin. Even though they signed as individuals and not as Meimad members, their support led the media back to Rav Amital. They tried to wrest a public declaration of support for Rabin from him, but he refused. To some he said, "I don't tell people who to vote for; I'm not a *chasidishe rebbe* who tells his followers how to cast their ballots." To others he added, "I have not found a party with which I can identify one hundred percent." He refused all interview requests prior to the election because he did not want anyone to get the false impression that he intended to run. He only broke his silence after the elections, to explain why Meimad did not run. "We failed in the last election; why try again?" he said to Menaḥem Rahat of *Ma'ariv*, "We got the impression that we do not have enough supporters to win a representative in the Knesset." In an interview with Gadi Monsa of *BaMaḥane*, he admitted that the debts that he had to pay back out of his own pocket after the failure of 1988 deterred him from running again.

Right after Rabin's victory in the elections, Rav Amital sent him a congratulatory letter in which he wrote, among other things, "your letter to me regarding religious education and the position I took, even if I did not express myself publicly, resonated strongly and surely had an impact on Meimad's supporters. I would be happy – as always – to put myself at your disposal and help however I can." Shortly after the elections, Ben-Meir and Rav Amital began meeting regularly with Rabin. At one of the first meetings, the Prime Minister said to Ben-Meir, "I will speak with Rav Amital about ideological matters and with you about political matters."

Rabin's new coalition included the left-wing parties and Shas, and excluded the right wing parties, including the NRP. The religious-Zionist public, left in the opposition for the first time, began to worry about the future of the settlements in Judea, Samaria, and Gaza, and about the future of religious education. Their concerns became stronger after the appointment of Shulamit Aloni as Minister of Education, and after the government decided, at its first meeting, to freeze Jewish construction in the disputed territories.

In interviews that Rav Amital gave around that time, he criticized the NRP for not joining the government. He told *BaMaḥane*:

> The NRP could have joined the coalition under the same terms as Shas, but they had foreign policy demands. Not just demands – they wanted to appear as though they had made diplomatic achievements, that the government would be presented as a right-wing government. Perhaps they're right from their perspective, but I see it as a bad sign. It sends a message to the public that their paramount value is Eretz Yisrael and that nothing else is important. Until now they've merely spoken about it, but now the proof is in the pudding. They're willing to give up on education, religion, everything. That's a very negative development.

At the same time, Rav Amital tried to assuage the fears of the religious-Zionist public arising from their loss of power in the state's religious and educational institutions. When secularist Uzi Baram was appointed Minister of Religious Affairs, Rav Amital said: "He'll concern himself with religion no less than Shaki or anyone else from the NRP would have." In an interview with Ron Goldberg of the local newspaper *Al HaSharon* he said that he had not lost any sleep over the fact that Shulamit Aloni was appointed Minister of Education. Shortly after taking over the ministry, she convened a "Council of Educational Sages" and included Rav Amital in it.

Three months after the elections, Rav Amital concluded that the time had come to renew Meimad's activities, though as a movement, not as a political party. *Haaretz* described the new organization as a lobby. Among the party activists mentioned by *Haaretz* were former Mizraḥi Bank CEO Aharon Meir, economist Ya'akov Gadish, and *Ma'ariv* journalist Avraham Tirosh.

In its new incarnation as a lobby, Meimad modeled itself after Gush Emunim: an ideological movement that managed to enrapture a generation and change the face of the NRP. The NRP, of course, did not like the Meimad initiative, if only because it was designed to show that it was possible to protect the interests of religious education even when the NRP was not in the government. NRP MK Shaul Yahalom described the lobby as a "satellite of the Labor party," comparing it to left-wing religious bodies like Oz VeShalom and Netivot Shalom. He claimed that the Meimad lobby had already failed in its attempt to protect religious education, citing as examples the cutback of thousands of teaching hours from the religious educational system and Minister Aloni's attempt to trim fifty million shekels from the budgets of religious boys' and girls' high schools. In response, Rav Amital wondered, "What does the NRP think? That they can fight the government tooth and nail while all of their interests are protected by a letter to me from Rabin? The letter has some weight, but it's not equivalent to Shas's six MKs."

Like the Meimad party, the lobby wished to present a different voice from the NRP on matters of religion and state. It did not take long for Rav Amital to drop a media bombshell, declaring in an interview with *Ma'ariv*'s Menaḥem Rahat that he proposed abolishing the offices of the chief rabbis. Elections for the chief rabbinate were set for February 1993, and Rav Amital's words, spoken five months earlier, created a firestorm. Rav Amital claimed that according to the vision of Rav Kook, the founder of the chief rabbinate, two qualities were demanded of a chief rabbi:

> It is not sufficient that the chief rabbi be a Torah scholar; he must be a *bona fide* halakhic authority. Secondly, he must have a public presence that allows him to articulate the voice of the Torah and offer messages in the realms of morality, mitzvot, and faith to the public at large. The combination of these two elements is exceedingly rare nowadays.

He proposed that the powers of the chief rabbis be delegated to a committee comprised of Supreme Rabbinical Court judges and the rabbis of the three largest cities. The presidency of the chief rabbinate would rotate among the members. "Judaism can be upheld in such a manner," he declared.

This attitude toward the chief rabbinate was not new for Rav Amital. During the elections for the office of chief rabbi in 1972, he voiced a pessimistic forecast about its future to Moshko, who was then promoting the election of R. Shlomo Goren as Ashkenazic chief rabbi. Rav Amital questioned Moshko's efforts: "You're wasting your energy," he told his surprised friend, "Someday the status of the chief rabbinate will decrease and it will not matter who heads it." "To my chagrin," Moshko admits, "he showed a lot of foresight on this issue, too, and he was right."

Marriage was another area where religion and state intersected in which Rav Amital expressed a bold view that was not accepted at the time. The massive waves of immigration from the former Soviet Union, which began around then, brought hundreds of thousands of immigrants who were not halakhically Jewish. In order to marry under Jewish law, they often had to undergo fictitious conversions. In August 1992, Rav Amital said in an interview with *Al HaSharon*'s Ron Goldberg: "I think that there is a need to make civil marriage possible, so that there are no fictitious conversions. The fictitious conversions that people sometimes have to undergo in order to get married are far worse, in my opinion, than civil marriage. There has been a plethora of fictitious conversions, and the problem is only getting worse." Although Rav Amital limited his support for a civil marriage option to those otherwise disqualified from marriage, even this was a bold statement for a rabbi and Rosh Yeshiva. He repeated this statement on several occasions over the next few years, until 1997, when he went even further and expressed support for civil marriage for whoever wanted it. He explained his change of mind in Meimad's journal:

> Until now I supported the possibility of civil marriage being extended only to those disqualified from being married according to halakha, but now I believe that it is possible to make this option available to whoever seeks it. I believe that only a small minority within Israeli society, other than those who are halakhically disqualified, will forgo a wedding "in accordance with the law of Moshe and Yisrael." For this reason, allowing civil marriage will not cause any real damage to the Jewish character of Israeli society. On the contrary, many of those who choose the route of civil marriage today do so as a rebellion against religious coercion and the religious establishment. We may hope that with a lowering of the motivation to rebel, on the one hand, and the increased supply of young rabbis who conduct weddings in a manner that is compatible with young secular couples, on the other, the number of instances will shrink even further.

Nevertheless, Rav Amital distinguished clearly between civil marriage and Reform marriage, which he rejected outright: "On the other hand, I am vehemently opposed to granting legal status to Reform marriage and divorce." His proposal was thus that there should be two alternative tracks for marriage: a civil track and a religious track acceptable to all streams, i.e., Orthodox marriage.

More than merely calling for civil marriage, Rav Amital worked to advance the establishment of such an option in actuality. The initiative was kept secret; the Meretz party's Yair Tzaban, then Minister of Immigrant Absorption, only recently began discussing it openly:

> When I saw the distress of the immigrants from the FSU when it came to marriage, I consulted with Rav Amital because I saw it as a national problem. As a result of that consultation, we convened a meeting of six or seven rabbis, mainly establishment figures, at Rav Amital's home to discuss the matter. I promised to maintain due discretion, which I why I have not publicized this until now. The rabbis showed that they understood the problem and proposed all sorts of solutions. Some suggested that the idea of civil marriage be accepted with some reservations, or accepted only for those disqualified from halakhic marriage. Ultimately, though, even those in favor of a civil marriage option feared severe backlash, and so the initiative did not advance.

Several months after the decision to renew Meimad's activities, it was proposed that the movement should hold an inaugural conference in which Prime Minister Rabin would participate. Ben-Meir and Rippel organized the conference, which took place in March 1993 at Beit Sokolov in Tel Aviv. In addition to the Prime Minister, the conference was attended by the new Ashkenazic Chief Rabbi Yisrael Meir Lau and former NRP MK Avraham Melamed. In Rabin's speech, he reiterated his support for religious education, as he promised Rav Amital before the elections. Rav Amital was the keynote speaker. In his speech, he accused the Likud government of failing to deal with the mass immigration from the FSU:

> In recent years, we have witnessed one of the State of Israel's greatest historical failures. Notwithstanding efforts that were made, a historical opportunity to attract and absorb hundreds of thousands of Jews into the state was missed... we did not succeed in absorbing them due to economic problems. We did not succeed in solving unemployment, and we failed to impart to them a sense that this problem would be solved within a reasonable amount of time. This failure is not merely economic. It is a failure of values. In our scale of priorities, we have preferred adding settlements to creating a realistic opportunity to rescue hundreds of thousands of Jews. The value of settling Eretz Yisrael, the primary meaning of which, according to the Torah and the halakha, is the immigration of Jews to Eretz Yisrael to settle therein, has been limited to the occupation of another hilltop in Eretz Yisrael. It is unfortunate that this approach and this attitude especially characterize the adherents of religious Zionism. I'm afraid that in a few decades, Jewish history will not be able to forget this failure.

The harsh accusations that Rav Amital hurled at religious Zionism must be understood, *inter alia,* against the background of failed attempts at collaboration between the NRP and Minister of Immigrant Absorption Yair Tzaban of Meretz. Rav Amital claimed that the NRP must cooperate with the secular public to absorb the immigrants spiritually and culturally without trying to deal with the issue on their own. He contended that the most serious problem in Jewish society was the loss of Jewish identity. He understood this not as a religious problem, but as a Jewish national problem.

Regarding the political front, Rav Amital said at the founding conference that as an intellectual movement that was not running from the Knesset, there was no need for Meimad to take a stand on matters about which public opinion was divided: "I believe there is room in this movement for hawkish and dovish positions, as long as there is fundamental agreement about the movement's ideological outlook." These words were spoken in March, before a clear political-diplomatic plan was presented to the public. Six months later, the Oslo Accords burst

With former Chief Rabbis Yisrael Meir Lau and Eliyahu Bakshi-Doron.

onto the world scene. The ensuing public controversy sharpened Meimad's political demarcation.

At the end of August 1993, the existence of secret meetings between Israeli Foreign Ministry staff and PLO officials was disclosed. The meetings took place in Oslo, Norway, and resulted in the first diplomatic agreement between Israel and the Palestinians. In the Declaration of Principles, initially described as the "Gaza and Jericho first" agreement, the Palestinians committed to renounce terrorist activities and excise those clauses of the Palestinian Charter that called for the destruction of Israel. In exchange, Israel committed to recognizing the PLO, to withdraw from Gaza and Jericho, to allow for Palestinian self-government while withdrawing IDF forces from the cities of Judea and Samaria, and to commence permanent status negotiations. The government approved the accords on August 30, and on September 13 the signing ceremony took place on the White House lawn, and Prime Minister Yitzḥak Rabin shook hands with PLO Chairman Yasser Arafat. Reactions in Israel were mixed. Left-wing support for the accords was met with strong opposition and massive rallies by the Right. On the Palestinian side, Hamas and Islamic Jihad attempted to torpedo the accords by orchestrating terror attacks.

Meimad, the ideas-based movement that had until then avoided presenting a clear political program, faced a serious dilemma. The vast majority of the national-religious public vehemently opposed the accords. The NRP, sitting in the opposition, did not hesitate for a moment before coming out strongly against the Oslo process. As soon as the existence of the accords became known, it was clear that supporting it would transform Meimad from a centrist, ideas-based movement to a leftist movement. On the other hand, given its prior support for reaching diplomatic solutions and their willingness to concede territory, Meimad could not avoid expressing its position on the signed agreement.

Dr. Danny Tropper described the discussions within Meimad that led to their decision to support the accords:

> Even before Rabin and Arafat signed the agreement, we met – Rav Amital, Ben-Meir and I – and debated how to proceed. I opposed supporting the accords; Ben-Meir and Rav Amital were in favor. Rav Amital said to me, 'Danny, I don't understand you. Rabin is going to sign. That gives us two options: We can sign and try to influence things so that we don't lose everything, or we can join those who oppose. We have an opportunity to make a difference. Let's not give that up.' His practical consideration convinced me. I did not trust the Oslo Accords, but I was persuaded because there was a chance to make a difference.

Despite his decision to support the accords, Rav Amital had many misgivings, and understood the Right's protest. In a discourse he delivered at the yeshiva around then, he began by specifically noting the success of the right-wing demonstrations, which had echoed internationally. "The world must know that Rabin also has his opponents," he stated. Nevertheless, he expressed his disappointment that very few secularists came to the demonstration. Rav Amital told his students that his main concern was the preservation of the existence and security of the Jewish people in its land, "and therefore we should strive for a real peace, which will keep us away from the dangers of war." And yet, he still expressed

Meeting Prime Minister Yitzḥak Rabin together with Yehuda Ben-Meir.

his concerns about the accords and their impact on security and on settlements in Judea, Samaria, and Gaza. "We must make sure that the problems that emerge from the Declaration of Principles and concern for Jewish settlements are addressed," he stated, "but we must send a message to the government that the leadership of Judea, Samaria, and Gaza wants to reach an understanding with the government in the context of the present situation, not through mutiny."

Nine days after the accords were signed, Rav Amital and Ben-Meir met with the Prime Minister. A memorandum published by the movement after the meeting stated, *inter alia*, that Rav Amital and Dr. Ben-Meir expressed Meimad's appreciation of the Prime Minister and his government for their bold and responsible decision to sign the accords, creating a real chance for peace and the prevention of bloodshed. In their conversation with the Prime Minister, it was made clear to them that the government had no intent whatsoever – during the interim period – to harm existing settlements in Judea, Samaria, and Gaza, or to stop their natural growth by limiting construction. It was impressed upon them that the precise boundaries of the settlements would be determined through negotiation, and that the security establishment would consult with the residents of the settlements in the framework of the peace talks.

The Prime Minister told the pair that it was a foregone conclusion that Jerusalem would remain unified, and was not on the table. Regarding permanent status talks, the Prime Minister stuck to his position that rejected the establishment of a Palestinian state. Two weeks later, the first religious-Zionist conference in support of the Oslo accords was held at the initiative of Oz VeShalom and Netivot Shalom. Rav Amital participated in the conference, giving a speech right after Foreign Minister Shimon Peres. He admitted that despite his support for the accords, he had serious misgivings. "These agreements remain very far from the vision presented by the foreign minister," he said. He explained that his support for the accords stemmed from his deep anxiety about the possibility of war, and then expressed his fear that the accords would cause a political rift in the nation that would develop into a profound social rift. He cautioned against mutual delegitimation of the two sides of the religious-Zionist camp, and decried the characterization of settlers as agitators and trouble-makers, and of supporters of the accords as amoral. He also called on the government to find channels of dialogue with the settlers out of recognition that it could not give up on religious Zionism.

In October 1993, Rav Amital published an article in the settler newspaper *Nekuda*. Under the title "There is Hope for the Zionist Settlement of Judea, Samaria, and Gaza" he spelled out his position at length:

> For many years I have felt that time is not exclusively on our side. There is a real possibility that had we not signed this agreement now, we would be signing a much less favorable one with Hamas in a few years…
>
> Despite the accords' shortcomings, risks, and wide-ranging concessions, one cannot ignore their clear advantage: the settlement enterprise in Judea, Samaria, and Gaza is not included under Palestinian autonomy, and will remain under the full and exclusive protection of the State of Israel and the IDF…
>
> Despite these worries, the accords' prospects outweigh their risks, and every other alternative is more dangerous to the State of Israel than the accords.

He referred to the opposition's intention to stop the accords as "pipe dreams and wishful thinking." Rav Amital came out against denigration of the accords, writing that it only sowed despair on the right wing and harmed the settlement enterprise. He then addressed the internal debate within religious Zionism that emerged as a result of the accords. Regarding the halakhic question, he wrote his position that the mitzva of settling the land is no different than any other mitzva; sound discretion must determine the conditions under which they may or may not be fulfilled. He thus pronounced that "the public good, whose determination is in the hands of the country's leadership, should establish when this mitzva may be fulfilled, and when not."

In the ethical sphere, he reiterated his position that the people must take priority over the land. Responding to the battle-cry of those who opposed the accords – "Eretz Yisrael is in danger" – he argued that the people of Israel were in danger. Rav Amital also cautioned against a religious-Zionist spiritual crisis: "We have seen statements about the failure of Zionism. On [settler-run, uber-nationalist, pirate radio station] Arutz Sheva there are voices declaring the complete end of Zionism. It's only a short distance from there to hermetic retrenchment and alienation from the secularist public based on the claim that "the dispute is not about Eretz Yisrael; this is a dispute between Judaism and Hellenism" and the determination that "support for the accords comes from living without values." Rav Amital cautioned against conflating secularization and estrangement from Jewish values with a moderate political orientation: "Is everyone who views the accords as the only way out of the *Intifada* and prolonged ongoing conflict, with all its ramifications, devoid of values?" At the end of the article, Rav Amital warned against despair penetrating the community's heart, calling for greater commitment to faith in a higher providence "that causes the beginning of our redemption to flourish in ways that we do not always understand."

Rav Amital's article provoked numerous reactions, some furious. The most interesting came from within his own yeshiva. R. Ya'akov Medan, a *ram* at Yeshivat Har Etzion and a student of Rav Amital, published his response in *Nekuda*:

> Rav Amital *shlit"a*, the Rosh Yeshiva of Yeshivat Har Etzion, is my master and teacher, from whom I acquired the fundamen-

> tals of my Torah and my faith. What little love for Eretz Yisrael I have, and what smidgen of anticipation I have for salvation – are mostly the result of what I have absorbed of the great love for Eretz Yisrael, the messianic fervor, and the profound faith that I have seen in my *rebbe*.

Thus Rav Medan opened his essay.

He then went on to criticize his mentor's statements. With regard to the political sphere, he claimed that the agreement with the Palestinians would only increase the risks posed by Islamic fundamentalism, and he questioned Rabin's commitment to the continued settlement of Judea, Samaria, and Gaza. In terms of halakha, he argued that the crux of the dispute over giving up parts of Eretz Yisrael is not rooted in the question of handing over territory versus existential interests, but rather in the best way to fight for the existential interests of the people and State of Israel: "The claim of the Gush Emunim rabbis was that it is in the state's existential interest not to give land to the enemy." Finally, with regard to general outlook, Rav Medan argued that even the opponents of the accords integrate realism into the process of redemption; specifically because of their realism, they do not trust the Oslo accords: "Perhaps our realism differs from Rav Amital's, but it is there." Regarding priority scales, Rav Medan denied his *rebbe*'s contention that in this instance the existence of the people of Israel was pitted against the existence of its land. He claimed that it was premature to eulogize the right-wing outlook of religious-Zionism, quoting Rav Amital's *HaMa'alot MiMa'amakim* that "the settlement of the people of Israel in the land of Israel builds the kingdom of God." He concluded his article by joining Rav Amital's warning against allowing despair to penetrate the community: "These words are becoming of the great faith of their speaker." Rav Medan's response in *Nekuda* to Rav Amital's support for the Oslo accords was just the beginning of the dispute that erupted between them a month later, when Rav Medan began publicly protesting the accords.

November and December 1993 were particularly difficult months for the Jewish residents of Judea, Samaria, and Gaza. Not only were their increasingly potent protests against the accords unheeded, their lives were destabilized by a wave of terror attacks. On November 7, Efraim

Ayubi, Rav Druckman's personal driver, was shot to death while driving the rabbi to Ḥevron. Rav Druckman was also injured in the attack. Three weeks later, Shalva Ozana and Yitzḥak Weinstock were killed in a drive-by shooting in the Binyamin region, north of Jerusalem. Several days later, Mordekhai Lapid and his son Shalom were shot and killed by Hamas terrorists near Ḥevron. The attacks shocked the entire country, but specifically the religious-Zionist public, who reacted with a wave of passionate demonstrations. In a discussion with students, Rav Amital said that he would advise certain government ministers to employ a psychological counselor to teach them how to speak to the settler population during those difficult times. He related how he received numerous phone calls from anxious mothers of students, saying that the government had an obligation to open channels of dialogue with the settlers so that they would not feel like second-class citizens.

The primary focus of the right's protest at the time was the Israeli government's intention to arm the Palestinian police as part of the Oslo agreement. Under the headline "Don't Give Them Rifles," Rav Medan began a hunger strike with the goal of convincing the majority of the Knesset not to allow weapons to reach terrorist hands. For ten days Rav Medan sat in a protest tent in downtown Jerusalem, greeting supporters in his struggle, and teaching Torah to his numerous visitors. Alongside the hunger strike, a petition against handing over the rifles was circulated among Knesset members, and many rabbis, students, and alumni of Yeshivat Har Etzion, led by the yeshiva's *mashgi'aḥ* R. Yitzḥak Levi, participated in the effort to enlist signatories.

A few days after Rav Medan began his strike, Rav Amital came to visit him in the protest tent. He did not agree with Rav Medan's position and saw the handover of rifles as a mere symbolic gesture. "They would have obtained weapons with or without us," he said. Nevertheless, consistent with his liberal worldview, Rav Amital came to praise his disciple for leaving the *beit midrash* to protest what was troubling him. During Rav Amital's visit there were also students from other yeshivot who had come to show support for Rav Medan. To demonstrate his satisfaction with Rav Medan's public involvement, Rav Amital told those in attendance the story that he had repeated innumerable times, the story of the Alter Rebbe and the crying baby. When he concluded, he turned to Rav Medan and said:

> Reb Ya'akov, you know that I am fundamentally opposed to hunger strikes. I also read the political map differently from the way you do. But I cannot hide the fact that I am proud. The yeshiva's first student is fulfilling its educational message: when a Jewish child is crying, he closes his Gemara and takes care of the crying baby.

At the yeshiva's Ḥanukka party a few days later, Rav Amital asked his students to see his own actions as a form of attention to the baby's cry:

> True, I'm not on a hunger strike, but whenever I feel that I can say something to benefit the Torah, the Jewish people, or Eretz Yisrael, I do not hold myself back. Whenever I think I can minimize *ḥillul HaShem*, increase the honor of Heaven, bring individuals closer, save Jews from bloodshed, or save part of Eretz Yisrael, I do not hold myself back; because I too was taught to hear the baby's cry. I wish that even those who completely oppose my opinions would feel a smidgen of pride that they have a Rosh Yeshiva who is attentive to the baby's cry, just as I am proud of our friend R. Ya'akov Medan. Although it's in poor taste for someone to speak about himself, I allow myself to say this because of its educational import.

Chapter Eighteen

"How Can I Thank You?"

There were times when gentile hatred of the Jews was directed in particular toward Jews who observed Torah and mitzvot, and not towards Jews who accepted upon themselves the religion of their host nation. This is no longer true. The Jew is hated for being a Jew, irrespective of his actual beliefs. When Jew-hatred ignores the opinions and actions of the individual Jew, then the love of the Jewish people must be directed at every Jew qua Jew, without regard for his views and deeds. It is unthinkable that non-Jews should regard a particular person as a Jew, and we should relate to him, God forbid, in a negative and alienated manner. In Auschwitz, they did not check people's Tzitzit before sending them to the gas chambers; should we check Tzitzit before regarding someone as a brother?

Jewish Values in a Changing World,
2005, p. 187–88

Concern about excessive concessions in the context of the permanent status negotiations and the desire to take part in the shaping of the agreement led Rav Amital and Yehuda Ben-Meir to draft a proposal for the permanent agreement in the spirit of Meimad. Their proposal won the appellation "the Blocs Document" and was presented to the public in February 1994. The plan expressed consent to the establishment of a demilitarized Palestinian entity throughout Judea, Samaria, and Gaza, but with emphasis on the preservation of Israeli sovereignty over large settlement blocs and territorial contiguity between them and the rest of Israel. Regarding security, the document set forth that there would be no military presence in the territory between the Jordan River and the Mediterranean Sea except for the Israel Defense Forces. The IDF would defend the borders with Jordan and Egypt, and the air force would be responsible for the entire airspace of Eretz Yisrael. Meimad's Blocs Document was very similar to the Allon Plan, submitted by Minister Yigal Allon to Prime Minister Levi Eshkol a month after the Six Day War.

On the morning of Purim 5754 (1994), Dr. Barukh Goldstein, an emergency physician and a resident of Kiryat Arba, broke into the Yitzḥak Hall of the Cave of Makhpela and opened fire on a crowd of Muslims at prayer, killing twenty-nine and wounding dozens more. Rav Amital spoke to the media about the terrible *ḥillul HaShem* caused by the murders. He emphasized that the fact that these people were praying when they were massacred only exacerbated the *ḥillul HaShem*. Over the next days, Rav Amital was shocked to hear expressions of support for the massacre coming from several quarters. When he was asked to address this phenomenon on the Voice of Israel's Reshet Bet radio program "All Talk," he began sobbing in the middle of the broadcast and told host Razi Barkai that he "gets sick" when he hears about teachers and students observing a moment of silence for Barukh Goldstein. "All of Israeli society must now undergo an upheaval," he stated, "I hear religious Jews denigrating the massacre and then adding 'but…' That's not

Jewish. Such a reaction is immoral and not Jewish. There are some things that must not be rationalized – the massacre at the Cave of Makhpela is one of those things."

In early May of that year, Avigdor Kahalani, Emanuel Zisman, and Yehuda Harel established a movement called the Third Way. Members of this movement broke away from Labor to set up a centrist alternative that supported the peace process but wished to keep Israeli sovereignty over settled and strategic areas such as the Golan Heights. Rav Amital, who saw similarities between the new movement and Meimad, gave it his blessing. Since it was obvious that the Third Way was a political organization that would run in the next Knesset elections, Rav Amital rejected the suggestion that Meimad join the Third Way, though he agreed to speak at its opening convention. In his speech he said that in his opinion the Third Way is the only realistic way to advance the diplomatic process. Regarding the support of some Labor MKs for a return to the 1967 armistice lines and the evacuation of all settlements, he said, "Whoever thinks that it will be possible to forcibly evacuate 120,000 Jews or more from their homes is living in a fantasy world." He also denounced talk of leaving Jewish settlement blocs under Palestinian sovereignty.

In mid-May, the IDF withdrew its forces from Jericho and the Gaza Strip in the framework of the Oslo Accords. The left marked the day as a holiday. Rav Amital, who supported the accords, opposed the outbursts of joy and expressed mixed feelings about leaving Gaza. In an interview with *Ma'ariv*'s Menaḥem Rahat the day after the IDF's pullout from Gaza, he said:

> Yesterday, it would have been appropriate to recite two diametrically opposed *berakhot* (benedictions): "*HaTov VeHaMeitiv*" – "Who is good and bestows good" – to mark this milestone on the path to peace and reconciliation with the Arabs of Israel, and "*Dayan HaEmet*" – "the true Judge" – on the pain entailed by disengaging from areas of Eretz Yisrael. I certainly was not happy yesterday, even though abandoning Gaza and its troubles was necessary.

At the yeshiva's Yom HaAtzma'ut banquet that year, Rav Amital said that one could not properly assess the significance of the contemporary State of Israel without historical awareness. He expounded on this theme in light of a Talmudic passage discussing the sin of the spies:

> I heard a rumor – and I hope that it's not true – that an important religious Zionist rabbi expressed some doubt as to whether *Yom HaAtzma'ut* should be celebrated this year. The moment I heard it, a teaching of our Sages (*Ta'anit* 29a) came to my mind: "'And the people wept on that night' (Num. 14:1) – Rabba said in the name of Rabbi Yoḥanan: That night was the night of Tisha B'Av; the Holy One, Blessed be He said: 'Your weeping was baseless, so I will set for you weeping for generations.'" A person who sees only "that night," only today, only now, has questions and doubts. But a person with a sense of history knows, like Rabbi Akiva when he saw the fox emerging from the place of the Holy of Holies (*Makkot* 24a-b), that "Old men and women will yet sit in the open plazas of Jerusalem" (Zechariah 8:4). Only someone with a deep historical awareness can understand the significance of such a scene... After two thousand years, children play in the streets of Israel, in the courtyards of Jerusalem! Can this be a natural phenomenon, after two thousand years?

During the summer and fall of 1994, the attacks by Hamas intensified, and consequently so did public protests against the Oslo Accords. The rift between the settlers and the Prime Minister, who ignored their protests, reached a crescendo – and Rav Amital found himself torn between a population that was very dear to him and a Prime Minister that he admired. On the one hand, he deplored the violence emerging from the fringes of the rightist camp and the restraint shown by its leadership toward the extremists, but on the other hand he did not spare the Prime Minister, criticizing his alienating and derisive attitude toward the settlers. In an interview with Yisrael Segal of Kol Yisrael in July 1994, after another angry protest, he said: "We see this phenomenon that the leadership follows the extremists, but I also have claims against the Prime Minister. Rashi comments on this week's *parasha* that anger can lead to error. By responding angrily, Rabin added fuel to the fire … I understand his rage, but Ḥazal demand a more considered reaction from a leader."

Rav Amital and the Prime Minister met again in September. Rabin mentioned that the government would insist that some communities be concentrated into settlement blocs that would not be included in the Palestinian autonomous regions. He cited Gush Katif in the Gaza Strip as an example of a bloc that would remain under Israeli control. Rav Amital asked Rabin to speak frequently about the future of the settlements in Judea, Samaria, and Gaza, so as to reduce the tensions between the government and the settlers.

Hamas suicide bombings began in October 1994. Twenty-two civilians were killed in an attack on the number-five bus line in Tel Aviv. That same week, Cpl. Naḥshon Wachsman was abducted and murdered. Several weeks later, three IDF officers were killed in a suicide bombing at Netzarim Junction in the Gaza Strip. A week later, another soldier was killed at the same spot. In January 1995, twenty-one soldiers and civilians were killed in a suicide attack at Beit Lid Junction, near Netanya. The unstable security situation seriously eroded support for continuing the Oslo process, and Rabin's public standing progressively weakened.

Rav Amital sent Rabin a letter in January 1995 in which he expressed deep concern about the security situation. "Unfortunately," he wrote, "the impression that the Palestinian Authority is not doing

(photo: Ya'akov Schenkman)

Meimad renews its activities as a political party, 1993. With Prime Minister Yitzḥak Rabin at the founding conference.

enough to fight terror is getting progressively stronger. We believe that improvement to the security situation must go hand in hand with the advancement of the peace process. We support the peace process, but we do not see how it can be advanced without taking security needs into consideration."

In an interview with newspaper *Al HaMishmar*'s Roni Sharon, Rav Amital stated, "The Rabin government is losing the public, and all of the polls show it. The government, and especially the Foreign Minister, generated expectations in the wake of the Oslo Accords that were simply too high. They sold this idea to the public that the accords would solve all the problems, and it's not happening." Nevertheless, even though he called for a temporary freeze on the implementation of parts of the accord and to postpone the release of Palestinian prisoners, he continued to express faith in the process.

As the security situation deteriorated, a new front in the struggle between the government and the settlers opened in January 1995. After the violent protests of Arabs and Leftists, the government announced that it had cancelled its tender to build on Tamar Hill in the town of Efrat, the largest city in Gush Etzion. The settlers responded that they would petition the Supreme Court and in the meantime hold mass rallies against the decision. In an interview with *Ma'ariv*, Rav Amital stated that Rabin was again acting unwisely: "Rabin, who approved the construction in Efrat and then retracted, is causing serious diplomatic damage to Israel." Rav Amital also protested the building freeze in Judea, Samaria, and Gaza in a letter he sent to the Prime Minister. He reminded Rabin of the commitment he made, right after signing the Oslo Accords, not to hinder the natural development of the settlements during the interim period. He warned him that accepting the stance of the Meretz ministers, who called for the complete stoppage of construction in Judea, Samaria, and Gaza, would erode public support for the peace process. At some point the Prime Minister's Office contacted Rav Amital, Yinon Aḥiman – the head of the Efrat Regional Council, and Moshko – Efrat's founder, in an attempt to find a solution to the Tamar Hill issue. Rav Amital played a role in the compromise reached between the settlers and the government. Instead of building on Tamar Hill, approval was granted for immediate construction on Zayit Hill, another of Efrat's hills.

As tensions mounted between the settler population and Rabin, hostility toward Rav Amital for supporting the Oslo Accords intensified as well. One morning, a large sign was hung from a house in Alon Shvut on which was written "Yasser Amital." Members of the Amital family who lived in the community were very hurt when they woke up in the morning and saw the scathing inscription. A resident made sure that the sign was gone before Rav Amital saw it.

Anonymous letters cursing, insulting and threatening Rav Amital poured into his home and into the yeshiva. It was not the first time that Rav Amital was threatened. In 1989, after Meimad's run for Knesset, an anonymous rabbi called Rav Amital at home and introduced himself as a member of the Sicarii – a band of Jewish zealots who had been active in the revolt against Rome in the first century CE. He called Rav Amital a "traitor" and a "religious defeatist" and threatened that members of his organization were plotting against him. Rav Amital and his wife did not get too upset by the threats, but they reported the call to the police.

Among even his closest friends, it was hard for some people to come to grips with Rav Amital's support for the Oslo Accords. Meir Ḥovav, his friend from Yeshivat Ḥevron and from the army, harshly criticized the move, but Rav Amital preferred not to respond. Ḥovav considered writing an open letter criticizing Rav Amital, but another friend advised him to write a personal letter first. Ḥovav accepted the advice and sent Rav Amital an eight-page letter explaining why he considered the Oslo Accords a catastrophe and why he deemed it forbidden to support them. He claims that he never got a satisfactory response: "He only answered my claim that rabbis should not get involved in politics, writing that he was shocked that I didn't understand what a great sacrifice he was making and how his actions were a *kiddush HaShem*. The issue of *kiddush HaShem* always held special significance for him." Rav Amital concluded his response to Ḥovav with the following: "Our friendship is as strong as it ever was, and I don't think that our disagreements can harm it. I propose that we continue our friendship as before and stop discussing issues where our opinions differ."

Some of Rav Amital's closest friends disagreed with him but decided right away not to discuss politics with him. Yedaya Hacohen, a yeshiva board member who had known Rav Amital for close to forty years, attests that he never debated politics with Rav Amital because he did not want to jeopardize their friendship: "The friendship was more important than voicing my opinion." Moshko, the Chairman of the Board of the yeshiva, also felt that Rav Amital's support for Oslo was misguided, but refrained from discussing it with him. "We were so close that I didn't need to tell him my opinion. He already knew it. I admired and respected him so much that I did not want to hurt him. I also knew that I had no chance of changing his mind."

That summer, the rift between the Rabin government and religious Zionism deepened. Prior to Yom HaAtzma'ut, R. Moshe Zvi Neriya, the head of the Bnei Akiva yeshivot, composed a new version of the Prayer for the State of Israel recited each Shabbat in Zionist synagogues. In the new version, the sentence petitioning God to protect the leaders of the state was replaced with "Protect the state from its leaders, ministers, and counselors, and direct us with good counsel before You." Rav Amital leveled criticism at the new formulation. "Liturgy doesn't change," he told Shaḥar Ilan of *Haaretz*, and added, "I believe that every lawful government elected by its citizens to determine what is good for the state also has the right to make mistakes. The possibility of a mistake was there forty-seven years ago, too. That's not a reason to alter a prayer."

Rav Amital was bothered not by the change in the liturgy, but by its motivation. He never attributed much sanctity to the Prayer for the State of Israel. For many years, the prayer was not recited at Yeshivat Har Etzion except on the High Holidays and Yom HaAtzma'ut. Rav Amital explained that from his perspective, the entire liturgy is a prayer for the state and there is no need for a special prayer (for the same reason, he did not feel it necessary for the yeshiva to commemorate Israel's Holocaust Memorial Day, Yom HaShoah; "For us, it's always Holocaust Remembrance Day," he told his students, "We don't need a ceremony or a flag"). Another reason for Rav Amital's hesitancy about the Prayer for the State of Israel was its similarity to the various prayers on behalf of gentile governments recited by Jews throughout the Diaspora. It was only after *ḥaredi* circles began citing Yeshivat Har Etzion as an example of a place that did not recite the Prayer for the State of Israel that Rav Amital decided to add it to the yeshiva's Shabbat services. However, he instituted that the prayer be recited by the entire congregation and not, as was customary elsewhere, by the *ḥazan* alone, in order to distinguish it from those exilic prayers for the prevailing regime.

In July 1994, another public debate broke out about the Oslo Accords and split the national-religious yeshiva world. Fifteen religious-Zionist rabbis convened at the home of R. Avraham Shapira, then the Rosh Yeshiva of Merkaz HaRav, to deliberate the proper course of action for a soldier who receives an order to evacuate a military base in Judea or Samaria as part of the implementation of the Oslo Accords. The rabbis ruled that evacuating IDF bases and turning them over to gentile powers violates a biblical injunction, as it negates the mitzva of settling the land and also endangers the existence of the state. The ruling, issued in the name of "The Rabbinic Union for the People and Land of Israel," provoked a public firestorm. Rav Amital expressed severe reservations about the halakhic ruling, cautioning that it was liable to drag the state into anarchy and detach religious Zionism from the state:

> Whether or not a religious soldier participates in the evacuation of the base, his refusal or non-refusal will not prevent the evacuation of that base. It would at most be a demonstration of protest. As such, a call to disobey orders is a terrible thing. Tomorrow, non-religious soldiers will refuse to protect settlements over the Green Line.

In an article entitled "A Political Opinion in Halakhic Garb," published by Meimad in its periodical, Rav Amital analyzed the rabbinic ruling at length, from a halakhic perspective. He wrote that even if one believes that the evacuation is forbidden, a participating soldier would at worst be indirectly assisting a forbidden act. Thus, he argued, there was only a doubtful rabbinic prohibition in this instance, which would be overridden by the terrible damage that would be caused to the unity of the nation and the army. He also opposed the rabbis' determination that the evacuation of army bases puts lives in danger: "Just as in medical matters one must consult doctors, who are assumed to possess professional expertise, so too in matters of security the authority to define a situation as a security danger rests with the government of Israel and the heads of the army." In addition to his critique of the rabbinic ruling,

Rav Amital predicted that the ruling would not prevent the evacuation of any army bases. He said that in any event the soldiers involved in the evacuation would be non-combat soldiers, among whom there were very few yeshiva students, if any.

The day after Rav Amital came out against the ruling, Rav Shapira was quoted in *Yediot Aharonot* calling rabbis who oppose the refusal of orders "*rebbelach*, small-time rabbis who kiss up to the government and rule in favor of obedience to the government, permitting what the halakha forbids, on the basis of cherry-picked adages." Whether or not Rav Shapira was referring to Rav Amital, he never attacked him directly. Rav Amital recounted that he happened to run into Rav Shapira around that time, and Rav Shapira asked him, "Granted, I disagree with you; but why haven't you made your voice heard?"

Already in the 1980s, when Rav Amital began speaking out in favor of territorial concessions for peace, an event occurred that illustrates the unique relationship that Rav Amital had with Rav Shapira. Rav Shapira had just been installed as Chief Rabbi, and he convened all of the *hesder* Rashei Yeshiva in his office to discuss how they could help improve the image of the chief rabbinate. He also discussed current events, expressing opposition to rabbis who support the relinquishment of parts of Eretz Yisrael and calling them "weak of faith." Rav Amital asked to speak next. He said:

> Ḥazal say, "A good guest says, 'Everything the host has done, he has done just for me.'" I therefore imagine that the purpose of this whole gathering is to dissuade me from voicing my opinions and to impose your authority on me. But with all due respect, you know that I am not obligated to listen to you. My rabbis ordained me and authorized me to teach and express my views.

Rav Amital related that despite his harsh statements, Rav Shapira praised him for speaking up.

In the summer of 5755 (1995), Israel held talks with the Palestinians with the purpose of reaching a new agreement. Public opposition reached a new peak, and Rabin's public stature reached unprecedented lows. Even within Meimad, some activists began expressing outrage at

Rabin's attitude toward the settlers, and some refused to invite him to one of the movement's conferences. But Rav Amital remained adamant about staying in touch with Rabin. At the beginning of July, he wrote a letter of encouragement to the Prime Minister: "I wish to express my sincere admiration of your steadfast insistence on the security of all residents of Israel, and the residents of Judea, Samaria, and Gaza in particular." Rav Amital reminded Rabin of his agreement in principle to the plan for settlement blocs in Judea, Samaria, and Gaza, and expressed faith that his support for these blocs and his concern for the security of the settlers were ever-present during his negotiations with the Palestinians. "I am convinced that the way you are leading this process, in accordance with these principles, guarantees the success of the negotiations and the nation's support for them."

Rabin replied to Rav Amital with a heartfelt letter: "I thank you and confess: given the turbulence of the past few days, I found encouragement in your letter. I was moved by your earnest words and can assure you that I will do whatever possible to keep my promise to you, your colleagues, and the entire people of Israel. How can I thank you?" Rav Amital viewed Rabin's letter as evidence of the Prime Minister's isolation and his need for words of strength and encouragement.

On 4 Tishrei, 5756 (September 28, 1995), the signing ceremony of the Interim Agreement on the West Bank and the Gaza Strip, also known as Oslo II, was held in Washington, DC. Under its terms, Palestinian control over Judea and Samaria was expanded, and arrangements between the sides were formalized for an interim period of five years, until the signing of a permanent status agreement. Due to the deterioration of the security situation since the signing of Oslo I, the new agreement caused even greater controversy. Meimad debated whether or not to support Oslo II. Three days after its signing, the Meimad secretariat met at Rav Amital's home. They raised many concerns about the agreement, but ultimately, under Rav Amital's leadership, they decided to support it. Their subsequent press release stated:

> Despite the national and personal pain entailed by relinquishing any tract of land in Eretz Yisrael, we take a realistic view of

> the short- and long-term risks that face the State of Israel, of the exceedingly high natural growth rate of the Arabs of Judea, Samaria, and Gaza, and of the lack of realistic alternatives. Therefore, we view this agreement, with its concession of densely populated Palestinian areas of Judea, Samaria, and Gaza, as a step in the right direction, toward peace for the people of Israel and the good of the land of Israel.

Meimad also called on religious Zionists who opposed the agreement to focus their efforts on formulating a permanent status agreement in a way that would secure the interests of the settlement enterprise in Judea, Samaria, and Gaza. "Continuing the struggle for the complete rejection of the Oslo Accords is unrealistic and has no chance," the press release continued.

The Prime Minister greatly appreciated the support, telling Rav Amital, "My own party has not yet given me support, yet you already have."

The Knesset approved Oslo II by the razor thin margin of one controversial vote: the vote of Deputy Minister of Housing Alex Goldfarb of the Yi'ud party, which had splintered off from the secular right-wing Tzomet party. On the day of the Knesset vote, a mass rally against the agreement took place at *Tziyon* Square in Jerusalem. The IDF began pulling out of Palestinian cities in Judea and Samaria during October. The frequency of right-wing protests increased, ratcheting up the tensions on the Israeli streets.

Against that backdrop, Rav Amital, Yehuda Ben-Meir, and other Meimad leaders met with the Prime Minister. Rabin told them that he already had a general plan for a permanent status agreement. Eitan Haber, Rabin's bureau chief, recounts that it was one of the only times that Rabin agreed to discuss the matter: "Rabin understood that Rav Amital's continued support for the process depended on his being apprised of the plans for a permanent solution," Haber recalled. Rav Amital invited Rabin to visit Gush Etzion, but the latter declined, saying: "Why should I come? So they can call me a traitor?" That was the final meeting between Rav Amital and Yitzḥak Rabin.

Two weeks later, on Saturday night, 12 Ḥeshvan (November 4),

Rabin was murdered at Kings of Israel Square in Tel Aviv. Rav Amital was home at the time. He heard about the assassination on the radio. In those first few minutes, he hoped with all his heart that the assassin was an Arab, not a Jew. His fear of the *ḥillul HaShem* that would be caused if the murderer was a Jew was far greater than his concern for a deterioration of the security situation if the murderer turned out to be an Arab. But it was not long before the murderer was identified as Yigal Amir, a right-wing, *kippa*-wearing, *hesder* yeshiva alumnus.

The State of Israel was in shock. The assassination brought to a boil the alienation of right from left and secular from religious. Four days after the assassination, Meimad and the NRP organized a joint "soul-searching" conference. The well-attended conference at Jerusalem's Beit Agron garnered coverage by all media outlets. Speakers included Rav Amital, MK Zevulun Hammer, R. Ḥayyim Druckman, Yisrael Harel, and R. Yoel Bin-Nun. Rav Amital opened his speech with a call to the leaders of the left to prevent incitement against the national-religious public. "Each camp must engage in introspection about the terrible polarization of the Israeli public. We will do our part." He then described the attack on the Prime Minister as an "attack on the Kingdom of Israel at the moment of the first flowering of its redemption." He then called for the rending of hearts, if not garments, over the great *ḥillul HaShem* that was compounded by the fact that "the deed was done by someone who regards himself as a religious man, and uses the Torah to justify his actions." Although many had begun calling for the indictment of rabbis who were sharply critical of Rabin, Rav Amital said at the conference that in his opinion there was no direct link between their words and the incident. However, he added the rabbinic injunction (*Avot* 1:11), "Sages – be cautious with your words."

At the same time, Rav Amital said that the Torah had a different standard of culpability on these matters. He developed this theme further in a speech at the yeshiva:

> On the national level, I don't know who is responsible, Right or Left, for using more inflammatory language. But in the *beit midrash*, measuring with a Torah standard, I know. When a man is found dead in the field, the Torah requires the elders of the neighboring

> city to state: Our hands have not spilled the blood (Deut. 21:1–9). The sages explain that their declaration of innocence means that they did not send off the victim without provisions and without escort. Rashi elaborates: Perhaps he left the town without food and, out of hunger and desperation, attacked another man and was killed. This possibility, far-fetched as it seems, will preclude the elders from declaring their innocence if they did not provide him with food when he left. This is the Torah's measure of culpability! Those who spoke of the "reign of iniquity" ("*memshelet zadon*"), who called the government a "Judenrat," who questioned the legitimacy of the government, who publicly issued the ruling concerning disobeying orders in the army – are they less culpable than the elders who failed to provide a traveler with provisions? Is the connection more far-fetched? Can they truly say "Our hands have not spilled this blood?"

Turning to the subject of soul-searching, Rav Amital said at the conference that it was necessary to make several changes in the national-religious camp. He called for an end to the exploitation of halakha in a political context. "The concept of halakha is too broad and sacred to be given over to the discretion of young men and women who do not possess the requisite breadth of knowledge to render Torah decisions on such matters… halakha has become, as it were, a tool to stake out a right-wing political position." He further argued that as a result of their national-religious education, religious youths were unable to think complex thoughts. He called for an end to the delegitimation of alternative views within religious Zionism and of Israel's democratically elected government. Speaking about peace agreements as a destructive *ḥurban,* he argued, is evidence of weakness of faith. Rav Amital then called for an end to invective against government officials and to viewing the secular left as being devoid of values. "We now face a major struggle – the struggle over the Jewish image of the state. In that regard, we were dealt a mortal blow… how much harder will we have to work now to demonstrate the Torah's pleasant ways?" he asked. In concluding, he expressed faith in the national-religious public's power to "rise to the occasion and occupy its proper place in the State of Israel."

In an interview he gave to Aryeh Bender of *Ma'ariv* after the conference, he expanded on his critique of the religious school system:

> The assassin is proof that our youth is accustomed to primitive thinking. This murderer is convinced that by perpetrating this act he has saved the world. How can it be that such a young man, a law student, arrives at such a conclusion? This is because, unfortunately, we are educating a generation with slogans and a simplistic approach.

A week after the assassination, as part of a series of attempts at reconciliation between the religious and secular publics, Rav Amital and author A.B. Yehoshua issued a joint manifesto in which they praised the soul-searching that had begun among the national-religious and cautioned those affiliated with Labor against exploiting the tragedy to place collective blame on the national-religious camp.

The tragic circumstances of the Rabin assassination granted renewed legitimacy to Rav Amital and Meimad in certain segments of the religious population. The soul-searching conference organized jointly by Meimad and the NRP represented the first time that the NRP acknowledged Meimad as a relevant religious-Zionist movement. The assassination also inspired a wave of phone calls to Rav Amital's home and to the Meimad offices, many of them urging Rav Amital and his colleagues to reconsider running for the Knesset in the next elections. Rav Amital did not rush to make any pronouncements, but he did issue a response: "Perhaps we need to think about that." He spoke to *Ma'ariv* about this change of attitude toward him: "All of a sudden, I found myself once again in demand in the religious-Zionist camp. For years they had viewed me as a strange bird. I was alone; they didn't understand me, or didn't want to understand me."

Shimon Peres was appointed acting Prime Minister immediately after the Rabin assassination. In an attempt to mend at least some of the social rifts that the assassination had widened, Peres offered Rav Amital to be a minister in his government. Peres also tried to include the NRP in his coalition, but the Meretz faction torpedoed the attempt.

(photo: Ya'akov Saar, Government Press Office)

Pledging loyalty as a minister of the Israeli government

Rav Amital and Peres first got acquainted in the mid-1970s, when Rav Amital served as liaison between the *hesder yeshivot* and the Ministry of Defense, Peres's ministry. Their respective roles resulted in joint meetings, familiarity, and mutual admiration. Yet Peres's offer after the assassination is more properly understood as being on behalf of the murdered Prime Minister. The esteem that Rabin had for Rav Amital caused him to consider, on several occasions, appointing him to a public role. Eitan Haber confirms that the initial idea of appointing Rav Amital as a government minister was articulated by Rabin. "In the period before the assassination we hatched the idea of appointing Rav Amital Minister without Portfolio. Had he not been murdered, Rabin would have approached him about it. After the murder I gave Peres the idea."

Rav Amital did not deliberate long. His only concern was that it would keep him away from the yeshiva. Once the media reported the possibility of his appointment as a minister, he was pressured to accept the proposal, and he agreed. Two things loomed large when he answered the call: the hope that his joining the government would lessen, even if only a little bit, the *ḥillul HaShem* caused by the assassination, and the sense that he would be able to bring a Jewish message into the government. He distinctly recalled Abba Kovner's lament about the secular public's unwillingness to accept spiritual lessons from the national-religious public due to its radicalization. He hoped that his messages, as

(photo: Ya'akov Saar, Government Press Office)

Group photo of the Peres government with President Ezer Weizman.

a minister and a rabbi, would find open ears in the secular public and positively affect Judaism's image.

The left praised Rav Amital's appointment. Under the headline, "Rav Amital – to the Government," *Haaretz* devoted its editorial to promoting the appointment: "The idea of including Rabbi Yehuda Amital in a Labor-Meretz government deserves praise… Including Rabbi Amital in the government will show everyone that the Labor-Meretz government does not reject the participation of the religious in fateful decisions and is not apathetic to the distress of the settlers, but is also unwilling to forego its objectives or its political path only to appease those who vehemently oppose it."

Within the national-religious population there were mixed feelings. The leadership of Judea, Samaria, and Gaza expressed doubts about the idea, claiming that Rav Amital, given his left-leaning opinions, could not serve as a bridge and mediator between the settlers and the government. Ḥagai Segal, of Ofra in Samaria, in an article he published in *Ma'ariv* entitled "An Emissary without a Public" ("*Shali'aḥ beli Tzibbur*") wrote: "Over the past twenty years, religious Zionism ran counter to the opinions of Rav Amital and ignored his melancholy rebukes… Including Rav Amital in the government will not only fail to appease the Bnei Akiva population, it will further infuriate them."

Yisrael Harel, Chairman of the Judea, Samaria, and Gaza Council, was even more vitriolic. In an interview with the Voice of Israel, he addressed the intention of using Rav Amital to mediate between the government and the settlers: "His Volvo, secretary, and budget will certainly keep Rav Amital otherwise occupied, because we will not cooperate with him." Harel's comments hurt Rav Amital. He welcomed being attacked for his opinions, but Harel painted him as a hedonist who wanted to be a minister so that he could have an official government vehicle. Ironically, Rav Amital already had a Volvo; skidding on the wet road to Gush Etzion convinced him to buy a safe car to drive to yeshiva. Right after the interview, Rav Lichtenstein called Yisrael Harel, unbeknownst to Rav Amital, and told him that he should apologize for insulting a Torah scholar. Harel accepted the rebuke; he went back on the Voice of Israel and apologized for how he expressed himself, but he reiterated that he did not renege on his opposition to appointing Rav Amital as a minister. "Appointing a special minister to liaise with Judea, Samaria, and Gaza, who will act as a 'supervisor' of the settlers, as a sort of 'Big Brother,' is intolerable from our perspective … Given the opinions he quite scathingly expressed in recent years, he is not the right person to forge ties with us."

The NRP also expressed opposition to the appointment, which was a political threat to them. They feared that Rav Amital's government position would increase Meimad's popularity in the religious-Zionist public and lead them to try running for the Knesset again. Rav Amital humorously told *Ma'ariv*: "They say that there are three opinions within the NRP about my expected appointment: some vehemently attack me, some maintain that it's better to ignore me, and a third group thinks it's worthwhile to join the government as long as it keeps me out."

On the other hand, there were many religious-Zionist voices – even from the right wing – that supported Rav Amital's appointment. Dozens of rabbis and public figures signed a large notice published in *Haaretz* praising the appointment. The publication of the notice was the brainchild of Adv. Aviad Hacohen, an alumnus of Yeshivat Har Etzion. Among the signatories were: R. Eli Sadan, the head of the premilitary academy in Eli; R. Dov Begun, the head of Makhon Meir who, like Rav Sadan, was within the orbit of Yeshivat Merkaz HaRav; R. Avi Gisser, rabbi of Ofra; and Yinon Aḥiman, the head of the Efrat Regional

Council. Even R. Shlomo Aviner, the rabbi of Beit El in Samaria and one of the leading rabbis in all of Judea, Samaria, and Gaza praised the appointment. Secular intellectuals who signed the notice included the poet Yehuda Amiḥai and authors Gail Hareven, Ḥayyim Be'er, A. B. Yehoshua, and Amos Oz. Poet Ḥayyim Goury called Rav Amital to wish him well. The heads of the kibbutz movement and some of its prominent thinkers, including Muki Tzur, Avraham Shapira, and Shai Zarḥi, praised the appointment.

Rav Amital won almost the complete support of Yeshivat Har Etzion. As opposed to his support for the Oslo Accords, which dismayed many of the yeshiva's rabbis, his entering the government was seen as the order of the day. R. Ya'akov Medan and Moshko, opponents of Labor government policy who expressed their consternation with Rav Amital's support for the Oslo Accords, signed the notice supporting his appointment. Rav Lichtenstein, as expected, fully backed his colleague. Speaking to the yeshiva the day after Rav Amital was sworn in as a minister, he said:

> At the present time, with so many difficult problems on the agenda, Rav Amital was asked by the Prime Minister to be part of the government – with the explicit intent that something of the ancient Jewish spirit would be palpable within the government, with the understanding that this is a time for solidarity, with the hope that it would bring reconciliation and closeness and not, God forbid, vitriol and schism. They know that he is not someone who would, God forbid, dilute or cover up his Torah-imbued stances. Does anyone think that at such a time the door should be slammed on this offer? That we should say 'do what you want; we're remaining outside'? We will do no such thing here, certainly not when the subject is someone with national responsibility and historical vision like Rav Amital.

When Peres was asked why he decided to include Rav Amital in his government, he responded: "Every government needs inspiration. I believe that Rav Amital provides the inspiration necessary to maintain the nation's unity, diversity, and internal dialogue."

Chapter Nineteen

Minister of Inspiration

At the President's Residence, after the traditional portrait of the new government, I was reminded of something that my teacher R. Ya'akov Moshe Ḥarlap wrote: In the verse (II Sam. 22:51), "A tower of victory to His king, Who deals graciously with His anointed – with David and his descendants evermore," David referred to himself in the third person. He did not say "with me and my descendants." He was so intensely possessed by a sense of mission and destiny, that his private persona occupied no space. "King David" was not the main thing – the idea was the main thing. Alas, I cannot say, like King David, that I have no personal feelings. And yet my personal feelings have diminished, because it's not about me. It's about the mission.

From a discourse at Yeshivat Har Etzion, November 1995

On 29 Ḥeshvan, 5756 (November 22, 1995), eighteen days after the Rabin assassination, Shimon Peres's new government, including Rav Yehuda Amital, was sworn in. Rav Amital's appointment generated much interest in the Knesset. The next day, *Ma'ariv* reported that "It was quite atypical to see the esteemed, full-bearded, black-skullcapped rabbi sitting to the right of [Meretz leader and arch-secularist] Yossi Sarid." Rav Amital was overcome by a sense of mission and trepidation on the day he was sworn in as minister. "The people did not elect me," he told the media, "but I have been called upon and saddled with numerous hopes. I feel like the *shali'aḥ tzibbur*, who prior to Musaf on Yom Kippur says, with fervor and anxiety, '*Hineni*, here I stand, impoverished of deed, agitated, frightened by dread of He Who is enthroned by the praises of Israel.' He experienced a particularly emotional moment when, standing at the Knesset podium, he invoked the names of his parents who were killed in the Holocaust. After the swearing-in, the ministers went to the President's Residence for the traditional portrait. After the photos, a journalist asked Rav Amital if he was excited. "I forgot to get excited," was the terse reply. The next day, he explained to his students that his personal feelings diminished in light of what the nation was going through at that time. "It's not about me. It's about the mission, the rescue, so I really never had the sense of 'Wow, I'm a minister.' It's small potatoes compared to the truly important things."

Rav Amital was appointed Minister without Portfolio in the Prime Minister's Office. Peres did not precisely define Rav Amital's area of responsibility, enabling him to define it for himself. After consultations, Rav Amital and his staff of advisors formulated three realms of activity: deepening the Jewish identity of Israeli society, moderating tensions and generating solidarity between the nation's various streams, and improving relations between Israel and Diaspora Jewry. Yossi Ben-Gal, then Director-General of Meimad, was appointed Rav Amital's bureau chief. Adv. Avrumy Yishai, a yeshiva alumnus, was appointed personal assistant. The bureau had a staff of five aides and advisors: R. Michael Melchior, advisor on Diaspora relations; Udi Cohen, advisor on deepening Jewish identity; Beni Lehman, a psychologist who advised on bridging the rifts in Israeli society; Adv. Aviad Hacohen, legal counsel; and Yisrael Cohen, spokesman.

Several days after being sworn in, Rav Amital was invited to a meeting of the Labor faction. *Yediot Aharonot* reported about that meeting:

> There has not been such absolute silence during a Labor faction meeting for many years. It was not only in honor of Minister Rav Yehuda Amital, who was honored with a guest invitation; it was mainly because of the sense of "we're missing someone" that brought Rav Amital to the meeting in the first place.

The sharp transition from the yeshiva to the government was not easy for Rav Amital. The trappings of authority were completely foreign to him, and those first days provided his staff with quite a bit of amusement. Yossi Ben-Gal recalls the newly-minted minister's first lunch.

> We hadn't considered the possibility of ordering in, so we – the entire staff plus Rav Amital – went to the employees' cafeteria. I think he was the first ever minister of Israel to eat lunch with the secretaries... after one day I sensed that it was somewhat inappropriate, so I began ordering his food to the office.

Another protocol that Rav Amital had difficulty adapting to was riding in a secure government vehicle. The day after he began his new job, *Ma'ariv*'s headlines proclaimed "Minister Amital Forgot he has a Government Car and Hitched a Ride." Even after he got used to the new car, he never worshipped protocol; if he was concerned about being late for a meeting, he preferred traveling in a different vehicle. His assistant, Avrumy Yishai, recounts one such situation:

> We had to get to a meeting at the Holiday Inn, about a five minute drive from our bureau at the Prime Minister's Office. For some unknown reason, the driver did not answer his mobile phone. Rav Amital, who was meticulous about arriving at every meeting on time, asked me if I had a car in the lot, and I said I did. I had an old Subaru. It was quite a sight – a minister riding in an old, beat-up Subaru. But from his perspective, the main thing was getting there on time.

(photo: Avi Ohayon, Government Press Office)

A minister in the Israeli government. Meeting with Prime Minister Shimon Peres.

As Rav Amital expected, the most difficult thing for him, especially at first, was his isolation from the yeshiva. "On the first day, sitting in his seat in the office," Yossi Ben-Gal relates, "he asked me how to get to the yeshiva… it was as though his whole being was saying 'I have a *shiur* to give!'" The yeshiva's location across the Green Line required that the new minister go there with a security escort. The first few times, Rav Amital had a hard time waiting for the escort, and another time, the escort's car was delayed and Rav Amital continued on without him. In the wake of the Rabin assassination, security guards were assigned to each government minister. The yeshiva enjoyed each visit by Rav Amital, but they had difficulty adjusting to the security guards that went everywhere with him. Not every day does a Rosh Yeshiva give a *shiur* flanked by bodyguards. Yet Rav Amital insisted on visiting the yeshiva and giving *shiurim* to his students. These *shiurim* gave him the strength to continue fulfilling the public mission that he undertook. He told his students:

> For me, the yeshiva is a tranquilizer, a real pleasure. Every one of you is contributing by allowing me to continue. I know that for various reasons, not every student feels comfortable to come to me and shake my hand, but I sense your encouragement. I look at your faces and it gives me strength. It is very important to me.

Rav Amital's relationship with the media was different from that of the other ministers. In contrast to the average government minister, Rav Amital did not enjoy being interviewed. "He wasn't sufficiently aware of how to utilize the media," Ben-Gal relates, offering an example:

> At the time, the IDF was getting ready to withdraw from Bethlehem. In that context, the tunnel road that bypasses Bethlehem on the way to Gush Etzion was being paved. Rav Amital intervened when the road work had to be accelerated, and as a result, the Public Works Department invited him to the construction site to inspect their progress. He arrived to find the media and the head of the Gush Etzion Regional Council waiting for him, but instead of acting like any other minister and taking advantage of the photo-op or the opportunity to offer a sound bite, he ran off to make sure the tractors were really working.

Rav Amital's political honeymoon did not last long. A week after he took office, personal attacks began to emerge from the religious sector. The first salvos actually came from the *ḥaredi* Degel HaTorah faction. They claimed that by joining the government, Rav Amital would serve as a fig leaf for all actions undertaken by the government, which they described as "an apostate regime that harms religion." Mk Moshe Gafni, the party secretary of Degel HaTorah, told *Haaretz* that Rav Amital was "the worst sort of exilic Jew, who sucks up to the local aristocrat." Degel HaTorah's newspaper *Yated Ne'eman* wrote that Rav Amital would eventually be "cast out by his partners in shame and disgrace, like all flatterers." Rav Amital did not respond to the attacks. Two months later, he was attacked by R. Yitzḥak Peretz, the former chairman of Shas. At a conference in Kibbutz Lavi, Rav Peretz insinuated that by sitting in the government, Rav Amital was granting legitimacy to Reform and Conservative Judaism.

On the other hand, there were other voices in the *ḥaredi* camp as well. MK Avraham Yosef Shapira, a veteran politician from the Agudah party, warmly welcomed Rav Amital in a speech to the Knesset plenum. MK Menaḥem Porush, who had resigned from Agudah's Knesset faction two years earlier, sent Rav Amital a congratulatory letter after his ministerial appointment, and praised him for continuing along the path of his father-in-law, R. Zvi Yehuda Meltzer, with whom Porush had been acquainted. He even invited Rav Amital to a meeting. Nevertheless, Rav Amital surmised that Porush wanted to get close to Rav Amital so that he could remain in touch with Labor.

The right-wing camp and the religious-Zionist public waited to see how the new minister would address current issues. The first test came two weeks into his tenure, when news broke that Rabin had promised the Americans an Israeli withdrawal from the Golan Heights. The Golan Settlement Committee immediately alerted Rav Amital's office. Opponents of the withdrawal naturally turned to Rav Amital due to his support for the Third Way, which opposed relinquishing the Golan. The residents of the Golan asked Rav Amital to influence the government not to impose new arrangements on the Golan until after the elections slated for late 1996. Rav Amital placated them by reiterating his opposition to a complete withdrawal from the Golan. "I don't think Syria wants peace," he added, "but in any event, if an agreement consolidates, it must be decided by referendum or elections."

Rav Amital's next test came that same week. Deputy Defense Minister Ori Orr provoked outrage when he called for an end to the *hesder* arrangement out of concern that as a result of the rabbinic ruling to refuse evacuation orders, yeshiva students would take over the military. The religious-Zionist community looked toward Rav Amital to see how, as a member of the same government as Orr, he would react. Rav Amital reiterated his opposition to the rabbinic ruling, but in the same breath he undermined Orr's statement: "His scenario of a military coup is practically impossible. The *hesder* students comprise platoons within larger regiments and are incapable of taking over the military."

The strained relationship between Rav Amital and the national-religious public came to a head later that week. Religious Zionists had been under attack since the Rabin assassination, so the NRP organized a rally at Kings of Israel Square to boost the morale of their constituency. Rav Amital was invited to the rally, but to prevent discomfort on the part of many attendees, he was asked not to speak, and remain content with a seat on the dais. Rav Amital chose not to attend. He explained his decision to *Davar*: "I'm not insulted, but this is a sign that the NRP still has a long way to go to become moderate."

At the same time, after three weeks on the job, Rav Amital optimistically described his relations with the religious public as a minister: "True, there is a particular group within the religious camp that still has not recognized me," he told *Haaretz*, "but it is mainly among the leadership. On this matter, the leadership does not represent its constituents, most of whom support me and expect positive results from my participation in the government."

Over the following months, Rav Amital faced numerous situations in which he was expected to represent the interests of the national-religious public, and particularly the residents of Judea, Samaria, and Gaza. In February 1996, a dispute erupted within the government between Peres and the Meretz faction regarding construction in Judea and Samaria. A ministerial committee meeting that was supposed to discuss plans for expanding several settlements was cancelled at the last minute at the insistence of Meretz. News of the meeting's cancellation raised the ire of the settlers, and once again they addressed themselves to Rav Amital. The regional council heads of Judea and Samaria demanded that Rav Amital resign due to the construction freeze, and they were joined in their call by the Third Way – by then a political party, and Efrat Regional Council Head Yinon Aḥiman, who had signed the letter supporting Rav Amital's appointment. Rav Amital requested an urgent meeting with Peres and claimed that permission to build in the settlements to accommodate natural growth was a vital step that had already been agreed upon under Rabin. In their meeting, Peres promised Rav Amital that he would convene the committee as soon as possible and authorize construction.

All told, Rav Amital contributed significantly to the expansion of the settlements in Judea, Samaria, and Gaza during his tenure as minister. A new neighborhood in Alon Shvut and expanded construction in Efrat were made possible, among other things, by the permits he secured from the Ministry of Defense and the Ministry of Housing. He also worked to accelerate the paving of the tunnel road connecting Gush Etzion to Jerusalem. On the individual level, Rav Amital helped R. Ido Alba, who was serving a prison sentence after being convicted of racial incitement and attempting to manufacture and possess weapons. Alba's father was on his death bed, and Rav Amital ensured that the son would be able to visit.

Yet as time went on, it became clear to Rav Amital that most of the national-religious public was not satisfied with his ministerial appointment or activity. He began hearing displeasure expressed even by the alumni and students of the yeshiva. In February 1996, Yeshivat Har Etzion held a panel discussion with the participation of the Rashei Yeshiva and alumni in the field of education. The alumni voiced criticism of the behavior of their Rashei Yeshiva in the wake of the Rabin assassination. R. Yuval Cherlow said that he was troubled by the fact that they criticized the national-religious public as outsiders. He added that he felt they accused the religious population of things that they were not guilty of. Yeshayahu Yeḥieli expressed displeasure at the legitimacy that the Rashei Yeshiva granted to Minister of Education Shulamit Aloni. He also wondered if there was any chance of finding a common ground between all religious Zionist rabbis. Rav Amital responded that Yeḥieli was presenting things too simplistically. He admitted that he was pained by the national-religious public's attitude toward him, but he nevertheless declared that he did not regret joining the government. "I'm not interested in what they say or write about me, even if they write that I undermine their educational values. I'm willing to accept it all, if only to minimize the great *ḥillul HaShem*."

R. Moshe Ḥabbah, a yeshiva alumnus serving as a *ram* at Yeshivat Kfar HaRo'eh, was distressed that all of Rav Amital's pronouncements to the media on matters of state and religion were interpreted incorrectly; on certain subjects, they even portrayed him as a supporter of Reform. Rav Amital said to Ḥabbah: "You want to silence me, to keep me from saying anything, any new ideas, because they will be misinterpreted?" Ḥabbah explained that he wanted Rav Amital to express his opinions on other matters as well. Rav Amital responded forcefully: "Why do you think that I don't say those things? Why doesn't the religious public listen to me? Because over the years there has been a delegitimation of Rav Amital and his students, as is well known." Ḥabbah complained that all they hear from Rav Amital about the religious public is vilification. Rav Amital responded with real agitation:

> Because I said that there's no contradiction between halakha and territorial compromise, they pushed me out of the community. Now you have an excuse for my ostracism – I expressed myself too sharply. But what came first? Where have you been all these years? You were ashamed of me because I was in favor of territorial compromise. You went home and were ashamed to be my students, even though you knew you loved me. This didn't just start now.

Avrumy Yishai relates that he and Yossi Ben-Gal tried to plan events that would bring Rav Amital closer to the national-religious public. "We were very pained by the ostracism he suffered as a result of his ministerial appointment, but he refused to try planning special events that would bring him closer to the religious public. He said to us, 'I'm not here as an emissary of the religious public, but as an emissary of the entire people of Israel.'"

Rav Amital's complex relationship with the national-religious public reinforced his sense of isolation. R. Moshe Zvi Neriya passed away three weeks after Rav Amital became minister. It was important to Rav Amital to attend the funeral, so he asked Dr. Danny Tropper to accompany him. "He knew it would not be easy to stand there in a large crowd, many of whom thought of him as a traitor," Tropper recounts, "I was with him throughout the funeral, and I felt his loneliness. They didn't make catcalls at him because of his stature, but his estrangement illustrated to me the price he paid for choosing to deliver his messages."

Another aspect of Rav Amital's charged relationship with the national-religious camp found expression in an encounter he had with Arutz Sheva. During his visit to the United States, Rav Amital refused to grant an interview to an Arutz Sheva reporter. He refused because, as a government minister, he thought it was prohibited for him to grant an interview to a pirate radio station, but the station directors interpreted his actions as a boycott of its right-wing views. Upon returning to Israel, Rav Amital tried to legalize the broadcasts by defining it as a local radio station, based in Judea and Samaria. Station director Ya'akov "Ketzaleh" Katz was summoned to meet with Rav Amital, but he rejected the proposal because he did not want to limit the broadcasts to only those areas.

In contrast to his strained relations with the religious public, Rav Amital won the overt sympathy of the secular population. It began with the close circle of government ministers and the staff of the Prime Minister's Office, who adored Rav Amital and regularly expressed their admiration for him. Finance Minister Avraham "Baiga" Shoḥat asked Rav Amital, after a work meeting, for words of encouragement. The legal counsel at the Prime Minister's Office, Aḥaz Ben-Ari, sought opportunities to go to Rav Amital's office to converse with him. Minister Yossi Beilin passed a note to Rav Amital during a government meeting, saying "There's no greater *bittul Torah* than this," using yeshiva-speak for "waste of time." Minister Shulamit Aloni lauded Rav Amital for his appearance on Kobi Meidan's television program. She was especially impressed by what he said about faith after the Holocaust – with his characteristic candor, he said that he could understand those who lost their faith due to the Holocaust.

The larger media outlets published complimentary articles on Rav Amital's appointment and activities. Whenever he attended a conference, the broader population demonstrated their fondness of him. At a meeting with students involved in various youth groups, members of the ultra-secular, socialist HaShomer HaTza'ir asked him to speak to the government on their behalf; the Bnei Akiva members present at the meeting made no such request. The only time that Rav Amital was criticized by the secular press during his entire tenure was when he refused to sit on a panel with female Reform Rabbi Einat Ramon. Ramon told *Ma'ariv* that "He disappointed a large part of the Israeli public when he boycotted a woman for the sole reason that she serves in the Reform rabbinate." One newspaper headlined its article on this news item: "It seems that when it comes to women, liberalism has its boundaries." Rav Amital explained that he cancelled his participation in the panel because the organizers changed the panel's composition without informing him.

Rav Amital took great satisfaction in the bonds he forged with Diaspora Jewry as part of his ministerial activities. Given his view that the people of Israel take priority over the land of Israel, he ascribed importance to fostering cooperation and dialogue with Diaspora Jewry. After several consultations, he proposed a ministerial committee to examine Israel-

Diaspora relations. The government accepted his proposal and appointed him chair of the committee.

In early 1996, Rav Amital flew to Russia to participate in the first Russian Jewish Congress in Moscow. At the opening ceremony, he said: "The time has come for the State of Israel to ask itself not only what it can get from the Diaspora, but what the State of Israel can do to help Diaspora Jewry in its fight for Jewish continuity." At a Jewish Community Center in Moscow, Rav Amital met with forty students who served as youth counselors, telling them that in an era that emphasizes individual rights, it is necessary to deepen one's awareness of his personal commitments: "Each of us must find the way to personally contribute to his people and homeland."

Professor Aliza Shenhar, then Israel's Ambassador to Russia, accompanied Rav Amital wherever he went during his visit and was very impressed with him:

> I was very impressed by his understanding and by the sensitivity he displayed regarding the needs of a community that was just beginning to show signs of a reawakening after many years of repression and destruction of Jewish life. In general, throughout the visit I was amazed by his personality. I found in him the synthesis of incredible erudition, warmth, and understanding of others, even when they seem very different.

In early February 1996, Rav Amital visited the United States. Although the goal of the trip was to meet with heads of Jewish organizations and visit the Jewish communities of New York, Washington, Cleveland, and Miami, it was also used for diplomatic meetings. One of his more interesting meetings was with Vice President Al Gore. Rav Amital told Gore the story of his appointment and said that there is no contradiction between the religion of the Torah and the Middle East peace process. He also presented Meimad's Blocs Document to Gore. Another meeting that made a strong impression on Rav Amital was with Cardinal O'Connor, the Archbishop of New York.

The meeting with O'Connor reminded Rav Amital of another

meeting with a man of the cloth several years earlier. In 1975, Rav Amital participated in a conference of the religious-Zionist Mizraḥi movement in Switzerland. At the end of the conference, he was approached by a man who looked Jewish, was wearing a *kippa,* and spoke fluent Hebrew. He introduced himself as a Protestant minister and requested a meeting. At first Rav Amital was concerned, but after clarifying through the man's acquaintances that there was no cause for concern, he agreed. During the meeting, the minister told Rav Amital that he loves Jewish prayer and regularly visits the local synagogue. He asked Rav Amital to allow him to enroll at Yeshivat Har Etzion, but without converting to Judaism. Rav Amital responded, "I respect you, and I will arrange for you to visit the yeshiva, but to study there on a permanent basis is too much – for me and for you."

Rav Amital's visit to the US caused a media firestorm: A body of eight-hundred Orthodox rabbis called the Union of Orthodox Rabbis of the United States and Canada, or the Agudath Harabonim, issued a ruling prohibiting Jews from attending Rav Amital's lectures. A member of the union, Rabbi David Hollander, explained that the ban was due to Rav Amital's willingness to participate in a gathering at which Reform and Conservative rabbis were also in attendance. The ban provoked rage in Israel and the US. Rabbis and Rashei Yeshiva called Rav Amital's office in Israel to take exception with the ruling. One of those who came to Rav Amital's defense was Dr. Yosef Burg, who was president of Hapoel Mizraḥi. Enraged at the boycott of Rav Amital, he responded: "First they boycott the Prime Minister, and now they're boycotting a Rosh Yeshiva? What else needs to happen in this country for all this boycotting to stop?" Burg even offered to fly to the US himself to attend Rav Amital's lectures. Rav Amital was not agitated by the ban and did not change his plan. "I fear God, not rabbis," he said at a press conference. Smiling, he told the press how he had to calm down all of the senior politicians in Israel who read about the ban and quickly called him. He did not see any problem with the attendance of Reform and Conservative rabbis at his lectures since they were coming to hear the messages that he wished to impart. In his meetings with representatives of non-Orthodox denominations, he called on them to engage in educational

Meeting with American Vice President Al Gore at the White House as Minister in Charge of Diaspora Affairs.

activities among the secular public in Israel and not focus on political fights in the Knesset.

Rav Amital's attitude toward Reform and Conservative Judaism was straightforward. He vehemently opposed granting legal status to Reform weddings and divorces, but supported the inclusion of the various denominations in the school system and in the state's religious services system. "They should be allowed to engage in educational activities," he said, "presuming that they will be a positive Jewish influence on the secular public." Rav Amital did not reject collaboration with Reform or Conservative rabbis in instances where their religious affiliation was irrelevant to the activity. In the late 1970s, Rav Amital's friend Yehoshua Cohen, the Stern Gang veteran, established a research group to study religious aspects of the Holocaust. The group was registered as a non-profit organization, and when Cohen sought a director, Rabbi Dr. Pesaḥ Schindler, an American Jew who wrote a dissertation on Hasidic responses to the Holocaust, came highly recommended. When it came to light that Schindler served as director of the Center for Conservative Judaism in Jerusalem, Cohen decided to consult with Rav Amital about this sensitive issue. Rav Amital responded that in this instance the fact that Schindler affiliated with the Conservative movement was irrelevant. "If he has the right motivations, take him," he said. Amos Safrai, an alumnus of the yeshiva who collaborated with Cohen to set up the organization, relates that Cohen was so overcome by Rav Amital's courageous response that tears ran down his cheeks.

In many of the Jewish communities abroad that Rav Amital visited, he addressed audiences to his political right. Nevertheless, he was received everywhere with congeniality and warmth, and his public appearances were standing room only.

When he visited the Israeli embassy in Washington, he was disappointed to discover that there was no Tanakh anywhere in the building. He expressed his dismay to the embassy staff: "In every hotel room in this country you can find a Tanakh, but in the Israeli embassy there is not one?"

Upon his return to Israel, Rav Amital received a memo from the Prime Minister: "I have the honor of praising you for your impressive appearances before US Jewry. Please accept my admiration and gratitude." Even Binyamin Netanyahu, then the head of opposition in the Knesset, complimented Rav Amital on his appearances in the US.

Less than a month after his first visit to the US, Rav Amital flew back to North America, this time to Los Angeles. Even though Rav Amital encountered friendly crowds almost everywhere he went, the threat of violence meant that he had an LAPD escort wherever he went. Ultimately the fears were unfounded and the trip was entirely peaceful, with the exception of a single incident in which one Jew tried to disrupt Rav Amital as he spoke at a synagogue, until the congregants forced him away. The Israeli Consulate in Los Angeles used Rav Amital's visit as an opportunity to arrange visits to Orthodox synagogues that were refusing to admit any other minister. At one congregation, the leaders admitted to Rav Amital that this was the first time that a speaker expressed a political opinion in their synagogue that was not right-wing. In Los Angeles, Rav Amital met with Muslim leaders who wished to talk to him. They made it clear to him that according to them, there is no justification in Islamic law to kill innocents. Upon his return to Israel, Rav Amital received a letter from Yoram Ben-Zeev, the Israel consul in Los Angeles, which stated: "This was one of the most effective visits we have experienced, and we have already seen its fruits. The pleasant atmosphere that you exuded made your visit a pleasant experience for all of us."

Rav Amital's fourth and final trip abroad as a government minister took place at the end of April. He was invited to lecture at the convention of the Conference of European Rabbis in London, described as the largest gathering of rabbis in Europe since World War II. The visit was used as an opportunity to address congregations and Jewish high school students in England.

At one such school, a student asked Rav Amital what he thought about Operation Grapes of Wrath, which had just concluded a few days earlier. Operation Grapes of Wrath targeted terrorist infrastructure in Lebanon. On the seventh day of the operation, over one-hundred Lebanese civilians were killed when the IDF mistakenly shelled a UN installation in Qana. World reaction was furious. Rav Amital answered the student that as a minister of the government of Israel, which is responsible for the safety of the residents of the Galilee, he agreed to the operation so that the people of the Galilee would not become victims of Katyusha rockets fired by terrorists. However, he continued, a terrible tragedy occurred and a hundred innocent civilians were killed. Although it was accidental, Rav Amital stated, it was a *ḥillul HaShem* and required absolution. "It keeps me awake at night," he told them, "as a government minister, I share in the responsibility for that *ḥillul HaShem*." After his visit, one of the teachers called the embassy in London to report in her name and on behalf of the students that the minister's words at the school constituted a *kiddush HaShem*. "It was important for us to hear a rabbi saying, in connection with the peace process and as pertains to tolerance between religious and secular Jews, things that we are not used to hearing from the rabbis to whom we are exposed," the teacher wrote.

In the third area of his stated goals, deepening Jewish identity in Israel, Rav Amital recorded significant achievements. To formulate ideas and methods for imparting Jewish values, his office worked to establish a national council for Jewish education in Israel. Together with Education Minister Amnon Rubenstein, Rav Amital brought a proposal to establish the council for government approval. The government approved the council, which was indeed established and headed by Rav Amital, Minister Rubenstein, and Jewish Agency head Avraham Burg. It managed to hold two meetings before the June 1996 elections, which led to a change of government. The new Minister of Education, Zevulun Hammer, elected not to continue the council's activities.

Another achievement, which actually remained in place after the elections, was in the field of communications. Out of a desire to promote Jewish television content, Rav Amital met with the directors of the Israel Broadcasting Authority, the board of the Second Authority for Television and Radio, and representatives of the concessionaires of Channel Two. In order to stimulate the creation of Jewish programming worthy of broadcasting on the various channels, Rav Amital's office announced a project to script, direct, and produce Jewish-themed content. A budget of approximately one million shekels was made available to the project, administered by the Government Advertising Agency. More than a hundred submissions arrived at Rav Amital's office. A public committee set up for this purpose selected six projects that they considered worthy of financial support. The project continued even after Rav Amital's term as minister ended, and with its assistance several films were produced and broadcast.

In the area of legislation, Rav Amital initiated an amendment to the new State Education Law initiated by the Minister of Education, after it became clear that his version did not mandate the incorporation of Jewish heritage. The amendment contained a clause that established that public schools must impart to students "the values of the State of Israel as a Jewish and democratic state" and teach the history and traditions of the Jewish people. Minister Rubenstein accepted Rav Amital's proposal, and the Ministerial Committee on Legislation approved it.

Another law that Rav Amital moved quickly to amend was the Surrogate Motherhood Agreements Act, better known as the Surrogacy Law. During the course of a government meeting held in mid-December 1995, Rav Amital discovered that the proposed law, which had already been unanimously approved by the Rabin government and passed its first reading in the Knesset, could lead to concerns of halakhic illegitimacy (*mamzerut*). The original version of the law established that for the purpose of surrogacy, *in vitro* fertilization could be performed using the ovum or sperm of one of the intended parents and prohibited the use of the surrogate mother's ovum. The law did not forbid the use of donor sperm if both of the intended parents were infertile. Rav Amital raised the concern that in cases where both intended parents were infertile, the fertilization could be performed with sperm that would render the resulting child halakhically illegitimate. The Prime Minister listened to Rav Amital and instructed him to meet with Health Minister Ephraim Sneh and Justice Minister David Libai to amend the law as needed.

The next morning, headlines in *Yediot Aharonot* proclaimed "Anger at the Ministry of Health: Rav Amital Proposes Changes to the Surrogacy Law." Health Ministry officials feared that Rav Amital's reservations would sink the law's passage, and they were worried that chaos would ensue two weeks later, on January 1, 1996, when the existing regulations governing surrogacy would expire. The concern was that, absent a clear law, an unregulated market of "wombs for rent" would emerge. Ultimately, though, the matter was settled. After a halakhic consultation with Sephardic Chief Rabbi Eliyahu Bakshi-Doron – a former student from the Yeshivat HaDarom days – Rav Amital, together with the Health Ministry and the Justice Ministry, reformulated the law in accordance with halakha, and the government passed the new version. Several years later, Rav Amital met some of the people who had been helped to have children by that law.

Organ transplant was another area of medicine in which Rav Amital took an active interest. Even before being appointed minister, he worked to promote halakhic organ donation. As minister, he held a discussion on the matter at his office, with the participation of scholars, rabbis, and representatives of Adi, an organization that promotes organ donation in Israel. In the wake of the discussion, Rav Amital's office sponsored a one-day seminar – the first of its kind in Israel – on organ donation in Jewish law, with the participation of rabbis, doctors, and experts. Rav Amital, in an effort to encourage religious Jews to sign Adi organ donor cards, signed one himself. It remained in his wallet until the end of his life.

When it came to religion and state, Rav Amital remained faithful to his approach that opposed religious legislation. When he stated that he would not reject the participation of non-Orthodox denominations on local religious councils, it made headlines. "A religious council is not a halakhic or religious body, and therefore the religious denominations to which its members belong are of no special significance, as long as they do their jobs in good faith," he said.

Rav Amital was a minister for just under seven months. When he began, in November 1995, elections were expected a year later, but they were moved up to May, thus shortening his tenure. On the personal level, Rav Amital was happy to return to the world of Torah. Even as he served as minister, he visited the yeshiva nearly every week and delivered occasional *shiurim*. From the perspective of his ministerial activity, Rav Amital left with mixed feelings of satisfaction and lost opportunity. Much of what he planned to do was cut short and left in the planning stages. His office staff expressed this sentiment well when they entitled a booklet summarizing the office's activities "The Work is not Ours to Complete" (a play on *Avot* 2:19). But even after his term ended, he remained proud of the fact that he had joined the government. He believed that this step, like his reaction to the Rabin assassination, would yet have historical ramifications.

An assessment of whether Rav Amital realized the goals he set for himself at the time of his appointment yields mixed results. He did not succeed in moderating the tensions that flared up after the Rabin assassination; he did not manage to heal the rift between the government and the national-religious public. The heads of the settlements in Judea, Samaria, and Gaza were right when they claimed that he was not the man for the job. On the other hand, he carried out his ministerial mission in two other areas: he advanced numerous projects designed to deepen Jewish identity in Israeli society. More than that, just by sitting in the government he created a bond between secular Jews and their Jewishness. "One evening," Avrumy Yishai recounts, "after he completed his term as minister, I went with him to a movie theater in Tel Aviv where they were showing films produced with the money he procured as minister. As we left the screening, figures from Tel Aviv's bohemian artistic and cultural scene were standing there. Some of them came over to him and said, 'You, rabbi, represent a Judaism that speaks to us.'"

With his student from Yeshivat HaDarom, Rishon LeTziyon Rav Eliyahu Bakshi-Doron, on the occasion of the latter's visit to the yeshiva.

At the same time, many of Rav Amital's nearest and dearest believe that he did not realize his goals during his term as minister. One such person in Dr. Yehuda Ben-Meir, who said:

> I believe that Rav Amital himself at some point was sorry he joined the government. It's hard for a Minister without Portfolio to find expression in the government. The public has expectations of ministers that are hard to meet, especially for a Minister without Portfolio. True, his position gave him the opportunity to voice his opinions, but over time that diminished as well. In the final analysis, the role eroded his standing as a rabbi.

Rav Lichtenstein also characterized his colleague's tenure as unfulfilled hope:

> I do not see a fundamental problem with a Rosh Yeshiva serving as a minister, and I do not retract what I said when Rav Amital was appointed. At the time they said that he entered the government

> to serve as the liaison with the religious population, but in fact the religious world shied away from him. The hopes were not fulfilled. There are power struggles in the political realm, and not everything that he hoped for and anticipated came to fruition.

When asked whether he ever regretted, even momentarily, agreeing to become a minister, he responded: "The whole time, I felt it was not my natural place." He was motivated, he said, by a sense of duty.

Chapter Twenty

Between Party and Family

It is not enough to distance oneself from a place of strife; one must run away from it… The Gemara in Ḥullin *(89a) states: "Rabbi Ila'a said: The world exists only for one who keeps silent* [bolem] *during a quarrel, as it says (Job 26:7): 'He hangs the earth on nothing* (belima).*'" The world does not exist on the merit of men of action who disagree and argue about everything, but rather on the merit of those who successfully avoid controversy and strife. It is particularly important to avoid strife that is "for the sake of Heaven," regarding which there are no constraints, because a person thinks that everything is permitted to him, being that he is acting – in his own estimation – for the sake of Heaven.*

Jewish Values in a Changing World, 2005, pp. 211–212

The elections to the fourteenth Knesset were supposed to take place in November 1996, but at the beginning of February, when polls put Peres twenty percentage points ahead of his nearest rival, the Prime Minister decided to push the elections up to late May. Right after the announcement of early elections, Rav Amital, still serving as a minister, was asked whether Meimad would run for Knesset. At first he did not dismiss the possibility that Meimad would return to the political playing field, though he stressed that he had no intention of running.

As a minister, it was not possible for him to serve as Meimad's official chairman. He did not participate in their deliberations on the matter, but he made his positions known through the media. On February 18, the Meimad leadership convened and decided that the movement would register as a party in the meantime, in order to keep open the option of running, and simultaneously began negotiations with the NRP and Third Way, to investigate the possibility of running together. Rav Amital preferred that Meimad not run at all, and if they decided to run, he felt it would be better to join NRP. "It can moderate the NRP population," he explained in an interview with the radio station Reshet Bet. Nor did he discount the establishment of a united religious front, on

(photo: Roni Na'aman)

Meimad leadership at the President's Residence. Standing from right to left: Yossi Ben-Gal, Dr. Danny Tropper, Rav Amital, President Ezer Weizman, Moshe (Moshko) Moskovic, Yisrael Cohen.

condition that the authority to make decisions for such a front would be reserved for politicians, not rabbis. The Meimad leader's willingness to cooperate with the NRP surprised only those who did not really know Rav Amital. Despite his frequent criticisms of the NRP over the years, he continued to see it as his political home. As Meimad's chairman he saw no problem with going to NRP meetings. "You're right, it's not my party – but it's my family," he answered those who expressed wonder.

The negotiations with the NRP and Third Way did not succeed, and in March the Meimad leadership decided not to run in the elections at all and to remain an ideological, non-partisan movement. The 1996 elections were Israel's first direct prime ministerial elections. Voters cast two ballots – one for a party and one for a prime ministerial candidate. Even though it decided not to take an active part in the elections, at Rav Amital's behest Meimad backed Shimon Peres against Binyamin Netanyahu for Prime Minister.

Ten days before the elections, Meimad held its national convention with the participation of Prime Minister Peres. Some Meimad members did not look kindly on the invitation of Peres and refused to attend. Rav Amital insisted that Peres be invited – more on principle than because of politics. In contrast to the right-wing campaign that began a few days before the elections with the slogan "Netanyahu – Good for the Jews," Rav Amital wished to demonstrate that Judaism is not affiliated with the right wing exclusively. He told his party colleagues: "If Peres wins, great. If Peres doesn't win, it's good that we supported him to show that the religious public is diverse, and that not everyone identifies the Torah and Judaism with a particular political bent. If Peres fails, it's even more important that we exist."

A week before the elections, Rav Lichtenstein publicly endorsed the NRP. Having backed Meimad in 1988, he admitted in his endorsement that he disagreed with the NRP's political direction and emphasis in recent years, but stated that "any citizen who fears for and strives to deepen the preservation of the Jewish identity of the state should vote for the party that sets this challenge as its primary objective." In addition, Meimad co-founder Dr. Danny Tropper along with board member Dr. Ami Ze'evi endorsed the NRP. Rav Amital told his yeshiva students that he believed that one should cast his Knesset ballot for a religious party.

As was his wont, he did not endorse a particular party and refused to disclose his vote, but he presumably voted for the NRP. The two-ballot system made it easier for the moderate camp of religious Zionism to vote; many Meimad adherents voted for Peres as Prime Minister and the NRP for the Knesset.

In the May 29 elections, Binyamin Netanyahu upset Shimon Peres, winning the premiership by less than thirty-thousand votes. The NRP performed impressively, winning nine mandates and increasing its Knesset representation by fifty percent. It seemed that the assault on the national-religious public that began after the Rabin assassination caused it to close ranks, and increased electoral strength. In the right-wing government that was established, NRP leader Zevulun Hammer was appointed Deputy Prime Minister and Minister of Education.

The increased strength of the religious camp in the elections brought Rav Amital satisfaction. In an interview with *Haaretz*'s Nadav Shragai six weeks later, he said, astonishingly, that he preferred the right wing government that included the religious to the Labor-Meretz government in which he served as a minister: "The last government, which relied on Arab votes even with the support of Shas, would have caused the peace process to fail. The rift in the nation would have deepened, and it would have been impossible to make any sort of progress." In the same interview he stated: "I think that my term as minister was my final political adventure. I'm finished with politics, though you'll continue to hear my views."

Rav Amital indeed left the public arena after the 1996 elections, returning to the familiar confines of Torah. Meimad, the movement he founded, continued its activities, and its change in leadership led to a change in its character. When Yossi Ben-Gal vacated his position as Director-General of Meimad to manage Rav Amital's ministerial office, the vacuum he left was quickly filled by R. Michael Melchior, who was then serving as Rav Amital's advisor on Diaspora relations. Rav Melchior was appointed acting chairman of Meimad and later chairman of its secretariat as well. His emergence pushed aside the veteran activists who led Meimad as a party during the 1988 elections and as a movement during the Rabin government. Much to the chagrin of Ben-Gal, Ben-Meir, Tropper, and others, Melchior led Meimad into territory that was far more political. For most of Netanyahu's term as Prime Minister, with the NRP in the government, Meimad did not have a political option. But as elections for the fifteenth Knesset drew near, Melchior began preparing Meimad for a renewed run at the ballot box.

In February 1998, the Meimad council decided to renew its status as a political party. Rav Amital supported the decision. In an interview with *Ma'ariv*'s Menaḥem Rahat, he explained: "We came to the conclusion that without politics there is no media attention, and when there is no media attention, it's hard for us to get our message out." Meimad pinned its hopes on the direct election of the Prime Minister, which greatly benefited the religious parties in 1996. Casting two ballots meant that voters could express their political views in the prime ministerial ballot and their social views in the Knesset ballot. The announcement of Meimad's re-establishment came shortly after Rav Amital and Meimad proclaimed their support for a new social covenant between religious and secular. The covenant was shaped by Meimad members together with MK Yossi Beilin of Labor and MK Alex Lubotzky of the Third Way. Their support for the covenant reminded anyone who had forgotten that Meimad championed something beyond a political platform.

One thing about that third incarnation of Meimad: Rav Amital was finished with his personal involvement in the world of politics; he would not head the Knesset list again. The first person mentioned as a worthy replacement at the top of the Meimad list was Dr. Yehuda Ben-Meir. Rav Melchior also saw himself as a natural candidate to head the list. As the chairman of the movement's secretariat and the one who maintained the party, more than anyone else, after the fall of the Peres government, Rav Melchior did not try to hide his political ambitions.

When Meimad announced its reconstitution as a party, Knesset elections – planned for November 2000 – were still far away, but in January 1999, a no confidence motion caused the dissolution of the Knesset, and elections were called for May of that year. Since June 1997, the Labor head had been Ehud Barak. During the run-up to the elections, Barak formed a new political entity – One Israel – to replace the Labor party by merging other parties into it. The first party to join Barak's One Israel was MK David Levy's Gesher party, which had split off from Likud. A month after the decision to hold early elections, Meimad, too, joined One Israel. Rav Amital supported the merger because he feared another failure were Meimad to run alone, but also because he saw a positive ideological message of cooperation in the fact that they were running together with Labor.

Rav Amital had faith in Ehud Barak. They knew each other from the Peres government in which Barak was Foreign Minister and Rav Amital was Minister without Portfolio. Soon after entering the government, he showed Barak Meimad's Blocs Document and got the impression that he supported it. He viewed Barak as the successor to Yitzḥak Rabin, saying of him:

> He's a straight-shooter who speaks the honest truth. He is continuing the path of Yitzḥak Rabin and Shimon Peres, emphasizing the link between peace and security and striving to attain both despite the many obstacles along the way. We know that he is aware of societal problems and sensitive to social distress. These are cardinal Jewish values.

In the agreement between Meimad and Labor, two spots deemed realistic were reserved for Meimad on the One Israel list: the seventeenth and the thirty-third. It was also agreed that a Meimad person, not necessarily a Knesset member, would serve as a minister in Barak's government, if indeed Barak would be assembling the next government.

In the elections held by the Meimad council, Rav Melchior was chosen to fill the seventeenth spot on the One Israel list, and R. Yehuda Gilad was chosen to fill the thirty-third slot. Rav Gilad, the rabbi of Kibbutz Lavi and one of the Rashei Yeshiva of Yeshivat HaKibbutz HaDati at Kibbutz Ma'aleh Gilboa, was married to Rav Amital's daughter Dina. Aside from him, Rav Amital had two other sons-in-law on the Meimad council: R. Shlomo Brin, married to Tali, and Shlomo Yishai, married to Ayelet. All three had been active in the movement since its founding in the 1980s. All three were naturally very close with Rav Amital, and they were considered his ideological successors within the movement. The only son-in-law who was not active in the movement was Shmuel Karsch, Devora's husband. All four sons-in-law are alumni of Yeshivat Har Etzion, as is Rav Amital's only son, Yoel.

At a gathering of the Meimad council held three months before the elections, Rav Amital described Meimad's running in the election as redress of an intolerable and unjustifiable misrepresentation: "For many years, a Jew who supported the peace process wholeheartedly, Zionistically, and morally, had no real political home. Nobody truly and fully expressed his positions and values in the most important public arena – the Knesset. Today we can proclaim to the tens of thousands of religious-Zionist faithful: you finally have a home." Regarding the partnership with Labor he said: "This partnership is not a return to the historic alliance between Labor and religious Zionism. That alliance was based on the relegation of matters of religion and tradition to the religious while the secularists handled matters of state. In this way, Labor was freed from having to deal with the problem of Jewish identity, questions regarding connecting to Jewish tradition, and shaping the religious character of Israeli society. Today we call for the cooperation of religious and secular in strengthening the connection of every segment of the population to Judaism." He concluded by stressing the relevance of the Jewish character of the state to secularists: "Someone with refined senses can hear, at this noteworthy event this evening, the echo of an ancient call from the pages of Jewish history: 'We have a share in the God of Israel.' All of us – those who observe the mitzvot and those who do not – have a share in the God of Israel." At the founding convention of One Israel a few days later, Rav Amital said, "We do not want to be the peace camp's *kashrut* supervisors."

The merger of Meimad and Labor was opposed by Yehuda Ben-Meir, who believed that joining Labor would cause Meimad to lose its credibility among the religious public. Once the decision to join Barak's One Israel was made, despite Ben-Meir's opposition, he decided to leave the movement and publicly endorse the Center Party of Yitzḥak Mordekhai, Amnon Lipkin-Shaḥak, and Dan Meridor. "I supported them by not joining another party," he explained, "I figured that if I had to join somewhere, there was a greater chance of making a difference through the Center Party. It was a new party that would not provoke the ire of the religious population like Labor would." Ben-Meir made it clear that his support was not as a representative of Meimad, and Melchior made sure to emphasize that point to the media. The only one in no rush to push Ben-Meir out of the movement was Rav Amital. He praised Ben-Meir, saying that he would doubtlessly contribute to whatever party he supported. In an interview with *Ma'ariv*, he expressed satisfaction that Ben-Meir and Alex Lubotzky – who was also identified with Meimad's approach – had joined the Center Party. "If more Meimad members join more parties," he said, "it benefits the people of Israel." For Rav Amital, the main thing was always the message. The political apparatus was secondary.

The national-religious public once again had difficulty swallowing Meimad's support for the left's candidate and, this time, its association with the Labor party. As the elections drew near and the public atmosphere heated up, it only got more difficult. When Barak's staff released sound bites opposing government funding for settlements and yeshivot, a large measure of the ensuing rage was directed against Meimad, which was perceived as Barak's partner. Even when the slogans were moderated, the mood remained tense.

A week before the elections, Barak planned a visit to Yeshivat Har Etzion. Yeshiva students decided to absent themselves during the visit, as a gesture of protest. Several of them told *Hazofe* that they did not understand how their Rosh Yeshiva could endorse running on the same ticket as Labor MK Yael Dayan, known for her anti-religious views. "Ehud Barak stood behind his party's anti-religious incitement, which continues even as he is invited to visit the yeshiva," the students lamented in the pages of *Hazofe*, "We will not be here when the yeshiva is visited by the man who invented the slogan 'Money for education – not for yeshivot or settlements.' We're both a yeshiva and a settlement." Barak ultimately cancelled his visit to the yeshiva.

The May 17 elections resulted in Ehud Barak's victory over Binyamin Netanyahu for the premiership. One Israel won twenty-six Knesset mandates, and thus Rav Melchior became Meimad's first elected parliamentarian. Barak formed a government, and Meimad had to choose who from among its ranks would serve as a minister. The natural candidate was Professor Avi Ravitzky, but once it became known that Meimad would not get the education portfolio but the social and Diaspora affairs portfolio, he gave up the appointment. Four people initially planned to contend for the appointment: Rav Melchior, Dr. Danny Tropper, Alex

Lubotzky – who had returned to Meimad from the Center Party, and Yonatan Bassi – who later headed the Disengagement Authority during Israel's pullout from Gaza. "I submitted my candidacy," Tropper recounts, "because I contended that someone else, not Melchior who was already in the Knesset, should be appointed minister, so that Meimad would be represented by two people. I cautioned that without two figures, Meimad would become a one-man party." Rav Amital backed Melchior's candidacy, believing that if Melchior did not receive a significant position within the movement, it would not survive. He viewed Melchior as someone capable of strengthening the party, and so he wanted to boost his status. Tropper was asked by Rav Amital to rescind his candidacy, but he wished to remain a candidate so that he would have a chance to speak before the vote. When he got up to speak, Tropper announced the withdrawal of his candidacy at Rav Amital's behest, but reiterated his warning that choosing Rav Melchior for the task would be a mistake. "I think that Rav Amital backed Rav Melchior's appointment because of his organizational abilities as well," Tropper said many years later, "Rav Amital and I lived through the trauma of those debts we accrued in the 1988 elections. The financial burden was heavy for him, and he was concerned that it would happen again."

Ultimately, the other candidates dropped out as well, and Rav Melchior became minister. To a large extend, Tropper's prediction came true: Melchior turned out to be a seasoned and talented politician, but Meimad increasingly became the party of one man. Slowly, two clear camps formed within Meimad: the camp of Rav Melchior and his people, and the camp of most of the movement's founders – Tropper, Ben-Meir, Rav Gilad, Rav Brin, and others. The differences between Melchior and the others found expression in several areas. Melchior did not put much stock in Meimad's activities within the national-religious public. For Rav Amital and the other founders, Meimad's significance was as an alternative to the NRP within the national-religious population. They wished to maintain dealings with the NRP, and frequently examined the possibility of reintegrating into the party it broke away from. Melchior, who, like almost all of Meimad's founders, was from abroad, was never part and parcel of the religious-Zionist community, and therefore he did not always engage in dialogue with it. At one point, he even passed a resolution in the movement's institutions defining Meimad as a joint religious-secular movement.

Another difference emerged in the political sphere. Rav Melchior's views turned out to be further to the left than most of Meimad; this found expression in the numerous crises that erupted between Meimad and Prime Minister Barak.

The first significant crisis between Barak and Meimad occurred a year after the elections, during the Camp David summit. A few hours before the Prime Minister flew to the summit, a positive meeting took place between him and the Meimad leadership, along with several other rabbis. In addition to Rabbis Melchior and Amital, Rabbis Lichtenstein and Breuer attended as well. The rabbis wished to show support for Barak but also to ask that during the course of the summit, if diplomatic concessions were demanded, he stress the pain that such concessions would entail.

Despite Meimad's support for attending the peace talks, the summit exposed differences between Rav Melchior and Rav Gilad regarding the solutions proposed at the talks for Jerusalem's Old City and the Temple Mount. Ultimately, Meimad presented a unified front. When it became known that Barak was about to give in to Arafat on Jerusalem, Rav Amital and Rav Melchior wrote Barak a letter firmly demanding that he not concede anything of the capital:

> We beseech you out of concern for Jerusalem's future, and hope that the agreement that will be signed gives proper consideration to the importance of Jerusalem. The special connection between the Jewish people and the Temple Mount must be expressed in any agreement. The Jewish people have no holier place. At the same time, we are willing to take Muslim sensitivities into consideration and extend the status quo. There is no place for the use of flags and national symbols, which are unrelated to the sanctity of the site. We wish to add that foreign sovereignty within the walls of Jerusalem shall not be accepted…

Foreign Minister Shlomo Ben-Ami reported after the summit that Barak presented the letter to President Clinton and translated it for him, saying, "You see, even the moderates cannot accept such concessions." He claimed that the letter helped induce Clinton to stop pushing Barak to make concessions regarding Jerusalem.

Upon Barak's return to Israel, Rav Amital praised his desire to make peace, as well as his proclamation to the world that he would not sign a document that gives Arabs sovereignty over the Temple Mount.

Rav Amital's attitude toward the Temple Mount was always different from his attitude to other territories liberated in the Six Day War. He viewed the Temple Mount as a red line that could not be crossed, and keeping the mount as a supreme value for which an individual must be prepared to give his life. Six months after the Camp David talks, the media reported that in contrast to what had been previously thought, Israel indeed expressed willingness to give up its sovereignty over the Temple Mount. In a discourse delivered at the yeshiva after this report, Rav Amital stated that the sanctity of Jerusalem is greater even than the sanctity of life and the value of peace. He continued:

> ... a declaration that we are in principle not prepared to relinquish the Temple Mount is of great significance, and any Prime Minister – in the present and in the future – should swear his allegiance to our sovereignty over that site.
>
> We must retain our sovereignty over the Temple Mount for nationalistic reasons, not for halakhic or religious ones. Firstly, the Moslems have claimed all along that the Temple never existed on that site, and if we transfer it to them they are likely to perceive our move as an admission to that claim. Moreover, transferring control of the Temple Mount into Arab hands represents, in effect, a severance from our historical Jewish identity.

He went on to explain the importance of preserving a Jewish identity shared by religious and secular alike:

> In his *Tzidkat HaTzaddik*, R. Tzadok HaKohen of Lublin writes that there are those among our nation whose sole characteristic defining them as Jews is their own self-definition:

> The crux of Judaism is being called by the name of Israel ... even if only by virtue of the fact that he is known as a Jew, that is sufficient ... for them to be joined together as one nation, and not divided to join with the other nations and to be included among them.
>
> A person's self-definition as a Jew means, first and foremost, a feeling of belonging to historical Judaism. If, heaven forbid, we relinquish our sovereignty over the Temple Mount to the Arabs, we will be cutting with our own hands the thin thread that binds all parts of the nation, nullifying the single element that binds those Jews who are not Torah-observant to Judaism.

The issue of whether it is halakhically permissible for Jews to set foot upon the Temple Mount nowadays is a matter of dispute. Most rabbis forbid it, but Rav Amital, beginning in the early 1970s, was one of a handful of rabbis who permitted it (within certain boundaries). When R. Ovadia Yosef was Sephardic Chief Rabbi, R. Mordekhai Eliyahu asked Rav Amital to join him on a visit to Rav Ovadia to attempt to persuade him to remove his opposition to ascending the mount. Rav Amital assented, but the two of them were unable to change Rav Ovadia's mind, which was also the official position of the Chief Rabbinate. When Rav Eliyahu replaced Rav Ovadia as Sephardic Chief Rabbi, he changed his position and began to oppose ascending the mount. In his later years, Rav Amital too stopped supporting visits to the Temple Mount. He feared that as awareness of the issue grew, women would also want to ascend the mount, which would require them to immerse in a *mikveh* beforehand. The fourteenth century Spanish authority R. Yitzḥak b. Sheshet (Rivash) instituted a ban on unmarried women immersing in a *mikveh*, so ascending the Temple Mount would pose a halakhic problem for women. Rav Amital explained his change of position: "When I supported ascending the mount, it was not yet too popular. Only individuals were going."

Not long after the Temple Mount crisis, Meimad and Barak had another falling out that enraged Rav Amital no less. Although the Camp David talks failed, they created a coalition crisis that led to the departure of Shas, the NRP, and Natan Sharansky's Yisrael BaAliya party. To stabilize his government, Barak decided to launch a new agenda, and at the end of August 2000 he announced his intention of creating a civic-secular revolution, in which he planned to eliminate the Ministry of Religious Affairs, complete Israel's constitution, and institute civil marriages. The religious population was in shock; they immediately turned to Meimad, Barak's religious partner. At first Barak managed to calm tensions by explaining to the Meimad contingent that he was not planning a secular revolution, merely social reform that would barely affect the status quo on matters of religion and state. But almost immediately afterward, he came out with new proclamations, which were hard for Meimad to swallow: he announced that within weeks the number of busses that ran on Shabbat would be increased significantly and that the national airline, El Al, would fly on Shabbat. This declaration angered Rav Amital and the rest of Meimad's leadership. The signed agreement between Meimad and One Israel explicitly stated that any legislation initiated in the realm of religion and state would require Meimad's consent. Barak's announced civic revolution was a blatant breach of the agreement. The day before Rosh HaShana 5761 (September 30, 2000), Rav Amital and other Meimad figures met with Barak; the media characterized the meeting as "difficult." Rav Amital expressed his deep disappointment with the Prime Minister's conduct. *Yediot Aharonot* reported that Rav Amital said to Barak: "I am frustrated, angry, and disappointed with you." On this matter too, Rav Melchior was far more forgiving than Rav Amital and Rav Gilad. He also expressed disappointment with Barak, but in contrast to the demands of some party members, he did not think it justified leaving the government.

The "revolution" was ultimately revealed to be Barak's political spin, but it was not long before the next crisis loomed. A new Intifada broke out in October 2000. Yet despite awful terrorist attacks, and without the backing of his parliament, Barak insisted on holding diplomatic talks with Palestinians. Rav Melchior saw no reason to raise a ruckus over it. R. Yehuda Gilad, on the other hand, attempted to pass a resolution through the Meimad council demanding that Barak establish a unity government, but the attempt failed. Nevertheless, it was resolved that Rav Melchior would vote in the cabinet against the Clinton Peace Plan, a framework agreement proposed by the American President in late December 2000 which included relinquishment of the Temple Mount.

The collapse of the Camp David talks, the continued uprising, and the formation of a Knesset majority to topple the government, convinced Barak to call for a new election. He immediately resigned the premiership to ensure that the elections would only be for Prime Minister, not for the Knesset. An election date was set for February 2001, with Barak running against Likud Chairman Ariel Sharon. As the elections neared, polls showed a clear advantage for Sharon. A disagreement arose in Meimad regarding the continuation of the partnership with Barak and his Labor party. Against a minority that demanded an end to the partnership, Rav Amital and most of the party membership believed that it would be inappropriate to pull out of One Israel a moment before the elections, when defeat appeared imminent. Rav Amital, who was still rankled by Barak's civic revolution, commented: "Our partnership with Barak is dead. Supporting him is a symbolic gesture."

Nevertheless, a group of members led by Rav Gilad demanded that they not explicitly declare their support for Barak's candidacy. Rav Melchior again toed a line more loyal to his political patron and wanted the party to strand by Barak's side openly; his position was rejected. Meimad's resolution not to declare its support for Barak, their partner in One Israel, was considered bold.

Sharon won the election and established a national unity government. The change in government temporarily papered over the differences of opinion within Meimad. Rav Melchior served as Deputy Foreign Minister, and in June 2002, after the resignation of several Labor MKs, R. Yehuda Gilad entered the Knesset, doubling Meimad's representation. As an MK, Rav Gilad often voiced opinions that differed from those of his colleague, Rav Melchior. He focused on social matters and on issues of religion and state. Given his disappointment with the leaders of Labor, he made no special effort to demonstrate loyalty to their party.

Rav Gilad did not remain an MK for long. Labor left the government in November 2002, and Sharon called new elections in January 2003. Amram Mitzna was elected as Labor's new chairman. His election reopened discussions within Meimad. Mitzna, whose ideas were to the left of Binyamin Ben-Eliezer, his predecessor as Labor chairman, expressed his opposition to entering into a unity government after the elections. He also declared his intention to unilaterally evacuate the

With Deputy Foreign Minister Michael Melchior (left) and author Elie Wiesel (center).

Gush Katif settlements in the Gaza Strip. Despite Mitzna's stances and the lingering disappointment of the partnership with Labor under Barak, Melchior wanted to continue the partnership with Labor. The movement's original members opposed. Ben-Meir, Rav Gilad, Rav Brin, R. Shmuel Reiner, and many others preferred looking into other options over continuing the partnership with Labor. They explored the options of joining Amir Peretz's One Nation party, running independently, and abandoning the political arena to focus on the theoretical plane. Rav Melchior stood his ground.

The Meimad council convened in November 2002 to decide whether to continue its partnership with Labor. Rav Amital did not attend that council meeting and did not wish to express his position in a movement-wide forum. The movement he had founded was torn between its political leader and its original members, the most prominent of whom were members of his family. At the end of a stormy meeting a vote was taken; Rav Melchior won. The movement's old-timers, led by Rav Gilad, resigned from the movement. Rav Melchior continues to claim that their departure was motivated in part by personal considerations.

Rav Amital did not back the departure of his sons-in-law and close friends. He did not intervene in the movement's decision-making apparatus, but he made his peace with the decision that was reached. His inclination was to agree with Rav Melchior and continue cooperating with Labor; looking at the situation pragmatically, he did not think that any of the political alternatives presented had a chance of success. Nevertheless, as during the struggle over the ministerial appointment in the Barak government, his main reason for supporting Rav Melchior was his belief in the latter's organizational capabilities. He believed that without Rav Melchior, Meimad would be completely wiped off the political map.

On the eve of the elections, he visited Meimad's convention, attended by Mitzna, and expressed his support. At the same time, he praised his son-in-law, R. Shlomo Brin, for an article he published in *Nekuda* explaining why he left Meimad. In the article, he listed three reasons for Meimad's failure: Barak's political conduct, the shattering of the Oslo Accords, which Meimad had supported, and the political conduct of Meimad under the leadership of Rav Melchior. Rav Brin accused Rav Melchior of turning Meimad into a "political brand associated with his name alone."

In the January 2003 elections, Sharon's Likud defeated Mitzna's Labor (direct election of the Prime Minister had been repealed by then). Rav Melchior was elected to the Knesset, and when Labor joined the coalition prior to the implementation of the Gaza Disengagement Plan, he was appointed Deputy Minister of Education. Tovah Ilan, one of the heads of the Religious Kibbutz Movement, replaced Rav Gilad as Meimad's number two, and she too served as a Meimad MK toward the end of that Knesset term.

In the summer of 2005, the settlements of Gush Katif were uprooted as part of Sharon's Gaza Disengagement Plan. Rav Melchior voted in favor of the plan. Rav Amital, in a talk to his students at the yeshiva, expressed opposition, arguing that since the move was undertaken outside the framework of a peace agreement, it would only increase terrorism. Nevertheless, he did not state his opinion publicly; as far as he was concerned, his public career was over. But the tension between the party he founded and his family did not disappear. Prior to the 2006 elections, his son-in-law Rav Gilad joined the centrist, anti-corruption Tafnit party established by General (Res.) Uzi Dayan. Gilad was slotted number three on its Knesset list. On the other side, Rav Melchior stuck to the partnership with Labor, then headed by Amir Peretz. Rav Amital attended the convention held by Meimad and Amir Peretz, but just before the elections Tafnit announced that Rav Amital supported it. Although he made it clear that, as usual, he had no intention of telling the media who he would vote for or making a public recommendation, after meeting with Uzi Dayan he agreed that the party could publicize his decision to support it. Rav Amital's support for Tafnit caused no small amount of stress for Meimad. They quickly elicited Rav Amital's fundamental support for their movement, and a denial that he had left it. Meimad's voters were confused by Rav Amital's split endorsement, even though each endorsement was different: his support for Meimad was based on values, not politics, which was nevertheless important for Meimad's struggle for the moderate religious vote. Despite his identification with his son-in-law's new political path, he preferred not to abandon his handiwork, Meimad. Rav Gilad believes that Rav Amital's double endorsement of Tafnit and Meimad expressed his fundamental attitude toward politics: "For him, the main thing is that the message gets out. It makes little difference to him what medium delivers the message to the public. He therefore viewed positively the fact that Tafnit was running as well as the continued partnership between Meimad and Labor."

After resigning from political activity, there was only one time that he insisted not just on getting across a message but on influencing political matters, even forcing his view on Rav Melchior. It was during the 2002 elections of the World Zionist Organization and its institutions. Avraham Duvdevani, head of the Settlement Division of the WZO, felt it important that Meimad run in the election on a joint list with the World Mizraḥi Movement, identified with the NRP, and he discussed the issue with Rav Amital. On the other hand, Rav Melchior wanted Meimad to run with Labor, its traditional partner in the Knesset. Rav Amital, in an uncharacteristic and unusual step, forcefully demanded that Meimad run with the NRP. His son-in-law R. Shlomo Brin recounts that Rav Amital even prepared a letter of resignation from the movement in case his request was not accepted. Rav Melchior surrendered, adopted Rav

Amital's position, and acted to ensure that the resolution to run with the NRP passed the Meimad secretariat.

The differences of opinion on this issue are further evidence of the differences between Rav Amital and Rav Melchior. Rav Amital never emotionally disengaged from the national-religious public or its institutions. Whenever there was an opportunity to join the forces of the religious camp – like within the institutions of WZO, in which political positions carry little weight – he preferred that to schism.

Even now that he has passed away, and more than fifteen years have passed since he completed his term as minister, Rav Amital still appears on Meimad's website as one of the movement's leaders. And although he stopped his involvement in Meimad's decision-making several years before his death, Rav Melchior continued to consult with him occasionally and to report the movement's activities to him.

Rav Melchior was again Meimad's lone representative in the seventeenth Knesset, elected in 2006. When asked to reflect on Meimad during that Knesset term, Rav Amital conceded that its status had indeed diminished, but in the same breath he cited its longevity approvingly: "We never had much of a foothold in the religious population. Only individuals went with us. The public wasn't ready for our messages, and yet Meimad still exists. The fact that we haven't disappeared – that's something, too." Rav Amital expressed his satisfaction with Rav Melchior's performance as Chairman of the Knesset Education, Culture and Sports Committee during the seventeenth Knesset. From his perspective, even if Meimad failed as a party, Melchior the politician continued to record successes.

Alongside its lack of political success, even Meimad's rivals admit that it has recorded no small number of achievements in the area of ideology and theory. Its ideas, particularly in the social realm, have become part of the religious-Zionist mainstream. Meimad's opposition to religious legislation has become the prevailing norm. Their willingness to re-imagine the relationship between religion and state through a covenant between religious and secular has taken pride of place in the outlook of national-religious leaders and Knesset members. The Gavison-Medan covenant – a framework agreement between Israel's observant and non-observant communities – created by Rav Ya'akov

Medan and non-religious legal scholar Prof. Ruth Gavison, and the Shabbat Law proposed by NRP's MK Zevulun Orlev, indicate that the ideas articulated by Meimad and by Rav Amital have been adopted by large segments of religious Zionism.

In the political sphere as well, Rav Amital identified certain of Meimad's ideas that succeeded in penetrating the general discourse. In the 1980s, Rav Amital opposed mixing halakhic considerations into questions of security and statecraft. Twenty years later, during the profound debate about uprooting the Gush Katif settlements, barely anyone used halakhic arguments. The rationale voiced by the anti-Disengagement "Orange" camp was primarily on the grounds of nationalism, civil rights, democracy, and security. Halakha did not play a central role in the Orange campaign, a change that Rav Amital viewed as positive.

Even Meimad's peace plan is not considered anathema as it had been in the 1990s. The Blocs Document that Meimad presented in 1994, according to which settlement blocs in Judea, Samaria, and Gaza would be annexed to Israel as part of a permanent status agreement while other parts would be given to the Palestinians, was considered staunchly leftist at the time and garnered marginal support from the national-religious public. By 2010 many right-wing religious-Zionists would be willing to accept a plan that ensures Israeli sovereignty over most settlements in Judea and Samaria, insists on territorial contiguity, and consents to the establishment of a demilitarized Palestinian entity.

On the other hand, it is impossible to forget Meimad's support for the failed Oslo Accords. Many in the national-religious camp have difficulty forgiving Meimad for standing by the leftist camp during the raging debate over the Oslo process. Meimad paid a political price for its support of the unsuccessful accords. Many of those who voted for it in 1988 had abandoned it by the mid-1990s due to its support of the Oslo Accords. Rav Amital himself paid a steep personal price for his support, although he believed until the end of his life that it was necessary to give the agreements, along with their promise of preventing bloodshed, a chance.

Chapter Twenty-One

Four Rashei Yeshiva

People of my age – or close to my age – have a problem. For almost half a century we've been repeating the same things, performing them day in and day out, watching the same phenomena for years and getting used to them. Sometimes we think that things can't be changed, that that's how reality has to be. It's a fact: five, ten, twenty years ago things were the same. But when you come into contact with young, energetic people, there's nothing that is self-evident. They don't let us get used to a routine. They ask about everything – what's this, why is that, what is the justification for what we're doing? What psychological, experiential and intellectual basis is there for prayer and for the commandments? These young people open a great gateway for their rabbis, and they are only able to do so because for them nothing is self-evident.[1]

1. Rabbi Yehuda Amital, *Commitment and Complexity* (Jersey City, NJ: KTAV Publishing House, 2008), p. 161.

When he finished serving in Peres's government, Rav Amital decided to retire – not only from political activity, but from the public sphere as well. Indeed, aside from the times he had to address political crises within Meimad, he did not want to voice his opinion. He broke his silence only twice. In February 2000, Rav Amital was shocked by statements made by Foreign Minister David Levy that Israel would retaliate against Hezbollah attacks and take "blood for blood, life for life, child for child." He viewed these statements as a *ḥillul HaShem*, and since the Foreign Minister's threats were met with silence on the part of the government, Rav Amital decided to take to the airwaves and called for the Foreign Minister to be sacked for his statements: "I would find it difficult to keep a minister who expresses himself thus in the government. This is a horrible moral and diplomatic failure, an act of blindness that calls the Foreign Minister's qualifications into question." He contended that Levy's statements should horrify anyone in touch with Jewish moral values. "It's hard to come to terms with moral decay of this sort." Rav Amital's words resonated, but did not lead to an apology by the Foreign Minister or an admonition by the Prime Minister.

The next time Rav Amital expressed himself publicly was in February 2006, after the demolition of houses in the settlement of Amona and the violent removal of right-wing demonstrators at the site. He was shocked by first-hand accounts of the brutal evacuation. He told *Haaretz*'s Yair Sheleg: "Just as I demanded a commission of inquiry into the events of Sabra and Shatila, I also demand a commission of inquiry into the events of Amona. There is no justification for the cruel manner in which the evacuations were carried out." Leftist circles were surprised at Rav Amital's forceful statements and criticized him for equating Amona with Sabra and Shatila.

These were Rav Amital's only public remarks during his final years. Other statements published in his name were generally quoted from talks he gave at the yeshiva. When, as on several occasions, he was urged to grant interviews or voice his opinions, he answered with a verse from *Shir HaShirim* (Song of Songs 5:3): "I have taken off my robe – shall I don it again?"

His abstention from the media did not stem only from his desire to end the political chapter of his life. He lost much of his trust in the media during the last decade of his life. He sensed that journalists turned to him not because they wished to hear his opinions, but because they wished to goad his former political rivals in the religious Zionist camp. He did not want to be used to cause commotion or harm religious Judaism.

He replaced the media with other tools in order to get his message out. Students who had summarized the discourses he delivered at the yeshiva frequently urged him to publish them for the broader yeshiva community, and he acceded. In 2002, his students published a booklet of five discourses delivered by Rav Amital on the tension between halakhic commitment and individual experience. In the booklet, entitled *Between Religious Experience and Religious Commitment,* Rav Amital warned of the hazards inherent in placing spiritual experience at the center of man's worship of God: "Acceptance of the Torah that is based only on willing assent, without a basis of coercion, is deficient." The expectation of experiencing a "connection" to mitzvot, he cautioned, could lead to selectivity, in which there is a need for "specific identification with each individual mitzva. Then what happens is that one is able to 'connect' to certain mitzvot, but with other mitzvot, one has less success." Rav Amital did not only point out the hazard; he suggested ways of dealing with the phenomenon. For example, in one of the discourses he suggested viewing commitment to mitzvot as loyalty to God, which is part of human nature: "Loyalty is something that a person can be proud of."

In another discourse, he proposed a different strategy:

> In light of the reluctance of the youth to identify with "obligation," we need to raise the banner of "responsibility." To a certain extent, responsibility is even more binding than obligation, but on the other hand it is a gentler concept that also gives one a sense of satisfaction: if a certain responsibility is placed upon someone, it means that he is worthy of it.

> In the words of Ḥazal, being responsible means being a guarantor: "All of Israel are guarantors for one another." This means that the Jewish people is a living web of humanity, in which every limb is concerned for the welfare of every other and is responsible to do its utmost to improve the other's situation. A sense of responsibility towards others means that a person does not look about for a cushion to sit on while his companions are suffering. Moshe sat upon a rock as the Israelites battled against Amalek because he felt himself a partner in their suffering. Likewise, we are required to feel a sense of partnership and to assume the responsibility of doing what we can to improve society as a whole. One who limits his concern to his own personal well-being – even by focusing on his spiritual well-being – is likened by the Gemara in *Avoda Zara* to someone who has no God.

Most of the booklet was collected from talks that Rav Amital gave at the yeshiva's annual Ḥanukka banquet. His annual Ḥanukka discourse became an occasion of interest to his students, and eventually beyond the walls of the yeshiva as well. In these discourses, he addressed current events and moods in religious Zionism, and changes in the national-religious Torah world. In the discourse from the 2002 Ḥanukka party, entitled "Religious Insecurity and its Cures," Rav Amital addressed a midrash cited in Maharal's *Netivot Olam* that records a debate about which biblical verse represents the greatest principle in the Torah. Best known is Rabbi Akiva's verse of choice, "Love your neighbor as yourself" (Lev. 19:18). Another opinion states that there is a more inclusive verse, which pertains to the daily burnt-offering: "The first lamb you shall sacrifice in the morning and the second lamb you shall sacrifice in the evening" (Ex. 29:39). Rav Amital explained, "Stability and consistency are a great principle in the Jewish system of education" and then added:

> I believe that the vacillation that characterizes our day stems from insecurity. I have nothing against quick fixes, but whoever thinks he can heal the ills of our generation through the songs of Rabbi Shlomo Carlebach, by merely intensifying emotions, is mistaken. The enthusiasm generated is fleeting. People will always need to

> seek out some new thrill. Torah study, on the other hand, is an everlasting value that remains with us long after we close the book.
>
> We must present two important messages. First, the Torah has not lost an iota of its charm; it is as relevant as ever. The problem lies not in the Torah but in what we have added to it. Second, quick fixes are not enough. We must return to the path of arduous study; we must toil and invest in the acquisition of knowledge. Only if we remember these two values and work towards their achievement, will we be able to ascend the path which leads to the House of God.

In the summer of 2002, Rav Amital compiled a list of twenty principles that he saw as the yeshiva's primary messages. At the request of his colleagues, Rav Amital gave a series of lectures on all twenty of these themes. The lectures were recorded, transcribed, and edited by R. Amnon Bazak, a *ram* in the yeshiva. In the fall of 2004, the lectures were published as a book, *VeHaAretz Natan Livnei Adam* (*But the Earth He has Given to Man*). The name of the book reflects its central message: responsibility. Among the book's most prominent themes are natural morality, the role of individualism in the service of God, sincerity and spontaneity in prayer, the importance of ethical behavior ("*derekh eretz*"), which precedes even the Torah, man's responsibility toward his society, and basic sensitivity toward all humanity, created in the image of God. The English translation of the book appeared in 2005 under the title *Jewish Values in a Changing World.*

In the spring of 2005, another work by Rav Amital was published: *Resisei Tal* (*Droplets of Dew*). This work, edited by Rav Amital's son Yoel, collected many of his Talmudic and halakhic novellae. Over the course of several months, father and son sat together poring over the issues addressed in the book. Rav Amital added two chapters at the end of the book in which he recorded his recollections about his mentor, R. Ḥayyim Yehuda Levi, and his grandmother, Dina. In the preface, Rav Amital explained why he agreed, after so many years of teaching Torah, to publish his novellae: "For various reasons, I was hesitant to publish this book, but my loyal students – my son and sons-in-law foremost among them – prevailed upon me that it would benefit my students in Israel and abroad, as well as our descendants as they grow in Torah and scholarship."

Another reason for the publication of *Resisei Tal* stemmed from Rav Amital's belief that a Rosh Yeshiva must be able to display Talmudic virtuosity. In an interview with *Nekuda* in late 2004, he criticized a recent phenomenon of Rashei Yeshiva not giving *shiurim* in halakha or Talmud:

> The ability to give an abstract *shiur* on halakhic matters was once a *sine qua non* for a Rosh Yeshiva. Now someone can be a Rosh Yeshiva without giving a single *shiur*. Someone recently asked me if I had seen the film "Ushpizin." He told me that you see a "real Rosh Yeshiva" in it. So I asked him if the Rosh Yeshiva in the movie gives a *shiur* on the Rambam…

Rav Amital did not deny that the publication of his Talmudic novellae was designed to lend gravitas to his statements on other subjects. "It's important to me that they hear my *shiurim*, so that they take me seriously," he remarked, "Nowadays there are all sorts of rabbis who are complete *amaratzim* (ignoramuses), and yet it doesn't stop them from making pronouncements in the name of the Torah."

Rav Amital turned eighty years old in October 2004. A year earlier, he began to be preoccupied with thoughts of what would happen to the yeshiva he built once he was no longer there. His sober and realistic vision once again prevailed: though uncommon in yeshivot, Rav Amital decided to name his successor while he still served as Rosh Yeshiva. "Experience has shown," he explained, "that in every yeshiva where a successor was not appointed in advance, the yeshiva split up into two or three yeshivot, or completely changed its format." He first shared his thoughts with his old colleagues, Rav Lichtenstein and Moshko. He then held meetings with every *ram* on the yeshiva's faculty, in order to solicit their views. The yeshiva administration decided to appoint a search committee. The committee included representatives from the administration, faculty, and alumni from Israel and abroad. They deliberated the issue for six months, without the involvement of the Rashei Yeshiva. The discussions were confidential – very few people even knew of the

(photo: Eliyahu Yanai)

Three partners: With Rav Lichtenstein and Moshko on Moshko's eightieth birthday.

committee's existence. Yedaya Hacohen, a member of the board, drove with Rav Amital every day from Jerusalem to the yeshiva and back, and they never broached the subject.

The search committee could not find a single candidate who would be able to replace Rav Amital, so they tapped two: R. Ya'akov Medan and R. Barukh Gigi, both alumni of the yeshiva who had been serving as *ramim* there for many years. They were asked to join Rav Amital and Rav Lichtenstein as Rashei Yeshiva. The committee made it clear that when the time came, another Rosh Yeshiva would be appointed as Rav Lichtenstein's successor, one who would have strong relationships with the yeshiva's English-speaking foreign students.

The committee elected Yedaya Hacohen to present its decisions to Rabbis Amital and Lichtenstein. As usual, they each reacted differently: Rav Amital glanced at Yedaya's memo for no more than a few seconds before agreeing. Rav Lichtenstein took the memo and said he would look into it before rendering his opinion. It did not take long, though, for Rav Lichtenstein to approve the committee's recommendation.

On 28 Elul, 5764 (September 14, 2004), Rav Amital and Rav Lichtenstein gathered the yeshiva students and informed them of the decisions taken and the changes they could expect. Rav Amital elaborated:

> I am not retiring, but with a view toward the yeshiva's mission and future, I wish to prepare for such a time that I will no longer

> be able to serve as Rosh Yeshiva. After the giving of the Torah, God said to the Israelites (Deut. 5:26), "Go back to your tents." There's a Hasidic saying that interprets this verse as follows: God said to the people of Israel, "You were so good during the revelation at Mt. Sinai, you said 'We will do and we will listen,' but now let's see how you do at home…"
>
> The guiding principle of the yeshiva has always been to concern itself not only with what goes on in the *beit midrash*, but mainly with how our students look once they leave the *beit midrash*. That same approach gave me the sense that I must concern myself with what will happen to the yeshiva once I leave…
>
> Thank God, I feel that I still have strength and I still have much to contribute to the yeshiva. Every *shiur* that I give, thank God, students still come, interested in what I have to say.

Rav Amital then explained the selection of Rabbis Medan and Gigi, praising them and their credentials, but adding: "We did not choose Rav Medan and Rav Gigi because they are greater than the others. Thank God, this yeshiva has a faculty full of Torah scholars worthy of being Rashei Yeshiva, and it can be said of every *ram* that he foregoes the honor due to him." He related that the *ramim* accepted the selection willingly and with love, and then he asked the students to accept the appointments as well, making it clear that the two new Rashei Yeshiva would serve alongside him and Rav Lichtenstein: "If Rav Lichtenstein and I could manage, the four of us will get along just fine."

Right after the dramatic speech, the students spontaneously burst into singing and dancing. News of the new appointments traveled fast and far beyond the yeshiva world – it is not often that an incumbent Rosh Yeshiva anoints his successors. Rav Amital's act was considered noble and admirable, reminding many of his decision thirty years earlier to invite Rav Lichtenstein to be co-Rosh Yeshiva.

It was not only the appointment of the new Rashei Yeshiva that was surprising – it was their identity as well. *Ma'ariv* picked up on Rav Gigi's Moroccan origins. Its headline proclaimed, "A First: Sephardic Rabbi to Head a Leading *Hesder* Yeshiva." The national-religious com-

(photo: Gershon Ellinson)

Four Rashei Yeshiva: Standing, from right to left: Rav Barukh Gigi, Rav Amital, Rav Lichtenstein, Rav Ya'akov Medan.

munity, however, was more interested in the appointment of Rav Medan. Many people were surprised that Rav Amital, the founder of Meimad, would be succeeded by the right-wing Rav Medan, one of the most prominent rabbis in the settler leadership, who often clashed with his mentor on political issues.

But those who knew Rav Amital were not surprised. They knew that political stances were not a major consideration in his assessment of his students. Shortly after the announcement of the new appointments, I interviewed Rav Amital for *Nekuda*. When I asked him how he would respond to questions about the differences between his worldview and those of his heirs, he replied: "The people who think like that are essentially talking about politics. They don't understand that politics are marginal here." When I posed the same question to Rav Medan, he answered: "It seems so natural and straightforward to me that I don't see any problem. I acquired my love for Eretz Yisrael from him; he's full of love for Eretz Yisrael. Our disagreements were on the tactical level, where we have full freedom of expression and freedom of action. This freedom is not due to indifference, but rather to the educational principle of respect for every person and every opinion." When I asked Rav Medan about his commitment to the path charted by Rav Amital, he told me a story that Rav Amital used to tell the students in the yeshiva's early years. The story is about a Hasidic *rebbe* who was named his father's successor but did not follow his father's path. When the old-timers asked him why, he replied, "I'm doing exactly what my father did. He did everything differently than his father, so I'm doing everything differently than mine…" On the other hand, Rav Medan went on to note that he would indeed try to emulate certain aspects of Rav Amital's leadership: "Freedom, space, and love for every proponent of Torah, even if he charts a different course, are the most important things I learned from Rav Amital, and I will act accordingly."

Rabbis Medan and Gigi were installed in Tevet 5766 (January 2006). At their investiture ceremony, which took place on Ḥanukka, Rav Amital noted that he was aware of the sensitive situation that the new Rashei Yeshiva were entering – serving alongside two long-standing Rashei Yeshiva. Addressing them, he said:

> One thing I promise myself even more than I promise you: due to this sensitivity, I will hold myself back in every way from teaching you and guiding you in the principles of leadership, of how to be a Rosh Yeshiva. I will enjoin myself to be a sage, not a prophet. What's the difference between a sage and a prophet? A prophet who suppresses his prophecy deserves death, but a sage may suppress his wisdom. I promise that I will suppress my wisdom, and I suggest that you do, too. One of the hardest parts of education is knowing when to teach and when to suppress the prophecy.

To illustrate the power of silence, Rav Amital told the audience about a student who, at the end of his time in the yeshiva, went to Rav Amital to thank him for his silence. The student told Rav Amital that he had previously done something worthy of reprimand, and he knew that Rav Amital had heard about it. For two years, as he went to wish Rav Amital "Shabbat shalom," he anticipated rebuke. The student claimed that Rav Amital's silence caused him to regret his actions more than any admo-

With young granddaughters Yael and Sari.

nition. "It's one of the hardest things to do," Rav Amital concluded, "to know when to speak and when to remain silent."

Rav Amital warned Rabbis Gigi and Medan that their new job would be very difficult and full of tension:

> There's only one positive form of tension in a Rosh Yeshiva's job, and I'm not sure that I still experience it. Several years ago I resolved that the moment I no longer feel tension before delivering a discourse or *shiur* to the entire yeshiva – I would retire. After forty years as Rosh Yeshiva, I must admit that I don't always experience that tension. This positive tension – I wish it upon you until the day you retire.

He also suggested to the new Rashei Yeshiva not to be deterred by mistakes: "If someone does nothing, he won't make mistakes. I also made mistakes – because I acted. There is no need to be afraid."

He concluded by discussing his own retirement: "Only God can take me away from the yeshiva. The vitality that God has given me even at my advance age would be harmed if I stopped coming to the *beit midrash*. So there's no reason to leave."

When Rav Amital turned eighty, Amos Safrai, the head of the yeshiva's alumni association, decided that the milestone should be celebrated with a special event. Rav Amital refused. He feared that the event would bear the characteristics of a personality cult, a phenomenon that he found revolting. Safrai persisted: "I said to him, 'Rabbi, you have so much you'd like to say, and your statements need a stage. You don't interview like you used to, so here's an opportunity to speak up; people want to listen." Rav Amital eventually relented, but only on two conditions: that there not be any overtones of a personality cult, and that the event not be funded by the yeshiva.

Safrai had learned Rav Amital's preferences over the years. In planning prior yeshiva events, he had internalized Rav Amital's likes and dislikes. While planning the yeshiva's twenty-fifth anniversary, some parents suggested hiring a professional emcee to run the event. Rav Amital vehemently disagreed. As Safrai recalls, "He banged on the table and threatened to cancel the event, saying that professional emcees cost money and like to hear themselves talk; 'We don't need an emcee's jokes to while the evening away,' he said. So I asked him who should be emcee. 'Are you mute? Do you stutter?' he replied, 'You should emcee!' And so it was."

Rav Amital's eightieth birthday celebration, which took place on Lag Ba-Omer, May 27, 2005, was organized according to the same principles. The entire program was produced by yeshiva alumni. Yitzḥak Recanati, an alumnus, produced a short film about Rav Amital's life; Aviad Hacohen edited and published an anthology of Rav Amital's moral teachings, *Kol Yehuda* (which appeared in English in 2008 as *Commitment and Complexity: Jewish Wisdom in an Age of Upheaval*); both emcees were yeshiva alumni; and the event had the musical accompaniment of an orchestra comprised of students and alumni.

Over fifteen hundred people attended the event, which was held on a Friday at Jerusalem's International Convention Center. Rav Amital's opening benediction – an emotional recitation of the *berakha* of *Sheheḥeyanu* – electrified the crowd. During the intermission, he ascended the stage again and addressed the audience: "Since many of you came from far away, anyone who feels they need to go home to prepare for Shabbat need not stay for the second half. I have already received your love; you're free to go." Rabbanit Amital viewed that statement as an expression of his general educational outlook: "It revealed what he really thought: you can go; you're not attached to me by an umbilical cord…"

The celebration took place several months before the Gaza Disengagement, and the mood of the national-religious public was already very tense. One of the speakers at the event was Bentzi Lieberman, Chairman of the Judea, Samaria, and Gaza Council and an alumnus of the yeshiva's ninth class. Lieberman noted that at critical junctures of his public activity, he often asked himself what Rabbi Amital would advise him to do. "It is clear to me that he does not agree with the content of my activity, but I believe he is proud that I am working for what I believe in."

Although Lieberman was undoubtedly correct, on the particular issue of uprooting Gush Katif settlements Rav Amital agreed with the Council of Judea, Samaria, and Gaza that the process was misguided. In an interview with *Haaretz*'s Yair Sheleg some two weeks after the birthday celebration, Rav Amital said of the Gaza Disengagement: "I am very unhappy with that plan, mainly because of its unilateral aspect. The fact that it is unilateral also adds to the pain the evacuees feel, because in this situation they also do not understand why they have to undergo the pain."

With his eldest granddaughter, Orit, on her wedding day.

The day before Tisha B'Av, 5765 (August 12, 2005), just days before the Gaza Disengagement Plan's execution, Rav Amital delivered a discourse in the yeshiva in which he criticized the faith expressed by some opponents of the disengagement that the plan would not be carried out because God does not want it. "Anyone who lived through the Holocaust cannot speak like that," he said, "to my great chagrin, I live in the real world. In Hungary, before the Holocaust, I heard rabbis saying similar things; since then, I don't prophesy about what God can or can't do. I try to cope with reality, not speculate on which reality God would prefer."

On 1 Elul, 5766 (August 24, 2006), Rav Amital went to *ma'ariv* at the main synagogue in Givat Mordekhai. It was a particularly dark night – the moonless night of Rosh Ḥodesh – and on his way home, Rav Amital failed to notice a new cement block that had been placed illegally near the synagogue to prevent cars from parking on the sidewalk. He tripped over the block and injured his knee. Medical examinations showed that he had broken his kneecap, and Rav Amital went in for surgery the next day. He was confined to a wheelchair for over a month, but on Yom Kippur he stood up to lead the services, as he did every year. The next day,

With great-granddaughter Roni.

With Rabbanit Miriam at the Yakirei Gush Etzion ceremony, 1998.

his injured knee began to get infected again, forcing Rav Amital to have another operation. His family recounts that throughout the ordeal, as his knee continued to swell and cause him pain, they never heard a word of complaint about his pain or physical limitations. At the bar mitzva of his grandson Itamar Yishai, which took place three days after his injury, he told the young man: "Your grandfather has gone through a lot in his life; a broken knee and an operation are small potatoes."

At precisely the same time, Rav Lichtenstein was recuperating from a hip injury caused by a fall. Rav Amital jokingly said that this, too, proved their solidarity as well as their differences: "Rav Lichtenstein's wife noted that even now we're different. I injured my knee, but he injured his hip..."

As Rabbis Lichtenstein and Amital recovered from their injuries, the two new Rashei Yeshiva, Rabbis Gigi and Medan, took on greater roles in running the yeshiva. Against this background of the temporary absence of the elder Rashei Yeshiva, Rav Amital's foresight in installing his successors while still going strong became even more pronounced. It prevented an unhealthy leadership vacuum as both original Rashei Yeshiva nursed their injuries.

After another two months of slow recuperation, Rav Amital gradually began returning to his activities. Within a few weeks he was giving *shiurim* at almost the same frequency as before the injury.

Leading yeshiva students in prayer at the Western Wall, Hoshana Rabba, 2007.

"An elder who sits and studies"

Between Rosh HaShana and Yom Kippur of 2007, Rav Amital posted a letter in the *beit midrash* in which he informed his students:

> With praise and gratitude to God, I have begun my fortieth year as Rosh Yeshiva. For thirty-seven of those forty years, I was joined in this capacity by my colleague, Rav Aharon Lichtenstein. At the

> end of this year, I will conclude, please God, my tenure as Rosh Yeshiva. Of course, I do not intend to leave the yeshiva, and as long as God gives me strength and health, I will continue teaching Torah, but in the capacity of an elder who sits and studies in the yeshiva.

His decision to completely retire from being Rosh Yeshiva coalesced over the summer of 2007. He felt that continuing to serve as Rosh Yeshiva alongside his young successors would hamper their ability to take full responsibility for running the yeshiva.

He concluded his letter with a request to the yeshiva students: "This year, God willing, I will join you for Simḥat Torah for the last time as Rosh Yeshiva. As such, the participation of each and every one of you in the yeshiva's celebration of the Torah will add do my joy and satisfaction." The students of the yeshiva responded *en masse*, returning from their vacations to celebrate Simḥat Torah in the yeshiva.

(photo: Ḥaggai M. Cohen)

"Vetaher libeinu...

Rav Amital had always been the star of the show on Simḥat Torah in the yeshiva. In one of the yeshiva's first years, he taught his students a stirring melody for "*Om Ani Ḥoma*," a liturgical composition for the *hoshanot* services on Sukkot, and instituted the custom of singing it at the onset of Simḥat Torah. He sang the same composition to a different tune during the dancing of *hakafot*. Occasionally, during the dancing, Rav Amital stood in the center of the circle on a chair or table as everyone gathered around, and he began singing the song that became his anthem: "*vetaher libeinu le'ovdekha be'emet*," "Purify our hearts to serve You in truth."

(photo: Gershon Ellinson)

… le'ovdekha be'emet"

On that final Simḥat Torah as Rosh Yeshiva, Rav Amital was asked by Rav Lichtenstein to speak briefly during the *hakafot*. Surprisingly, he spoke about the difficulty that he, as a Holocaust survivor, experienced during the Jewish holidays. "It's hard for me to say '*Ata veḥartanu*,' 'You have chosen us,' in the festival prayers," he told his students, "I also ask myself how worshippers at Auschwitz and Mauthausen could recite these words…" These feelings explain the emotion that overcame him as he led the High Holiday prayers whenever he reached those sections that describe the election of the people of Israel and God's love for his people.

Chapter Twenty-Two

A Simple Jew

Students ask me whether the State of Israel is indeed the "first flowering of our redemption." This time, I'll answer with a story. It is told about Reb Levi Yitzḥak of Berdichev that one year, as he led Ne'ila *on Yom Kippur, he suddenly stopped just before reciting the* berakha *of* Melekh sole'aḥ *("King Who pardons our iniquities and the iniquities of his people, Israel…") and was silent for several moments. The congregation waited with barely-controlled tension, but Reb Levi Yitzḥak continued to keep quiet. Suddenly, he blurted out the* berakha *loudly and quickly. Later, when he was asked to explain himself, he replied that in heaven, there was a terrible accusation against the Jews that was preventing the pardon of their sins. He therefore could not recite the* berakha. *Reb Levi Yitzḥak continued:*

> *I tried this way and that, but I could not overcome the accusation until I recalled an anecdote from my childhood and discovered a way out. When we were kids and there was something good to eat in*

> *the house that my mother did not want us to eat right away, we would go right up next to her and loudly recite the* berakha *of* shehakol *over the food. This would force her to give us what we wanted, for otherwise it would be a superfluous* berakha*… So I did the same thing in my prayers. When I saw that all hope was lost, I loudly recited the* berakha*: "King Who pardons our iniquities and the iniquities of his people, Israel" and didn't give God a choice. Now he has to forgive us, because otherwise it's a superfluous* berakha*…*

> *So, too, with the "first flowering of our redemption." Perhaps if we recite this phrase with special concentration in our prayers, it will indeed come true.*
>
> From a speech at Yeshivat Har Etzion's fortieth anniversary celebration, June 2008

In 2008, the yeshiva marked its fortieth anniversary. Throughout that year, Rav Amital participated in the various alumni reunions that the yeshiva organized. At one such get-together, Rav Amital wished to discuss the significance of a fortieth anniversary. He mentioned the foundational Hasidic story that he told at that first meeting with prospective students who asked what would make the yeshiva unique.

> I told them then that if we studied Torah but did not hear the baby's cry, then there was something wrong with our Torah study. We educate not only toward the love of Torah, but toward the love of the Jewish people as well. We are not disconnected; rather we are attentive to the cries of the world. A lot has happened over the past forty years; the problems have changed, but the yeshiva has always had something to say. Forty years ago there was messianic euphoria; now there's a lot of doubt, pessimism, and despair. The

Rav Amital at the 40th Year Celebrations

As part of the yeshiva's fortieth anniversary celebrations, re-enacting its founding at Kfar Etzion. To the left in the foreground is Rav Yoel Bin-Nun.

yeshiva was relevant then, and we're relevant now in a completely different world. That's a big deal.

Rav Amital added that this may have been Ḥazal's intent when they said (*Avoda Zara* 5b) that one does not know the mind of his mentor until forty years have passed, explaining: "If the master's words are still relevant to the student after so many decades, it's an indication that he indeed understood his teacher."

One such reunion took place right after the terrible attack on Yeshivat Merkaz HaRav, in which eight yeshiva students were killed. Rav Amital addressed the pronouncement of a *ḥaredi* rabbi that the attack occurred because of Zionism and the state. "How can someone say that after the Holocaust?" cried Rav Amital, "You have no answer for the millions, so you have the nerve, the *chutzpa*, to explain why this happened?" Rav Amital recounted how some youngsters asked him how such attacks can be theologically justified, and he responded that there is no explanation. "I told them to undertake some Torah study or philanthropic project and they would be able to hold on, but I didn't have an answer. Anyone who says he has an answer is lying. That's our generation's test. All of a sudden there are those who know God's mind, who know what's going on in heaven." He went on to argue that one

(photo: Gershon Ellinson)

Addressing an outdoor gathering at the yeshiva's 40th anniversary celebration.

of the reasons for the crisis in religious Zionism is the fact that rabbis spoke with certainty about God's will:

> After the victory of the Six Day Way they said that God, as it were, issued a halakhic ruling that Eretz Yisrael is the most important thing. That created expectations, and when those expectations were not fulfilled, there was disappointment. Following our sages and prophets, we try to understand, but we are not certain. God doesn't run the world with human reason. There is Divine providence that we cannot begin to understand. If people would realize that we cannot understand everything, that we are merely trying to make sense of things, it would solve a lot of problems.

The main event marking the yeshiva's fortieth anniversary took place the day after Shavuot, 2008. Hundreds of alumni gathered at the yeshiva campus for a day filled with *shiurim*, reunions, and discussions about the yeshiva's approach. At the end of the day there was a large assembly in Alon Shvut. Rav Amital, as was his wont for such events, spoke last,

(photo: Gershon Ellinson)

With the yeshiva's first two classes on the occasion of the fortieth anniversary celebration. Standing to the right of Rav Amital are Yedaya Hacohen, Moshko, and Ḥanan Porat. To his left is Rav Yoel Bin-Nun.

and as usual his speech played on the audience's emotions. His voice trembling, Rav Amital said:

> I will permit myself to say what I have not permitted myself to say for the past forty years. God has given me the privilege of being a Rosh Yeshiva. Since the times of Rabbi Akiva, there was no Rosh Yeshiva who taught Torah and then sent his students off to war, after which they returned to the *beit midrash*. This is a historic phenomenon. For forty years I have held that in; I have not had the courage to say it. I came from Europe alone, by the grace of God, and suddenly found myself needing to inject faith and optimism in the yeshiva after some students did not return from the war. They all expected me to boost morale and faith, and God gave me the strength. I can understand this in only one way – that I represent my teachers who were consumed at Auschwitz, and with them my peers. That's what gave me the strength to found and lead a yeshiva.

After his emotionally charged speech, Rav Amital called out to his students: "Let us celebrate together the fact that you were students at this yeshiva," and began singing "*Ve'ata banim, shiru laMelekh*" ("Now, children, sing to the King"). Within seconds hundreds of alumni and their children had burst into singing and dancing around Rav Amital.

On 28 Elul, 5768 (September 28, 2008), as had been planned a year earlier, Rav Amital gave notice that his tenure as Rosh Yeshiva of Yeshivat Har Etzion had ended. In a talk he gave in the *beit midrash*, he announced the appointment of R. Mosheh Lichtenstein as the new Rosh Yeshiva alongside the other three then serving. Rav Mosheh, the eldest son of Rav Aharon Lichtenstein, is an alumnus of the yeshiva and later served as a *ram*. Like Rabbis Medan and Gigi, he was selected, in a process that began with Rav Amital's request, by a search committee's recommendation to the yeshiva's administration.

Rav Amital emphasized that he was only retiring from the position of Rosh Yeshiva – meaning that he would no longer deliver a weekly *shiur klali* to the entire yeshiva – but would continue on in the capacity of an "elder who sits and studies in the yeshiva." "I will continue not because I must, but because I want to," he told his students, "In another two months I'll be eighty-four, not a young man, and will have been with the yeshiva for forty-one years. I know that in order for me to stay strong I must be in touch with students and with the yeshiva. I will continue to serve you faithfully, and I want you to know that the yeshiva is first and foremost about the students; the Rashei Yeshiva are here to serve the students."

Rav Mosheh Lichtenstein's investiture took place a month later, on 29 Tishrei, 5769 (October 28, 2008). In his address at the ceremony, Rav Amital felt the need to speak about why the yeshiva was not satisfied with just one Rosh Yeshiva:

> It became clear to us over time that the variety displayed by two Rashei Yeshiva with different styles of learning and leadership is of great value. It became one of the yeshiva's primary attractions. When the time came to turn the yeshiva over to the next generation, there was a problem: [Rav Aharon and I] came from two different *batei midrash* and two different worlds, but the new Rashei Yeshiva grew up in the same *beit midrash*. Nevertheless, I continually conveyed the message that the yeshiva must preserve its multifaceted character. We therefore decided to seek out Torah scholars worthy of serving as Rashei Yeshiva, but with different personalities and strengths. With these three new Rashei Yeshiva, we will be able to preserve the variety that made this yeshiva unique all these years. They represent different approaches in their leadership qualities and in their methodologies, and I hope that the singularity of this yeshiva will continue.

That entire year, Rav Amital continued giving *shiurim* and delivering discourses at the yeshiva and visiting during the week and for Shabbat. The desire of the younger students to hear him speak thrilled him anew each time. At one alumni reunion he told a story:

> First year students come to me and ask that I give them *shiurim*. I finish one *shiur* and they ask for another. It gives me strength. If I'm not elderly, if I still have an ounce of youthful vigor, it is only

> because of those young students who want to hear me. What do they want from an eighty-year-old Jew? Apparently what I have to say is still relevant.

On 15 Av 5769 (August 5, 2009), a student from the yeshiva's fortieth class, Uriel Liwerant, was killed in a tank accident during a training exercise in the Golan Heights. Rav Amital asked permission to eulogize his student, but when he got up to speak, he broke down crying and said: "How can I, at my age, eulogize a student?"

On Sukkot, 5770 (2009), Rav Amital's health took a turn for the worse. He experienced a relapse of a cancer that had long been in remission, and as a result experienced terrible pain and weakness. Throughout the holiday he stayed with his son Rav Yoel at Sha'alvim. Troubled by his medical condition, he told his son that he felt extremely feeble and asked that people pray for his wellbeing. Clear-headed as ever, he instructed that upon his death he should be eulogized by only three people, and that all three eulogies together not take longer than a half an hour. The next day was Hoshana Rabba, the last day of Sukkot, and Rav Amital went to the yeshiva as he did every year, to spend Simḥat Torah with the yeshiva students. But for the first time, he did not participate in all of the *hakafot* or lead the Musaf service.

The next month, Rav Amital was absent from the yeshiva as he underwent medical treatment. He came to the yeshiva only once, for an event in honor of R. Binyamin Tabory, one of the yeshiva's longest-standing faculty members, upon his retirement. When asked to speak, Rav Amital chose to address his striving to be a normal Jew:

> Over the past forty years, I have faced one challenge – to be a normal Jew, and more importantly, to have normal students and friends. Anyone with even the slightest spiritual interest also has a bit of insanity… I strive to be normal. Rav Tabory is one of the most normal of the people I've worked with – whoever understands this fully knows that it's a big deal. It's possible that he has a crazy side as well, but I only know his normal side. Thank God, I have been privileged to be a friend and colleague to such a Jew.

In November 2009, Rav Amital had a heart attack and was hospitalized. During his hospital stay he was catheterized, and his body became very weak. He returned home a week later, but completely stopped traveling to the yeshiva and even had a hard time going to the local synagogue. At the initiative of several yeshiva alumni living in Jerusalem, a *minyan* was organized at the Amital home each Shabbat, attended by alumni and old-timers from Givat Mordekhai. One of the regulars described it as a "*minyan* of love" of students for their mentor.

The first Shabbat that the *minyan* was held, Rav Amital was called up for an *aliya* so that he could recite the *berakha* of *HaGomel,* thanking God for having survived his latest hospitalization. He recited the *berakhot* on the Torah slowly and with feeling, particularly when reaching the words "Who has chosen us from all peoples." He was again overcome by emotion when reciting *HaGomel* – "Who bestows good on the unworthy; who has bestowed on me much good." R. Shaul Wieder, an alumnus of the yeshiva and a regular participant in the *minyan,* related how Rav Amital said each word slowly, heartrendingly, emotionally, clearly ascribing meaning to each word.

Each Shabbat that a *minyan* was held at the Amital home, a kiddush followed the services, during which the worshippers sang several tunes together. Among the regular tunes at the kiddush were several from the Modzhitzer Hasidic court, including "*Yismakh Moshe*" and "*HaKol Yeshabeḥukha.*" While they sang, Rav Amital would close his eyes and move his head in time. One such Shabbat he said to the worshippers: "I don't know what I did to merit you coming to be with me." Another time, he told them, with tearing eyes and all choked up: "You are giving me a free gift and unconditional love. I don't understand why." He meticulously thanked each worshipper individually for joining the *minyan* and would chat with the kids who came along with their fathers.

Throughout his illness, Rav Amital was surrounded by doting family members. Numerous students and alumni came to visit him and see how he was doing. Several alumni who had become physicians kept abreast of his health situation and assisted in his treatment. Two such students were Dr. Beni Gesundheit and Dr. Gabriel Breuer. Professor Sammy Adler, whose son studied in the yeshiva, was also involved in the treatment. Dr. Breuer was impressed by the noble bearing that

Rav Amital maintained throughout his illness: "Even when he was in intense pain, he never discussed it and always thanked me for everything." Something else that made an impression on Breuer was the complete harmony between Rav and Rebbetzin Amital, and between the two of them and the entire family that had enveloped them in love. Prof. Adler commented on the truthfulness and sincerity that characterized Rav Amital even during his illness: "During our discussions at every phase of the treatment he was straight as an arrow, free of rationalizations and evasions. I knew that every answer I got from him was true." Adler frequently discussed matters of Torah and faith with Rav Amital. During one of their conversations, Rav Amital showed him the Rambam's comments on the aphorism from *Avot* (3:16): "Receive everyone cheerfully." In his *Commentary on the* Mishna, the Rambam wrote: "One must receive every person – young and old, free and slave, every member of the human race – with cheer and good-heartedness." These comments made a deep impression on Adler. He copied and enlarged these words, framed them, and hung them in his clinic.

Dr. Beni Gesundheit, who kept abreast of Rav Amital during his hospitalization, recounts that despite his personal stature, he insisted that he not be given any special attention at the expense of other patients:

> When Rav Amital had a heart attack that brought him to the emergency room, I attempted to accelerate his case because he was in a state of life-threatening respiratory distress. An Arab patient who had injured his hand, but was not bleeding, stood nearby. Rav Amital insisted that the other patient be attended first, even though he was not in as much danger as Rav Amital, simply because he had been waiting longer.

During his hospital stay, Rav Amital endeared himself to the medical staff attending to him. Dr. Gesundheit tells how Rav Amital would take an interest in the wellbeing of the nurses and ask about their families. One of the nurses told Gesundheit, "Rav Amital gives meaning to my work." Dr. Gesundheit also regularly conversed with Rav Amital about matters of Torah, and reviewed ideas that often came up in Rav Amital's discourses. Rav Amital was very weak at the time and could barely speak, so he would listen to Gesundheit and react with a look of his eyes. "Throughout his illness," Gesundheit relates, "I witnessed how he fulfilled the verse (Eccl. 7:12) 'Wisdom preserves the wellbeing of its possessor.'"

Rav Amital's conversations with students and alumni who visited during his illness were generally connected to their various activities. One alumnus who visited regularly and participated in the *minyan* at Rav Amital's home was Dr. Yehuda Frankel, a psychiatrist by profession. Frankel, who advised Rav Amital on matters pertaining to his health, would share professional dilemmas with Rav Amital. In one of their conversations, he shared with Rav Amital a profound dispute within the world of psychology about the evil within man and within the world. He presented both sides of the debate: are evil, violence, and aggression reactions to loss, injury, and frustration, or is man inherently, *a priori*, and congenitally wicked? Rav Amital answered Frankel with a middle position: "I learned that God created man with two impulses: an impulse for construction and an impulse for destruction."

On Shabbat of the first day of Ḥanukka (December 12, 2009), Rav Amital was called to the Torah again at the *minyan* in his home, and again recited the *berakhot* with great feeling. After the services he told those present: "Gentlemen, I wish to mention that today is a very special day for me and my family. It's the day that we mark my *aliya* to Eretz Yisrael. Generally we celebrate with the whole family, but since today is Shabbat, you are in lieu of family." His son Rav Yoel, who was present that Shabbat, wanted to give his father strength, saying: "You'll make it up to us next year, God willing."

The next day, the second day of Ḥanukka, a group of foreign students from the southern hemisphere, who had just completed a year of study at Yeshivat Har Etzion and were about to head home, visited Rav Amital at home. Rav Amital read to them the opening passage of the Rambam's Laws of Ḥanukka, where he emphasizes the restoration of Jewish sovereignty for two-hundred years as the primary impetus for marking the holiday: "The kings of the Hasmonean dynasty," Rav Amital continued, "engaged in civil war and did not bring honor to Israel. And yet according to the Rambam, the very fact that there was a Jewish kingdom was a great thing." Rav Amital added that one of the lessons of Ḥanukka is not to be afraid of disseminating Judaism, even abroad. "God will help you make a difference," he told them, "You have studied in yeshiva and now must repay those who sent you. You must try and make a difference, organize *shiurim,* and study Torah with friends. God will assist you in this endeavor."

Just before Pesaḥ 5770 (2010), a well-attended dinner was held in Ramat Gan in honor of Yeshivat Har Etzion. Rav Amital was unable to attend due to his weakness, but he sent his blessings by way of a movie clip that a member of his family recorded. Speaking in a voice choked with emotion, Rav Amital said:

> I have been ill these past six months, going from hospital to hospital. Thank God, I'm alive only by virtue of clinging (*devekut*) to God. I am strengthened by the fact that God helps me. This very fact – that I have nothing but my clinging to God, is what gives me strength and keeps me going. Thank God, I have gone through many different periods, but it has become clear to me that without God's kindness I would have had nothing to seek out in the world.

Rav Amital thanked the dinner participants for their attendance and said that he was exhilarated because their attendance attested to the fact that the yeshiva's alumni really care about their alma mater. "That was one of my messages, that students who studied in the yeshiva would have a certain commitment to it."

Upon the return of the yeshiva students from their Pesaḥ vacation, Rav Amital wrote to them:

> Greetings to all my precious students,
>
> I am grateful to God for the great opportunity to have been one of the heads of our yeshiva, and I pray to God to heal me and enable me to be active again as Rosh Yeshiva in our important yeshiva. Happy is your lot for having elected to be among its students who choose to study Torah out of a real thirst for God's word.

On the eve of Yom HaAtzma'ut in April 2010, after a year-and-a-half absence from the *beit midrash*, Rav Amital attended the festive prayer service at the yeshiva. He slowly entered the *beit midrash* supported by two of his sons-in-law. The excited students burst out singing "They shall praise God for His steadfast love, and wondrous deeds for mankind" (Ps. 107:15) and continued to sing until Rav Amital reached his seat, where his co-Rashei Yeshiva, R. Aharon Lichtenstein and R. Barukh Gigi, awaited him. The three energized rabbis stood together as the students encircled them and sang. Mordy Miller, a young student, described in the yeshiva's newsletter the students' feelings during Rav Amital's visit: "We would push our way through the dancing to be as close as possible, as though saying, 'We have been waiting for you, Rav Amital, and you have come. Though we cannot embrace you, know that we, who yearn to be close to you, are thrilled to see you.'" Rav Amital too was keyed up by his visit to the yeshiva. His wife reported that he could barely fall asleep that night.

The Shabbat *minyan* at the Amital home continued throughout the spring and into the summer. One Shabbat at the end of June, the *minyan* was joined by R. Isser Klonsky, the rabbi of Givat Mordekhai. That same Shabbat, one of the regulars sponsored a kiddush in honor of the birth of a grandson. Rav Amital expressed his wish that the youngster grow up to be a simple Jew, with no haughtiness. It was the last time that the *minyan*-goers would hear Rav Amital speak. The next Shabbat, though the *minyan* took place, he was already too weak to speak. He expressed his gratitude to the participants with his loving glances.

On Monday, 23 Tammuz, 5770 (July 5, 2010), the family sensed that Rav Amital's days were numbered. Two days later, Rav Aharon and Dr. Tovah Lichtenstein came to visit Rav Amital. Tears flowed freely as everyone present sensed that this was a farewell visit. A little while later Moshe Moskovic, Rav Amital's partner in founding the yeshiva, joined them as well. As they prepared to take their leave, Tovah Lichtenstein thanked Rav Amital for inviting her husband to serve alongside him as Rosh Yeshiva.

That afternoon, Rav Lichtenstein gave a spontaneous talk in the *beit midrash* of Yeshivat Har Etzion, informing them:

> To our great sorrow, Rav Amital's health has continued to deteriorate; his strength is wearing away. In this situation, we must feel that we bear a common burden as we plead for divine mercy. There is not much that we can do, individually or collectively. But to bear that burden, to feel the pain in our gut, to reawaken our sense of gratitude and admiration for the man – which are pillars of our spiritual lives – this we can and must do.

On Thursday, 26 Tammuz (July 8) in the afternoon, the doctors informed the family that Rav Amital's remaining time would be measured in hours. The entire family gathered at the Amital home. During that night, Rav Yoel read the words of the deathbed confession in his father's ears. Rav Amital was fully conscious and followed his son's words with alert eyes. All night the family prayed at his bedside, with Dr. Beni Gesundheit at their side. At 3:20 A.M. on Friday, 27 Tammuz, 5770 (July 9, 2010), Rav Amital returned his soul to its Creator. He passed away in his home, in his own bed, surrounded by the sacred tomes to which he devoted his life, and by his beloved family.

Thousands gathered at the Shamgar funeral home that afternoon to escort Rav Amital on his final journey. Rabbis, government ministers, Knesset members, hundreds of students and alumni of Yeshivat Har Etzion, and many simple Jews who admired Rav Amital, crowded into the streets around the small funeral home to pay their final respects.

As Rav Amital had requested, only three people eulogized him, and they tried to keep to his second request that the eulogies last no longer than half an hour. "My brother, my brother, Israel's chariots and horsemen," cried R. Aharon Lichtenstein, Rav Amital's long-time colleague at the yeshiva, invoking a biblical verse (II Kings 2:12). And, in the words of David's lament for Jonathan, he wept and continued, "You have been very dear to me; I am greatly pained for you, my brother" (II Sam. 1:26). Rav Lichtenstein promised that the yeshiva's faculty and Rav Amital's students would make sure that "the Torah he imparted, the values he sharpened and clarified, and the worship of God that he taught, would prosper and flourish in the hands of his students, and his students' students, forever more." R. Yoel Amital devoted his eulogy to the centrality of the twin concepts of *kiddush HaShem* and *ḥillul HaShem* in his father's life, and to the principle of silence that guided him. He spoke about the thousands of students that Rav Amital influenced, and how he served as an anchor for people who were distant from the Torah and who became closer to it as a result of their relationship with him: "Thousands of people regularly cite sayings and aphorisms that they heard from you." R. Shlomo Brin, a son-in-law and close disciple, spoke about Rav Amital's spiritual and educational lessons, comparing them to fragrances that filled the world: "You filled the world with fragrance; we have enjoyed these fragrances. We inhaled them deeply." He then spoke about Rav Amital's love for simple people. "You did not distinguish between simple folk and men of renown. You had real love for the Jewish people."

From the Shamgar funeral home, the funeral procession made its way to the Har HaMenuḥot cemetery in Jerusalem. Due to the abbreviated eulogies and the approach of Shabbat, the funeral did not take long – apropos of a man like Rav Amital who tried, throughout his life, to avoid imposing himself on others. Just hours before the onset of Shabbat, they laid to rest Rav Yehuda Amital – Torah scholar, extraordinary teacher, Rosh Yeshiva, and public leader – who strove to be a simple Jew.

(photo: Gershon Ellinson)

Thousands attend Rav Amital's funeral in Jerusalem.

Afterword

Kol Yehuda: An Outline of Rav Amital's Religious Thought

Aviad Hacohen

Rav Amital's thought is built upon several foundations: love of Torah and fear of Heaven; love of the people, land, and state of Israel; erudition; originality; courage; humanism; and the wisdom of integration – the incomprehensible synthesis of past with present, Holocaust with rebirth, Torah with morality, halakhic erudition with philosophy, and universalism with particularism.

One who truly wishes to become familiar with the corpus of Halakha should absorb the teachings of a great sage and attempt to discover its defining characteristics. The sages understood that the many types of trees in the forest can – and should – be distinguished by their own individuality. They said, "The words of Torah are fertile and multiple." This is especially true in our generation, in which it seems as though everyone publishes his own insights, and the earth is full of the knowledge of God.

So many writings on Torah seem to be carbon copies of each other. At times one thinks one is reading novel words of Torah, but they turn out to be already familiar. Countless Torah scholars teach in the same style.

However, there are times that a single, unique voice rises above the cacophony and is not swallowed up in the general noise. As the voices of other sages reverberate, a single voice emerges – a still, small voice, singular in its clarity and beauty.

Such was Rav Yehuda Amital's voice. Over the course of many years, this voice was virtually hidden, known only to his students, but swallowed up in the tumult, and unnoticed by the public. When the noise of the crowd subsided a little, Rav Amital's unique voice emerged and made itself heard – an original voice, pure and clear, voicing its unique insights into halakha, *Aggada* and Jewish thought.

Originality is one of the outstanding features of Rav Amital's teachings. In this context it is worth noting a fine distinction regarding the halakhot of purifying waters, articulated by R. Yitzḥak Hutner, the author of *Paḥad Yitzḥak* and one of the great twentieth century Rashei Yeshiva: According to the halakha, any quantity of water connected to a natural spring suffices to purify, whereas water that has been gathered into one place – a *mikveh* – requires a minimum of forty *se'ah* in order to render something pure. This is because the significance of even a trace of originality trumps a large quantity of second- or third-hand material. This is the power of originality.

In the following pages, I wish to offer a basic outline of Rav Amital's unique mode of thinking. It is extremely difficult to encompass thousands of classes, halakhic rulings, and essays on Jewish thought into just a few pages. Rather, the goal is to offer the reader a small taste of the richness, uniqueness, and breadth of Rav Amital's *oeuvre*.

LOVE AND STUDY OF TORAH

Rav Amital did not merely study and teach Torah; he loved it, constantly and powerfully. From his youth he set his eyes and heart on the Torah, immersed in his studies at all hours of the day or night, whether at home or away, in times of peace and times of desperation and war.

The Torah is multifaceted. It contains multiple layers of meaning, from the straightforward to the esoteric. Even with the emerging popularity of the "New Age," when many – even in the ranks of yeshivot – turn toward esoteric and mystical aspects of Torah, and spend their days studying works of Jewish thought and Hasidut, Rav Amital continued to emphasize the traditional curriculum of Talmud study with the commentaries of Rashi and the Tosafot, supplemented by other medieval and modern commentaries. For Rav Amital, this was the foundation upon which other layers – halakhic codes, responsa literature, and works of Jewish though, ethics, and Hasidut – could be built.

As in other areas of life, Rav Amital viewed the inclination toward works of Kabbala and Hasidut at the expense of Talmud study as a form of evasion. Study of the Talmud with its medieval commentators is difficult and demanding, requiring intense and prolonged effort. There are no shortcuts – not in education, and not in Talmud study. Only after long months and years of effort will one reach significant achievements in Talmud study.

Rav Amital expressed this approach on various occasions. For example, in a discourse at Yeshivat Har Etzion he stated:

> Wherever one does not bring Torah, other things will enter. Nothing is neutral. There is no room for the statement, "I'm not a *lamdan* [scholar]." If you aren't a *lamdan,* if you don't engage in Torah study, you'll end up engaging in frivolous matters. We do not aspire to disconnect ourselves from communal matters and needs. We are aware of and involved in what is going on in the nation.
>
> The whole idea of *hesder* is an expression of this involvement. Indeed, I believe that one cannot be involved in secular society without a strong Torah foundation. Without Torah, we will be left with nothing.
>
> The foundation of the Torah is the Oral Law. "The Holy One, blessed be He, forged a covenant with the people of Israel only for the sake of the Oral Law" [*Gittin* 60b]. The foundation of everything is the Talmudic debates of Abaye and Rava. After them, there is room for studying Tanakh and Jewish philosophy, but the foundation is the Oral Law. It holds a special, magical

> secret. Anyone who tries a different route – basing his study mainly on philosophy, Tanakh, or other subjects – is doomed to failure. One of the strategies of the evil inclination is to instill the feeling that "the *beit midrash* is the answer to everything," that you don't need to make any effort; that the *beit midrash* will create the atmosphere and influence you. Certainly, the atmosphere helps. But someone who builds his life on atmosphere alone ends up living in the air – *luftgescheft* – and has achieved nothing. A person must apply himself. He cannot simply follow his mood. He must arise to serve God, whether he feels like it or not. He must get to the *beit midrash* on time and open his Gemara, no matter what mood he's in.

True to his ideals, Rav Amital expected his students to continue studying Talmud in-depth even after they left the yeshiva. For him, it was insufficient to engage in the most popular contemporary form of Talmud study, *Daf Yomi* – the daily study of a page of Gemara which tends to move rapidly through the most complex of Talmudic discussions.

> It is important for a person to continue with in-depth Torah study his entire life, even after he has left full-time study in the *beit midrash*. This is not only because this is the highest level of Torah study, but because it is in this way that the service of God finds expression in its fullest intensity. In a world where so much importance is attached to the intellect, a person cannot possibly fulfill his obligation through Torah study that does not require great intellectual effort. The brain, the seat of the intellect, is man's most important organ. Should we content ourselves with serving God with our hands and other limbs – taking the *shofar* in our hands and blowing it with our mouths, donning *tefillin* and eating *matza* on Pesaḥ – and let our brains lie idle, uninvolved in His service?...The service of God will not survive in our day if its bearers are devoid of Torah scholarship. It is impossible to live a serious religious life without deep Torah learning.

Rav Amital viewed the importance of Talmud study with a historical perspective and broad vision, encompassing vast segments of time and space:

> A person who studies Torah "takes" God with him and creates a bond with Him. Even if we are unable to explain exactly how this bond is created, history proves that without intensive Torah study, nothing will remain. Jewish communities in which there was no Torah study, no occupation with the Talmudic debates of Abaye and Rava, did not survive. Go and look at all the curricular experiments that have been conducted to this day, go and visit all the various *batei midrash*, and you will see that the only institutions to survive are those where Gemara was and continues to be studied.

SCHOLARSHIP

As mentioned above, Rav Amital's thought is strongly connected to his time and place. Many other Torah sages immigrated to Israel like Rav Amital, but their Torah remained, for most of them, the Torah of exile. One cannot tell by looking at their Torah whether it was composed in the Holy Land after the restoration of Jewish sovereignty, or in some Diaspora community where Jews were a persecuted and despised minority.

Rav Amital's Torah is not like that. One example among many relates to the Laws of Kings as codified by the Rambam in his *Mishneh Torah*. The Rambam details the laws governing a Jewish king at war and distinguishes between mandatory and optional wars. What is an optional war? "A war against neighboring nations to extend the borders of Israel and to enhance his greatness and prestige." (*Mishneh Torah*, Laws of Kings 5:1)

Some *Rishonim*, such as R. Menaḥem HaMe'iri (fourteenth century Provence), explained that this referred to two types of optional wars: one "to extend the borders of Israel" and the other "to enhance his greatness and prestige."

This explanation seems fundamentally problematic. Is it conceivable that the king's desire "to enhance his greatness and prestige" would justify waging war, which entails pain, suffering, and bloodshed?

Some commentaries, such as that of R. Avraham de Boton,

Leḥem Mishneh, explain that the enhancement of the king's prestige is not merely a public relations ploy, but a deterrent that provides protection from potential enemies.

Like other commentaries, Rav Amital does not like this explanation: if this is what the Rambam meant, he would have said so explicitly.

In his attempt to resolve this difficulty, Rav Amital addresses another well-known law stated by the Rambam (ibid. 7:15):

> Once, however, he has entered into battle, he should put his reliance upon Him who is the Hope of Israel, their Savior in time of trouble. He should know that he is fighting for the Oneness of God. Therefore, when he risks his life, he should neither fear nor be affrighted... He who fights with all his heart, without fear, with the sole intention of sanctifying God's name, is assured that no harm will befall him and no evil will befall him.

Rav Amital emphasized that any waging of war – even optional war – must be with all one's heart and soul and for the sanctification of God's name, and that this law developed out of the Rambam's understanding of war generally.

According to the Rambam, the main objective of war is not defense or security related, but on the ideological and spiritual plane; at its root, war is fought against idolatry. When a nation accepts an offer of peace prior to the commencement of war, it is sufficient for them to accept the seven Noahide laws and acknowledge the unity of God. For this reason, the Rambam highlights the following (ibid. 4:9):

> [The king's] sole aim and thought should be to uplift the true religion, to fill the world with righteousness, to break the arm of the wicked, and to fight the battles of God. The prime reason for appointing a king was that he execute judgment and wage war, as it is written: "And that our king may judge us, and go out before us, and fight our battles" (I Sam. 8:20).

The wars of the Jewish people are not particularistic wars – they are universal. Even if their declared objectives are "to extend the borders of

Israel" or "to enhance the king's greatness and prestige," their ultimate aim is not to conquer for the sake of conquest or out of political necessity, but, first and foremost, for the sake of their moral and spiritual significance – to sanctify God's name.

This lesson must become the credo of each individual soldier: "He should know that he is fighting for the Oneness of God." Moreover, Rav Amital emphasized that even in the case of an optional war, the authority to go to war depends on the ratification of the High Court of seventy-one judges: since war is only permitted when the underlying goal is the supreme moral value of "sanctifying and unifying God's name," it stands to reason that the decision to declare war is not based merely on military considerations, but on spiritual and moral considerations. Therefore, the military echelons must be joined in this decision by the rabbinic sages of the High Court, who take no less of a responsibility for the results of the war.

The military force may only do battle when this objective, the sanctification of God's name, animates the spirit of the fighters. Without it, the general prohibition on warfare remains in effect.

Rav Amital concluded this shiur with a very subtle allusion: "Without a doubt this understanding has ramifications in the realm of Jewish thought. This, however, is not the forum to discuss the issue at further length."

Did this halakhic approach, which emphasizes the spiritual and moral ramifications of war, help shape Rav Amital's political approach and worldview, or did his political approach lead him to discover meanings within traditional sources that others glossed over? It is hard to know. Either way, the religious and ethical worldview proposed by Rav Amital went hand in hand with his political thinking.

RAV AMITAL'S LIBRARY

One of Rav Amital's identifying marks was his extensive library, which reflected the breadth of his knowledge and interests within the sphere of Torah and in the worldly realm. This was true of both his physical library – the overloaded but well-organized bookshelves that covered most of the walls of his apartment in Givat Mordekhai – and his "spiritual" library – his own glosses and novellae on those works that he had been delving into for decades.

Rav Amital's bibliophilia was self-evident; his love for books left its mark on his Talmudic teachings and works.

Many Rashei Yeshiva engage in Torah their whole lives, but the scope of their studies remains relatively limited: the Talmud, the *Mishneh Torah,* and some medieval and modern commentaries and novellae that became primary texts of the yeshiva world: the commentaries of Nachmanides (the Ramban) and R. Shlomo ibn Adret (the Rashba), *Ketzot HaḤoshen,* the novellae of R. Akiva Eger, R. Yonatan Eyebeschutz's *Urim VeTumim,* the novellae of R. Ḥayyim Soloveitchik, the volumes of R. Avraham Yeshaya Karelitz's *Ḥazon Ish,* and R. Elḥanan Wasserman's *Kovetz Shiurim.*

Rav Amital used all of these works regularly, but as usual he was not satisfied with the commonplace. He added to the classic Talmudic corpus dozens of works containing gems of Talmudic commentary that had been all but forgotten.

Rav Amital was especially fond of the volumes produced by Hungarian sages, which he had studied as a young man. Long after the Lithuanian, especially Brisker, style of Talmudic scholarship had conquered the yeshiva world, Rav Amital continued to study and offer gems of erudition from the vast corpus produced by Hungarian scholars. Alongside the classic novellae of the Ḥatam Sofer, Rav Amital also exposed his students to other sages who they otherwise may never have heard of, such as R. Moshe Shmuel Glasner of Cluj, author of *Dor Revi'i,* whose novellae pertain primarily to *Ḥullin* – a tractate rarely studied in yeshivot.

Along with works of commentary, novellae, halakha, and responsa, Rav Amital spiced up his teaching with works of Jewish thought and philosophy – another indication of his originality. In general, Rashei Yeshiva excel at Talmudic casuistry but stay away from philosophy and theology, and unfortunately give no expression to the latter in their erudite tracts. And vice versa: philosophers and theologians construct entire metaphysical systems but do not delve into legalistic Talmudic discussions. Rav Amital was not limited in that way. One who studies his work of Talmudic erudition *Resisei Tal* or peruses summaries of the *shiurim* he delivered in the yeshiva over the years will find references to classic Talmudic works alongside works of theology and philosophy and wonderful but now obscure Talmudic and halakhic works that for some unlucky reason or another never became popular in the yeshiva world. The most technical halakhic minutiae are discussed alongside broad ethical principles.

Rav Amital possessed an intense and consistent love for responsa literature. His library contained hundreds of volumes of responsa from which he mined hidden treasures. His writings are filled with references to responsa, integrating works ancient and modern, from East and West. Yet his writings also included, woven into the same cloth, the great works of Jewish thought and philosophy, from the medieval Rabbeinu Sa'adia Gaon, Rabbeinu Yona of Gerona, and Rabbeinu Baḥya, through the early modern Maharal of Prague, to the twentieth century Rav Kook and Rav Soloveitchik. Such a broad range is rare in the world of the *beit midrash*.

THE COURAGE TO BE LENIENT

Rav Amital's vast knowledge of the works of the *Rishonim* and *Aḥaronim* alike served him well when it came to issuing halakhic rulings. Although Rav Amital never served in a formal rabbinic capacity or undertook to be a formal halakhic decisor, a *posek*, he was often called upon to render decisions on his students' queries. Here too, Rav Amital displayed a rare combination of capabilities vital for the task of rendering halakhic decisions: profound knowledge of the entire halakhic corpus and intimate familiarity with worldly affairs – the application of the eternal Torah to the exigencies of life, here and now.

One characteristic of his practical halakhic rulings, following the approach of *Rishonim*, was their leniency. "[God] has given the earth to man" (Ps. 115:16), not to angels, and the halakha therefore must be applied realistically, in the actual world, not in an imaginary ideal world.

Rav Amital's approach to halakha was not, God forbid, frivolous. He knew, however, that the world of halakha is complex and multifaceted, with many approaches, in which stricter is not necessarily better. Sometimes, by imposing stringencies in one area, the *posek* may cause his petitioners to be lenient or errant elsewhere; the costs of stringency in such cases outweigh the benefits.

A study of Rav Amital's written halakhic rulings (many other rulings were issued orally) show that his ear was always attuned to reality and to the conditions of the time and locale. For example, he allowed soldiers in the field to perform their ritual hand-washing using canteens with narrow openings or to have breakfast prior to prayers so that they could join their peers in a *minyan*. Similarly, he permitted taking a Torah scroll in a portable ark into the field when there was no alternative.

Here too, when issuing practical halakhic rulings, Rav Amital's integration of Talmudic erudition with broader themes in Jewish thought is apparent. One example is his approach to the frequently discussed question of including public Shabbat violators in a *minyan*. Rav Amital was well aware of the vast literature from previous generations, but he was also familiar with the particular local situation: he was aware of the broad implications that could result from the exclusion and rejection of such people, especially in the army. Here too, he made use of his vast knowledge of responsa. He begins his responsum with the significant declaration: "Nowadays, particularly among soldiers, we are commanded to seek any justification to draw near and not, God forbid, to push away." Immediately thereafter, he cites R. Yehuda Aszod, a leading mid-nineteenth-century Hungarian *posek* who articulated similar reasoning 150 years earlier in his collection of responsa, *Yehuda Ya'aleh*. In this instance as well, Rav Amital supports his halakhic ruling with philosophic writings, citing the Rambam's "Essay on *Kiddush HaShem*" along with other sources to allow public Shabbat desecrators to join a *minyan*.

In the same spirit, Rav Amital permitted – again, based on a thorough study of the issue and relying on earlier authorities – offering food to people who would not ritually wash their hands or recite *berakhot*. With his awareness of reality and his broad-mindedness, relying on purely halakhic sources such as R. Moshe Isserles and the Ḥazon Ish as well as philosophical works like Rav Kook's letters, Rav Amital determined that any such act whose purpose is to sanctify God's name and bring Jews closer together can be permitted when there is no other alternative.

One who studies Rav Amital's responsa will recognize that he does not take the halakha lightly – just the opposite. It is not that he is lenient regarding the laws of Shabbat; he is stringent when it comes to *ḥillul HaShem* and mistreatment of a fellow human being.

From a theoretical and ideological perspective, Rav Amital was revolted by exaggerated displays of stringency – whether authentic or contrived – which were inappropriate to the spiritual and religious level of those who proudly took them on. He recoiled from pride in external, artificial things that are not backed up by any substance. As one who had studied under an earlier generation of Torah sages, Rav Amital knew the power of humility and being content with less – even when it came to service of God.

Rav Amital gave expression to this extreme – and negative – gap between external stringency and inner substance on many occasions. For example, he one described a "new custom that has come to this country:"

> We have never before seen such a phenomenon in the religious-Zionist community. Young men wear large knitted *kippot*, long sidelocks, sockless sandals, and untucked shirts – true "*Ḥasidim*." It is as if they are proclaiming, "I am religious. Even if my *kippa* flies off in the wind, my long sidelocks will pull me and bind me to the religious camp." Long sidelocks and *tzitzit* that dangle at one's knees have no halakhic-religious meaning; however, they grant one a certain sense of security and express a certain type of fervent religiosity and ultra-Orthodoxy.
>
> I hear of *Hesder Yeshivot* where the students don *tefillin* for Minḥa prayers. *Tefillin* add holiness. Halakhically, this practice is not arrogant or otherwise inappropriate; in fact, technically, the opposite is true. But I belong to a different generation. I have been fortunate enough to pray with some of our greatest sages: R. Shlomo Zalman Auerbach, R. Yitzḥak Weiss (author of *Minḥat Yitzḥak*), R. Isser Zalman Melzer and R. Aharon Kotler, and I never saw any of them recite Minḥa wearing *tefillin*. No one in the previous generation would have considered wearing *tefillin* for Minḥa when the greatest sages did not, despite what the technical halakha may suggest. Thirty years ago, I was told by Rabbi Bergman, the son-in-law of Rav Shakh and a close disciple of the Ḥazon Ish, that he once decided to build a *sukka* according to all the specifications of the Ḥazon Ish: a *sukka* without any nails. On the eve of Sukkot, he suddenly thought, "How can I have a super-stringent *sukka* when my grandfather did not?" He immediately took some nails and fastened them into his *sukka*.

As the educator of generations of students, Rav Amital wished to ascertain where this tendency toward stringency came from. After extensive contemplation, he blamed it on the lack of confidence characteristic of many members of the younger generation, for whom added stringency is a sort of veneer:

> Our generation has lost faith in its predecessors and feels the need to "start from scratch." Suddenly, all kinds of new customs are being rediscovered in the *Mishna Berura*. Religious behavior of this kind has its drawbacks; stringencies can be a sign of weakness. A student of mine who teaches in one of the *Hesder yeshivot* recently told me, "When I see students who wear *tefillin* for Minḥa, I know that there are other students who skip Minḥa entirely."

Perhaps Rav Amital's unconventional view on external stringencies was instilled in him in his youth. In his hometown, service of God was natural, in the Jews' veins. There was no need for artificial reinforcements.

Indeed, one of the messages that Rav Amital wished to impart to his students was aversion to the "religious anxiety" that constantly discloses itself in the life of modern man. It originates in uncertainty and lack of self-confidence in one's service of God and culminates with purposeless stringency, frequently on matters that our forefathers never dreamed of. Rav Amital wrote:

> The importance of tension in life notwithstanding, a person must guard himself against excessive tension and anxiety in his worship of God. Just as in every other aspect of life exaggeration is seen as abnormal, so too in the observance of mitzvot. This stands in contrast to the prevalent view that equates excessive meticulousness with fear of Heaven. The Rambam, in his *Shemona Perakim* (chapter four), notes that a person should strive to reach the level at which he can easily follow the golden mean in all his character traits, instead of constantly struggling with his baser inclinations. Excessive anxiety and suspicion are liable to lead to total paralysis. Here, too, a person must find the proper balance.

THE LAND OF ISRAEL AND THE STATE OF ISRAEL

Alongside his love for the Torah and the Jewish people, Rav Amital deeply loved the Land of Israel. Nevertheless, on this issue – as was typical of him – he refused to see the Land of Israel as the most important thing. With his profound and complex vision, he emphasized that the Land of Israel is but one of three legs of the eternal triad of the People of Israel, the Torah, and the Land of Israel. Without minimizing the importance and sanctity of the Land of Israel at all, Rav Amital was able to find the proper balance between these three cardinal values. In a generation that expected everything "now," he was able to keep perspective.

As a result of his positions, which balanced the pressures of the moment with future security needs, Rav Amital suffered many insults and paid a heavy public price. Yet despite everything, he continued to speak his mind. Throughout his life, he expressed great love for the Land of Israel – a love that cannot be summed up in mere words, but was implicit in his actions. From the moment of his arrival in the Land of Israel, he took an active part in defending it during its wars, and in establishing a foothold in Gush Etzion. Even when agitating for peace, he was motivated by a real concern for the fate of the Jewish people and the Land of Israel.

It is small wonder that at a particularly emotional moment, during a speech he gave in the yeshiva on Ḥanukka 5754 (1993), at the height of the anti-Oslo protests, he disclosed some of his thoughts on this matter:

> The greatest hurt was when people suggested that I am deficient in my love of the land of Israel, God forbid. I was connected to the Land of Israel long before I knew the famous teaching of the Ramban (regarding the mitzva to settle the land of Israel; commentary to Numbers 33:53). When we were liberated from a Nazi labor camp, there was a group of about twenty of us Jews there. We had no newspapers, no radio; we didn't know what was happening in the world. But I said, "I'm going to the Land of Israel." They said to me, "Are you crazy? You don't know what's going on there!" But I answered, "I'm going." For me, the Land of Israel is not only a spiritual matter, not just a matter of sanctity. I feel it is my homeland in the simplest sense, and I'm not ashamed of it.

Nevertheless, Rav Amital's love for the Land of Israel never impeded his better judgment. For him, the importance of the Land of Israel did not depend on its borders, but on the realization of Jewish sovereignty and self-rule. A Jewish state in the Land of Israel would bring new life to the Jewish people individually and collectively.

As a religious thinker whose worldview was nurtured by the Torah, Rav Amital did not see the return of the Jewish people to its land as a solely political act or as an act of individuals, but as a collective act with a spiritual mission. In an essay whose title speaks for itself – "The Jewish People Come before the Land of Israel" – Rav Amital specified the mission's objectives:

> The mission of our people is to be a light unto the nations, not as exceptional individuals, but as an exceptional people. Beyond the mundane social, economic, and military problems, we must be a moral and ethical exemplar. The Land of Israel was designated as the territory for an exemplary Jewish society.

Only against the backdrop of this principle can one understand Rav Amital's anxiety about any immoral act connected – even only indirectly – to the State of Israel and its people. It forms the cornerstone of Rav Amital's famous declaration, after the massacres at the Sabra and Shatila refugee camps, that a great and terrible *ḥillul HaShem* had been perpetrated with the knowledge of the Israeli government. Rav Amital expressed public and unequivocal disgust at the bloodshed and the consequent *ḥillul HaShem*.

He reacted similarly to the murderous rampage of Barukh Goldstein at the Cave of Makhpela:

> Barukh Goldstein besmirched the Jewish nation and the Torah with the taint of shedding innocent blood. Beyond the moral and religious baseness of killing innocent people as they knelt in prayer, the terrible murder caused a *ḥillul HaShem* in the eyes of the entire world. Perhaps Goldstein perpetrated this massacre specifically because he viewed it as an act of "wiping out Amalek" (Deut. 25:19), out of a sense of dehumanization of every Arab. Our

> Sages recognized long ago that the entire Torah, when given over into the wrong hands, may become "a potion of death" (*Ta'anit* 7a). But it would have been difficult to imagine that a mass murder could be perpetrated in the name of the Torah, concerning which the Rambam wrote that "the judgments of the Torah do not bring vengeance into the world; rather, they bring compassion and kindness and peace into the world."

Similarly, Rav Amital emphasized the awful *ḥillul HaShem* of the assassination of Israel's Prime Minister Yitzḥak Rabin by a man purporting to be mitzva observant: "Have we become like Sedom, do we resemble Amora? The Jewish people, who taught the world absolute morality, beginning with the prohibition on murder; the Jewish state – the only democracy in the Middle East, a nation founded on the vision of redemption – now resembles some Third World banana republic" Rav Amital roared, arguing in favor of penetrating soul-searching. In contrast to other leaders, who were quick to shirk the mantle of responsibility, Rav Amital called for a real self-examination based, among other things, on seeing reality in its complexity, and not shallowly or superficially:

> Sadly, the *ḥillul HaShem* in this case is made worse by the fact that it was perpetrated by someone who regards himself as religious, and he justifies his actions by invoking commandments from the Torah. From a more general perspective, we are guilty in our education of an entire generation towards superficial thinking that is built on slogans and clichés. Our youth are incapable of perceiving and understanding a complex reality. In the yeshivot, they engage in Talmud study with deep, complex thought; at university they are taught to analyze a text in a complex, serious way; but in political matters, the public atmosphere educates towards shallowness and superficiality.

Rav Amital's historical perspective left its mark on his attitude to the State of Israel. He did not view Israel's national rebirth merely in political terms, but also – perhaps primarily – in spiritual terms, as being part of the "Kingdom of Israel." He regularly cited the Rambam's formulation in *Mishneh Torah* (Laws of Yom Kippur, 3:1) about the prayer of the High Priest: "He blesses Israel separately, praying that God save Israel and that their king not be removed." Commentaries on this passage tried and failed to find a source for the conclusion of this blessing. Rav Amital suggested that the Rambam, based on his understanding that the Jewish people need self-rule in order to survive, made his own addition to the blessing formulated by the Sages.

Rav Amital's vision differed from today's common conceptions, which focus on the "here and now," and as a result oscillate between the extremes of euphoric optimism and depressed pessimism. Rav Amital, by viewing things through the lens of history, saw things in a more balanced and measured way.

In one of his *Yom HaAtzma'ut* discourses, when he generally expressed gratitude to God, he said:

> My beard has still not turned white with age, and yet during the course of my life I have seen, as our sages have said, "a world built, destroyed and rebuilt" (*Midrash Lekaḥ Tov*, Gen. 6:9). I have seen Jews being led to Auschwitz; I have seen Jews dance at the establishment of the State of Israel; I have seen the great victories of the Six-Day War; I have traveled with soldiers to the Suez Canal. I have lived through an epoch, in the shortest span of time. It is hard to believe that in such a short lifetime one could witness so many changes.
>
> Today, the State of Israel stands at the focal point of world history. It is clear that we are living in a period of great change and, as such, it demands of us great deeds. It necessitates sacrifice; it hungers for creativity; it requires accomplishment; it compels us to take action. From day to day, from year to year, changes take place. To live in such a period, to really and truly live it; to see and understand the dynamics and intensity of Jewish history as it unfolds before us; to gaze upon the great events – upon each one, in and of itself, and upon all of them combined – while we maintain the correct perspective, knowing that it is just a part of the whole; to sense the process of redemption as it unfolds before our very eyes; to know our responsibility in this world, at this

> time and in this place; to perceive what it is that God demands of us, here and now – all this creates a grave responsibility which one can neither escape nor ignore.
>
> I am the man, poor in worthy deeds, who has seen communities in desolation, and who has merited to behold a land rebuilt: sorrow and sighing, while I was upon a strange and foreign land; gladness and joy, when I came up to Jerusalem. "I will declare Your name to my brethren; in the midst of a congregation, I will praise You" [Ps. 22:23]. This is God's promise: "For a small moment I have forsaken you, but with great mercies I will gather you" [Is. 54:7]. One thing remains clear: "Upon Mount *Tziyon*, there will be a remnant" [Ob. 1:17].

This view of the establishment and functioning of the State of Israel as a *kiddush HaShem*, guided Rav Amital when he sought to articulate the religious and spiritual significance of the State of Israel:

> I believe that we merited a Jewish state only because of God's desire to sanctify His name in the aftermath of the terrible *ḥillul HaShem* of the Holocaust. The establishment of the state and its military victories against the Arab armies that rose up against it constitute a response of *kiddush HaShem*. Precisely for this reason, the obligation to sanctify God's name has special significance in our time for those of us who live in the State of Israel, the entire establishment of which stemmed from this principle. This is why, on various occasions over the years, I have felt obligated to protest against instances of *ḥillul HaShem*. This was the only cause for which I felt a need to speak out publicly.

Here too, Rav Amital's worldview guided him toward his public activism and can even explain his foray, brief as it was, out of the rarefied environment of the *beit midrash* and into the cold, alienating public arena.

The religious perspective through which Rav Amital interpreted events allowed him to not only see them in their proper proportion, but also to assign to them the proper religious and theological meaning.

Rav Amital frequently leveled severe criticism at those circles –

certain *ḥaredi* and national-religious groups – that acted as though they understood God's calculations. More than once, rabbis from these circles offered ostensibly religious explanations for current events, calamities in particular. Thus, for example, they wished to claim that the Yom Kippur War resulted from the generation's lack of modesty; that the HaBonim disaster, a train wreck in which nineteen school children lost their lives, was the result of Shabbat desecration in Petaḥ Tikva or non-kosher *mezuzot* on the homes of the victims; that the Gaza Disengagement was the result of various sins.

Rav Amital vehemently opposed any attempt to rationalize catastrophes:

> The major failing of many of these people is that they did not experience the Holocaust or the events leading up to the establishment of the State of Israel bodily, in the flesh. Someone who experienced such events would never attempt to rationalize current events. We have no explanation for the Holocaust, but we have an explanation for the attack on Merkaz HaRav?
>
> Such pretentiousness, according to which mortal man can become intimate with God and understand His machinations, is fundamentally invalid. This flawed conception leads some such people to be convinced that *Mashiaḥ* is just around the corner. A religious perspective that lacks historical perspective is fundamentally invalid and is likely to lead to tragic practical and religious consequences.

In Rav Amital's opinion, to a large degree the crisis of religious Zionism was caused by this type of vision that lacked perspective. The greater the expectations, the greater the disappointment. When messianic and other expectations are inflated sky-high, but come crashing down when they are shown to be empty and hollow, a terrible crisis is created, resulting in disbelief and a crisis of faith. The outcome of this reality is made several times worse in light of the fact that some of the main spokespeople for religious Zionism are precisely the ones who lack the historical perspective that Rav Amital so often spoke about.

Rav Amital's attitude toward the Land of Israel, like his attitude toward halakhic practice, was not extreme or uncompromising. It was the result of many years of in-depth study of Jewish sources, Jewish history, and the contemporary *zeitgeist*. Rav Amital's approach dictated that fateful questions such as the attitude toward the Land of Israel should not be decided based solely on emotions; they must be considered with common sense, balancing between various values to reach a considered and intelligent decision.

In his balanced and considered calculus, Rav Amital looked not only at the value of the Land of Israel and the struggle to keep it whole (which, in the eyes of his contemporaries, was a dominant – even cardinal – value), but also at the equally important value of the Jewish people and their Torah. He wrote: "In the realm of ethics and values, the crux of the argument concerns the question of whether, in the composite of the Jewish people, the Torah, and the Land of Israel, no one value has more weight than another, or whether we must have a hierarchy of values in which the Jewish people rates highest."

Rav Amital's answer to this question was unequivocal. It draws nourishment from within the multivocal and complex world of Jewish thought and learning, which rarely sees things in terms of black and white:

> The very principle of a hierarchy of holy values, with one higher than the next, is a fundamental one in Torah and in halakha, as set forth at the beginning of Tractate *Kelim* [1:6–9]. The need to arrange a hierarchy of values arises from the fact that in reality, it is not always possible to fully realize all three values. Sometimes the implementation of one value conflicts with another. To those who claim that "The Land of Israel is in danger," we counter that "The Jewish people are in danger," and that the value of the Jewish people takes precedence over the value of the Land of Israel.

As a faithful disciple of R. Avraham Yitzḥak Kook, Rav Amital was not captivated by the charms of those who pretended to be Rav Kook's students while occasionally misinterpreting his teachings. With his profound and intimate familiarity with Rav Kook's voluminous writings, Rav Amital was well aware that they, too, were not all cut from the same cloth:

> It is astounding how the vision of redemption espoused by Rav Kook, the crux of which was the spiritual revival of the Jewish people in its return to the land, has become limited, in recent years – among those who regard themselves as his students and disciples – to the commandment of settling the land exclusively. Everyone should take a look at his masterwork *Orot* and note how much space is taken up by the subject of the Land of Israel (not to speak of the specific issue of the boundaries of the land), as opposed to the subject of "the spiritual reawakening of the Jewish people."

Within his basic approach of seeing reality as rich, complex, and multifaceted, Rav Amital charted his own course regarding the struggle for the Land of Israel:

> One cannot simply dismiss any opinion that is different and anyone who does not think like everyone else. I, for example, am considered a great heretic because I do not believe that it is forbidden to relinquish so much as a centimeter of the Land of Israel even when human life is at stake. All of the religious-Zionist rabbis today subscribe to this prohibition, while I think differently. I am considered an even greater heretic because, in my view, it is worth relinquishing parts of the Land of Israel in order to rid ourselves of the yoke of two million Arabs who will join the other million Arabs [who are Israeli citizens], while the number of Jews in the country stands at a mere four-and-a-half million. I do not try to influence anyone. I do not attempt to sell my wares – neither within the yeshiva nor anywhere else. But one has to know that there are people who think differently; one can't just dismiss everything.

This bold approach, which deviated from the national-religious mainstream, caused shock – and no small amount of criticism – among many of Rav Amital's students. They did not understand how their mentor could turn away from the comfortable consensus to strike out on his own lonely path.

As a man of truth, Rav Amital was not afraid of or deterred by criticism. Even though it occasionally caused him personal grief, he adhered to his path, thereby teaching a valuable lesson to his students.

HUMANITY

A basic feature of Rav Amital's teaching was its humanity – its simple, heartfelt compassion that required no tradition or prooftext. It was engraved upon his heart, and its implications for Torah and *menschlichkeit* were far reaching.

Rav Amital was fond of saying, "All sacred Service of God cannot nullify simple human feelings." He would often reinforce this teaching with a pithy statement from the Kotzker Rebbe. Commenting on the verse (Ex. 22:30) "You shall be holy people to Me," he observed, "God is saying, 'I have enough angels. I want holy *people*.'" It is no coincidence that he called one of his books *VeHaAretz Natan Livnei Adam* ("He has given the earth to man," translated into English as *Jewish Values in a Changing World*). He taught that even if "the heavens are God's," He gave the earth to man, and the Torah is a living, reality-based, this-worldly document, not something theoretical that applies only to angels.

This worldview is not restricted to his philosophy; it has practical expression as well. Rav Amital noted:

> There has been a tendency in recent years to idealize great rabbis, to the point of total disregard of their human feelings and weaknesses. The Torah presents the opposite approach: every person has a human side, which must not be denied. Even the prophets had doubts and difficulties. The Torah recognizes that man lives in this world, and it has no expectations that one behave as if he were living in an ideal and unreal universe.

POSTSCRIPT

Rav Amital's teachings are filled with brilliant insights. Halakha and *Aggada*, philosophy and spirituality combine to form a single fabric – not a set of disparate parts that happen to coexist, but an organic combination whose whole is greater than the sum of its parts.

Love of Torah and fear of heaven; the people, Land, and State of

Israel; erudition and originality; courage and humanity – these all joined together in an astounding mosaic of Torah, morality, and philosophy. His works seamlessly incorporated life wisdom with *menschlichkeit*, pouring the old wine of tradition into the new vessels of modern life, creating hope for the future.

Rav Amital's foresight went well beyond the "here and now," contemplating Jewish history with sober vision and a broad perspective.

In Rav Amital's teachings, the Torah's power is not time-bound; it spans all generations. The Jewish people are not sprinters, but marathon runners spanning epochs and continents, past and present, destruction and rebirth, the universal and the particular, the Jewish people and Jewish sovereignty.

Rav Amital had an ear to the ground, listening for the cries of his generation, yet his heart and mind were not captivated by every stylish and opportunistic caprice. Balance and discretion, complexity and moderation, are clearly discernible in his teachings.

Rav Amital's unique personal history was an integral part of his personality, leaving a profound mark on his teachings. Discernible are his love for the old *beit midrash*, natural, straight, Jewish life, unembellished by anything counterfeit, and simple, innocent faith. In addition, he possessed admiration for Torah giants, a boundless love for Torah, and complete immersion in the treasures of the Jewish spirit – Talmudic learning, philosophy, and ethical thought – cultivated by generations of Jewish creativity.

This was all accompanied by constant, considered, balanced, and sober contemplation of current events. The ever-present shadow of the Holocaust did not impede his judgment. The great, unanswerable questions of the Holocaust coexisted in his mind with praise and gratitude for the great miracle of the return of the nation to its homeland and the restoration of Jewish sovereignty.

Taken together, all of these elements subtly influenced Rav Amital's unique teachings, investing them with an ever-present charm. The illumination embedded in his teachings accord one who studies them with something of that joy – the joy and creativity of their author.

DR. AVIAD HACOHEN, a longtime student of Rav Amital, is dean of the Sha'arei Mishpat College of Law, a senior lecturer in Law at the Hebrew University of Jerusalem, and a fellow at Van Leer Institute, Jerusalem.

For Further Reading:

Rav Yehuda Amital, *Jewish Values in a Changing World*, ed. Amnon Bazak, transl. David Strauss (Jersey City: KTAV, 2005).

Rav Yehuda Amital, *Resisei Tal,* ed. Yoel Amital (Alon Shevut: Yeshivat Har Etzion, 2005).

Rav Yehuda Amital, *Commitment and Complexity*, ed. Aviad Hacohen, transl. Kaeren Fish (Jersey City: KTAV, 2008).

Moshe Maya, *A World Built, Destroyed and Rebuilt: Rabbi Yehuda Amital's Confrontation with the Memory of the Holocaust*, transl. Kaeren Fish (Jersey City: KTAV, 2005).

Memorial page: http://www.haretzion.org/about-us/rav-amital-ztql

Articles in English by Rav Amital:
http://vbm-torah.org/rya-articles.htm

Eulogies:
http://www.haretzion.org/component/content/article/73-hespedim

Index of Personages

About the Author

photo: Eric Sultan

Elyashiv Reichner, a resident of the Negev city of Yeruḥam and a graduate of its *yeshivat hesder,* is a journalist at the newspaper *Makor Rishon.* His most recent book is *The Orange Campaign: The Fight for Gush Katif* [Hebrew].

The fonts used in this book are from the Arno family

Maggid Books
The best of contemporary Jewish thought from
Koren Publishers Jerusalem